D1569409

THEOLOGICAL METHOD
AND IMAGINATION

THEOLOGICAL METHOD AND IMAGINATION

Julian N. Hartt

A Crossroad Book
THE SEABURY PRESS · NEW YORK

1977

The Seabury Press
815 Second Avenue
New York. N.Y. 10017

Printed in the United States of America

Library of Congress Cataloging In Publication Data
Hartt, Julian Norris.
Theological method and imagination.
"A Crossroad book."
1. Theology—Methodology. I. Title.
BR118.H37   200'.1'8   76–49901   ISBN 0–8164–0335–X

CONTENTS

INTRODUCTION

I

When the integrity, coherence, and authority of the spiritual life of a society have been called into question, thinkers of various persuasions and interests are sure to ask how, or perhaps whether, a treasured common life can be reconstituted. They want also, of course, to learn what has gone wrong, where the slippages are between the basic schematisms of that society and the great world beyond. But the question of highest priority is how to reconstitute a viable, harmonious, and fertile common life.

Now "called into question" does not necessarily mean that those basic schematisms of belief and behavior are defenseless under withering philosophical fire; or that the battlements of this city of man have been undermined and rendered worthless by philosophical "sappers." A lively supposition is abroad that anything that greatly matters is not likely to be seriously affected by philosophical artillery, unless it is the childhood religious faith of tender souls from Fundamentalist hinterlands who have come to college believing all sorts of things long since jettisoned by enlightened souls, such as majors in the philosophy department.

So even if one does not agree with Hegel that the philosopher is not licensed by his muse actually to change the world rather than properly to understand it, we should probably all agree that the meaning of life in a given society can be called into question by a great many different forces. The present age is much taken with apocalyptic visions of the world's end, but in the interstices of these crises we know there are many nondramatic destructive forces at work.

For instance, one day it dawns upon ever so many people that there is little to be gained now by hearing and repeating the old truths or by

vii

preserving the old loyalties. For as they now experience the world and reflect, however dimly and fitfully, upon it, the old truths seem neither to illuminate it nor give fertile or clear signals about how to relate to it practically. Here the words of the psalmist come to mind:

> By the waters of Babylon,
> there **we** sat down and wept,
> when **we** remembered Zion.
> On the willows there
> we hung up our lyres.
> For there our captors
> required of us songs,
> and our tormentors, mirth, saying,
> "Sing us one of the songs of
> Zion!"
> How shall we sing the Lord's song
> In a foreign land? (Ps 137)[1]

Of course the old songs can be sung simply to preserve the hallowed febrile memories of the lost world, and perhaps also to keep alive in the hearts of the young some sense of what that world was. But how often the young join the ranks of the cruelly mirthful tormentors and say, "Sing us one of those silly old songs of your dear dead past."[2]

But there are seasons of much more radical doubt, doubts that reach far beyond the plausibility of old songs sung in a foreign land. These are doubts about the traditional routes to truth and wisdom. Now the persistent refrain is not, "How implausible are those old stories!" The thrust of this far more radical doubt is rather more like this: "Why did any thoughtful person ever suppose truth and wisdom could be reliably and predictably attained in those old ways? O yes, some of the old truths may have had something in them, something that may have been valid in that world from which we are now separated once and for all. So we do not say there was nothing but superstition in what they held to be worthy of all acceptance. What we say, what we insist upon, is that they had no method for screening fancy out of fact, for properly distinguishing engaging or intimidating myth from hard knowledge, for critically weighing the traditions of their fathers affecting the right conduct of life. No doubt they hit now and then upon some nuggets of wisdom; but they lacked a rational method for determining the proper goals of human life and thereafter for the selection of the proper instruments for their attainment."

So Descartes does not simply throw out as so many untruths the dogmas—religious, metaphysical, scientific, ethical—he had been religiously taught. Instead he wants to know how any of these things can be rationally assented to—or rationally denied for that matter—unless one has achieved fundamental clarity on the right method of inquiry.

Something like this is to be said also of Kant. It was no part of the critical philosophy to destroy traditional religious beliefs as such: beliefs about the reality and sovereign goodness of God, about the dignity and immortality of the human soul, about the principle of radical evil in the heart of man, and about the true lordship of Jesus Christ. But the structure, indeed the mentality, of argument which philosophical theology over many centuries had developed and defended as the indispensable foundation for certain of these beliefs, and the ecclesiastical institutions devised in Christian history more to enslave than to liberate man: these all had to go. For he had now in hand the right method for exhibiting the nature of the mind itself and its relationships to the world. And therefore a rational reordering of life was at last possible: a synthesis in which beauty and righteousness would crown the human edifice of which a rationally determined and determinate knowledge of the natural world was the foundation. Not that science could at last unlock every mystery of man's being in the world, but that both what we ought to be and what we may legitimately hope for derive from a sure knowledge of the mind itself reducing the flux of experience to an intelligible world.

And now in our own time two new forms of radical doubt have been fixed upon the old truths, upon the received structures of meaning and value. One of these is new only in its logical sophistication. I mean the revisions of Humean systematic skepticism. The other is existentialism.

Let it be said at once that Humean systematic skepticism is not designed to throw out everything hitherto revered as wise, true, holy, and good. The thrust of this form of radical doubt appears in this way: What sort of fact-ascertainment is possible for the proper appraisal of religious, metaphysical, and ethical assertions? Hume saw very clearly that there might be excellent reasons for preserving certain beliefs and the institutions built around and upon them. But these would be reasons of social utility, or perhaps just reflections of the constitution of human life, which to honor is the part of wisdom, but to translate into a metaphysical wonder is the part of folly.

As for existentialism (if I may be momentarily indulged in a journalistic appellation) as a form of radical doubt, it intentionally attacks both the substance of traditional beliefs and the methods hitherto employed to ascertain the dimensions, the destiny, and the good of the human condition.

I have no intention here of presuming to evaluate any of these programs of radical doubt. They are cited, rather than analyzed—least of all, refuted—simply to make sure we realize that they are important elements in the general situation in which Christian theologians are trying to reconstruct their enterprise. In a time when from all quarters of the intellectual world people are demanding methodological revisions, or at least the revelation in depth of what is involved in methodological commitments, it is little to be wondered at that theologians should take up the hue and cry. But there are other reasons also.

II

The general considerations so far adduced affecting the stability, coherence, and fertility of the spiritual life apply *a fortiori* to Christianity because for many centuries it claimed, and with considerable force of evidence, to define, actually to *be*, the meaning of "the spiritual life." But now by common consent (which does not necessarily argue common understanding) our world is secular and its dominant spirituality is secularistic. At the very least this means that Christian institutions do not have the power, had they the mind and heart, to define the options even of their own professed adherents; that is, to define the legitimate range of options of Christian expression in "precept and example"—in creedal espousal and styles of life. Church theologians can be as dogmatic as ever they please, or feel divinely inspired to be. That will not induce the multitudes to believe that their pronouncements are true or their prescriptions valid. Homiletical thunder from the pulpit or from the theological rostrum is not commonly followed by lightning that does the slightest damage to the massive institutions and ingrained patterns of behavior of the American people.

So the truths which traditionalist theologians proclaim seem to be the sounds of voices carrying uncertainly across a great abyss. To change the metaphor: Between the purveyors of the old truths and the multitudes run the broad swiftly moving waters of Babylon. Let those who will, or who cannot help themselves, sing the old songs on the farther shore. On the near shore, where all the action is, we hear only the oddments and fragments of the old songs. And these residues, these echoes, defy translation into the new verities, aspirations, and life-styles of the secular world.

And again, to the radical doubters it is the cognitional routes which seem fatally wrong; it is as though the singers of the old songs on the farther shore supposed that the sheer repetition of once blessed and fertile words could now establish, miraculously, solid connections with a greater world that was never, even in its richest evocations and most sophisticated arguments, more than suppositious. Take for instance that once blessed magisterial word "revelation." In that old dead world, gone beyond restoration if not beyond recall, that word both identified and certified a great range of truths and duties upon which a global human reality could be—was, in large fact—actually constructed. But what remains of its splendor, its power, its cogency? "Revelation" now hardly means more than a presumptuous claim that certain "truths" are forever immune to rational criticism. Pronounced infallible, they are understood to be incorrigible. In other theological contexts "revelation" signifies some moment of experience, some disclosure of meaning, so subjectively precious and potent that it has the force of God transcendent speaking person-to-person.[3]

It is no part of the agenda of radically serious doubt to quarrel with meanings buried in subjective affectivity; for what truth-weight is to be assigned to and assayed in reports of such meanings? The fundamental quarrel is with any and every prescription of a route from such revelational wonders to a description and explanation of the real world. So if all a person means when he says that God has revealed something to him (and there is no known limit to the variety of things thus signified and dignified)[4] is that some experience has made all the difference in the world to his life, it would be grossly unfair as well as philosophically pointless to doubt what he says unless we know him to be a dedicated liar. But if this confessor goes on to say that the real world is God's creature, that its whole history lies within his governance, and that he will bring it in due time to his own glorious consummation, it is entirely legitimate to ask, not only what that means but how anybody could go about to ascertain its truth or its falsity. Unless, of course, he is still testifying rather than asserting: unless, that is, he really means, "Well, hang it all, this is the way I see it, the way I see the whole thing; and there's an end on it." So again we must note that the only legitimate philosophical quarrel with religious *testimony* is: (1) Is it honest? and (b) Is it pertinent to a moot issue?

III

Radical doubt in the modern world has always been the prelude to a reconstruction of the world of human meaning. This is true of Descartes, of Hume, of Kant, of the best of the existentialists, and of Husserl, who must accept a considerable part of the responsibility for the emergence of existentialism. There are, of course, very wide differences of opinion and strategy among these powerful minds. But the radical doubter is, above all, looking for a way to certify what he takes to be the indispensable truths and goods of the human condition. This is as true of the existentialist as it is of Descartes, though it is still a popular sentiment that the former is out to save his own Dasein.[5]

Thus the radical doubter must be profoundly concerned with a spiritual malaise that infects the general society. He must be deeply alarmed by inauthentic doubts and by neurotic anxieties about the human situation. Note here the great differences between Descartes and Montaigne. Note also the differences between Hume and Kant. Hume was a firm believer in many of the values of his society. A social revolution was no part of his agenda. The real revolutionary has to be so very right, his doctrines must be so very true, that he is willing to change the shape of the human world to fit an ideal abstract design. But if custom, rightly reflected upon, is the guide of life, and if custom can be relieved of a monstrously heavy superstructure of dogmatic metaphysical beliefs, then there is no place for the revolutionary except in the madhouse if he is living, and in a footnote if, mercifully, he is dead.

But Kant saw that the rational foundations of man's knowledge of nature had to be defended against Humean skepticism; and it little matters for this purpose that Hume himself at the outset proposed a "new science of human nature." For how can we rationally expect the higher values of the social order to flourish anew (a commanding hope of the

Enlightenment) if the very foundation of the intellectual life, of the mind itself, is shrouded in doubts that are as factitious as they are persuasive? Kant, as we all know, had ever before him what he took to be a paradigm of true science: Newtonian mechanics. But the notion that the prime item on his agenda was to certify *that* as true and absolutely true, is a profoundly serious misreading of the philosopher. Neither Kant's philosophy of mind nor his philosophy of nature is refuted, or even markedly discomfited, by the great revisions in Newtonian physics since his time; to say nothing of his ethical theories and his interpretation of religion.

IV

The condition of Christian theology in the present reflects all of these elements. Some say: There is no use proclaiming the Gospel to an age unprepared to believe that there is a Gospel—that there is a God from whom good news can be expected or has already been once and for all delivered for us and for our salvation. Still others say: That is all true enough, but it means that the theologian must first of all learn and take to heart the criteria of intelligibility which shape the meaning of this world. We cannot linger longer by the waters of Babylon moaning the old song. We have to learn what song will make sense to the Babylonians. True, as mere theologians we may not be able to show that these criteria of intelligibility are themselves intelligible. But is it not comforting that there is a general doubt in so many philosophical camps about being able to account rationally for the sentiment of rationality?

There are still other theological voices in other rooms; and they say: There are new pieties a-borning in this secular world. So the real methodological issue is to learn how to extract, refine, and express these truths. Perhaps they will have some agreeable echoes of the faith of our fathers. But echoes are epiphenomena. They must not, therefore, be taken to be the main business of theology.

And still others profess that the Gospel itself is everlastingly valid: It is, now and always, God's good news. But theologians have not yet successfully liberated its truth from archaic conceptual and symbolic forms. Hence the main methodological business is just that. If, therefore, "God acts in history" has become a largely vacuous proposition, we must —and as God helps us, we will—find language in which to express the Christian conviction that somehow and somewhere, at the heart of the great world, human life matters to Something, perhaps to Being; as, of course, at its best it matters to us. And perhaps the real meaning of this is that we should learn to care more about human life than a secularist society inspires us to do.

Finally, there is a small and ill-assorted minority of theologians (I am speaking of the Protestant world) who believe that the proper business of the theologian is to show forth the meaning of the faith without fear or favor: without fear of philosophical snipers and "sappers"; without favor to secularist powers deeply entrenched in church and world. For these theologians it is no part of the agenda to trim and mold the faith to fit the mind of the age. For in whom or what does that mind reside in such majesty, clarity, and power that we should bow before it and humbly petition to be absorbed by it? What is worse, suppose that the mind of the age is now divided against itself, and comes to light and voice only in shrill self-referencing fragments? Is it, therefore, Babylon that we need to be concerned with rather than that mighty river, time itself, which bears all her sons away, minds and all?

For this sort of theological stance the really prime methodological question is how to order the principles of the faith in such coherence, clarity, and pungency that the errors of the mind of the age can be seen in their true light, and repented of.

V

In this essay I do not propose to test properly all these methodological stances and programs. For this, if I may so, there is ample historical justification: Neither did Descartes nor Kant nor Aquinas nor Anselm nor Luther nor Schleiermacher. For each of these, the substance of things loved, seen, and hoped for reached far down into their methodological convictions and decisions and procedures.

In this essay I propose to look at a variety of things commonly judged to be foundational methodological concerns for theology. And I shall be looking at them from and out of a conviction that the "faith once and for all delivered to our fathers" is true and can be construed as true. Yes, and defended as true. But this is not the same as going about to explicate that faith. That is the work of systematic theology. That work outranks by a great deal any and all methodological concerns and bemusements.

VI

Why then methodology at all, as a discrete essay, since it certainly does not come first in the order of importance, except perhaps here and there in a wayward seminary? Certainly not because the air is full of methodological concerns and neuroses—though it is.

The reason is this: Methodology is part of systematics. Metaphysicians have always known this. The best of Christian theologians have always practiced it. This means that it is not enough, it has never been enough, to say "Here is the faith." One must also say—though it must be said in different ways in different places— "Here are the ways the faith makes sense." But to say that second thing entails a a range of responsibility for canvassing the ways in which things make sense; not all of the ways, God knows, but the ways in which the things that matter most make the most sense.

VII

And now a lexical warning. I shall persistently use the term "incorrigible belief." By this I do not mean such things as the affectional grip we have on things that matter most to us. Nor do I mean dogmas against which no amount or kind of criticism is permitted to fall. I simply mean logical-ontological convictions so fundamental that without them the very sense of life and world as shaped and shaping would disappear. We all have such beliefs, whatever our formal creeds. Moreover, we do sometimes surrender them. When we surrender them for contingent propositions, for empirical generalizations or for weighty formations of the the mind of the age, at that stroke, we surrender concrete individuality and become details of the social order. When we abandon one set of incorrigible beliefs for another sort, we have been converted. Whether or not that is a bad thing, depends, does it not, on what we are converted to? Conversion, therefore, is a very different matter from the variegated processes by which persons are assimilated into social structures, sometimes on "profession of faith." The objective of conversion is attainment or recovery of authentic individuality in the nexus of generic humanity. Social assimilation, whatever its linguistic and other emblematic banners, is the process of being *aufgehoben* into a false infinite. From such a fate alienation is the first indispensable step toward salvation. But it is only the first step.

The loss of authentic individuality (or historical agency, as I shall later argue) goes hand in hand with the loss of any fertile and vivid sense of generic humanity.

These, obviously, are systematic concerns. In any properly serious methodology, in theology at any rate—though I think this is true also of metaphysical philosophy and ethics—these and kindred things are bound to show up. That is as much a promise as a prediction.

EPILOGUE

The meta-concerns of philosophy are sometimes pursued, or at least celebrated, as though here at last, and thank God, really basic issues can be handled without showing one's hand on anything of substance. But, for example, are the arguments over the philosophical foundations of mathematics justly famous for their immunity to infections from the "real world"?

Therefore, it matters little whether or not this essay be viewed as a meta-something that sins against the true spirit of meta discourse. For I fear that that spirit has as much rational force as the mind of the age.

THEOLOGICAL METHOD
AND IMAGINATION

Chapter One

❧

BELIEFS, CASES AND REASONS

I

To be a Christian means to hold certain beliefs, for instance that "God was in Christ reconciling the world to himself" (2 Cor 5:19). To hold certain beliefs is to accept them as true. Christians tend to accept these beliefs because "that is what Christians do." Naturally one likes to suppose that one's beliefs are true. Just as naturally one wants to do the things regarded as required in order to belong to a company to which one aspires to belong. So it may well and early occur to even the most devout and sympathetic believer to ask: "But why do we believe these things, especially since some of them seem to fit so poorly with things we know to be true?"

Traditionally, theologians were supposed to have ready and convincing answers to such "Why" questions. This element of the theologians' portfolio is now hard to locate. They find it hard to claim any unique responsibility for answering that Why question. Perhaps it smacks too much of trying to offer rationalistic answers to misunderstood questions. More generally, theologians are likely to feel that it is up to parents, grandparents, pastors, church school teachers—the concerned laity generally—to provide the rationale for Christian belief and behavior.

This theological posture is not implausible. It connects with common observation and ancient practice. Commonly observed, being a Christian means talking as Christians talk and acting as Christians are supposed to act; the latter, of course, includes feeling guilty for improper behavior. So a child being trained in piety is set to learning these ways of talking and behaving and feeling. It would be wrongheaded to start him in the Christian business **by** trying to stuff his head with beliefs; that is, with carefully articulated propositions. Thus the ancient prac-

1

tice of the church was to treat the catachumen, whatever his or her age, as an infant having to learn the rudiments of a mother tongue. Perhaps this is what St. Paul means when he tells some of his readers that they must feed on the milk of the Gospel because they are not yet ready for its meat (1 Cor. 3:2).

So far we are dealing with garden-variety practical wisdom. Do we tell an infant that he must believe in Daddy if he wants to be accepted as a real member of the family? Hardly. He learns that Daddy is the name of a particular face, hand, and voice. Say "Daddy" and see what happens: the smile, the coo, the caress. If there is no one to be so named and summoned and clung to, the infant thus deprived may some day become a man who can do theological-conceptual wonders with the notion of fatherhood, but he will have missed the heart of the matter. In the infant's world, the question is not whether Daddy exists and is good. The question is whether Daddy's presence and goodness can be trusted.

The homely illustration is not intended to dispose of the possibility of using *belief* to make strong and important reality claims. This can be seen by stretching the illustration in several directions.

One. "Where is Daddy now?" Answer: "He has gone away but he still loves you." Rejoinder: "I don't believe that." Question: "You don't believe what?" (Not a very bright question, under the circumstances.) Answer: "I don't believe Daddy loves me." Response: "O, of course you do! Why do you say Daddy doesn't still love you?" Answer: "Because he went away and has never come back."

Obviously this child is not questioning the fact that Daddy has left him. He does not believe that the absentee Daddy still loves him. Perhaps he will believe again when the gifts and letters arrive, but only if he first believes that they come from his real Daddy rather than from a near liar, however loving that liar may be.[1]

Two. "Daddy doesn't love me because he just spanked me real hard." Answer: "O my dear, Daddy did that *because* he loves you." Rejoinder: "Then if I love him I should hit him back." Answer: "Dear heavens, no! Daddy spanks you only when you have been bad." Rejoinder: "But Daddy just *did* something bad—he hurt me."

Here the child is being asked to believe that his father is doing what is good for him, no matter how much it hurts. The child is not likely to believe that if his father never does things that feel good to him. Daddy is the known doer of some evil—spanking, frowning, or withholding goodies. He can be credited as *being* good only if he is known to be the *doer* of some good. It will not do to simply allege that Daddy, in fact, is the doer of all good.

Thus being a Christian means believing that God, the Father in heaven, "the Maker of the heavens and the earth," has through Jesus Christ made his goodwill toward men and to this person, oneself, abundantly, plainly, wonderfully, and practically known. So if one believes this, one ought to be prepared to act appropriately. Indeed, believing it is presumably the sufficient motive for characteristic action; that is, "doing good to all men, so far as in you lies." This is the appropriate way of relating (expressing) what one believes to be true of the ultimate world to the experienced world.

It does not follow from this that the full or real meaning of the metaphysical beliefs of Christianity is an oddly disguised ethical command or endorsement. If I ask, "What does God require of me?" I am Christian insofar as the answer to that question strikes me as being different in kind from what I require of myself, but different also from what Aunt Maud or President Ford requires of me. Even if it appears to me that God wants me to accede to Aunt Maud's unreasonable demands (which of course might make me wonder how well he knew her) or to the President's (which might make me wonder how well he cared for the nation), I cannot learn that either of these is the manifest will of God by asking Aunt Maud or the President. Each will have reasons for answering my question in the affirmative. But I ought not to be persuaded by anything other than a *religious* reason, which cannot be a general prudential consideration, such as it is a good thing to obey the Aunt Mauds of the world because they generally know what they are talking about or because they can hurt you in a variety of ways if you disappoint them. The only adequate religious reason, no matter from whom or what it comes, will be of the general form: The God in whom we believe as Christians commands us to do good to all people. Therefore, I shall have to see whether Aunt Maud's commands, or the President's, can be accommodated to that. In the meantime I can hope that Aunt Maud will overcome the habit of talking as if God worries more about her welfare than he does about her gardener's—or mine.

3

II

Why do theologians so badly want Christian belief extricated from the integuments of metaphysical beliefs? One answer to that is that "metaphysical" triggers melancholy memories of the Gospel in servitude to prideful philosophical systems that owed nothing to the Christian tradition except some choice linguistic expropriations—Hegelianism, for example.

There are other quite different answers, such as an interest in tidy logical housekeeping. That is to say that Christian beliefs ought to be carefully sorted into different baskets: (a) intelligible and convincing, (b) intelligible but no longer convincing, (c) unintelligible but persuasive, (d) unintelligible and unpersuasive. Now suppose widely influential philosophers declare that metaphysics *per se* is (d). What a terrible handicap that theology is saddled with which recommends a budget of metaphysical beliefs! It would be better in that day for theologians to be left only with (c) as the (rotten granite) rock of their salvation!

It may also be argued that metaphysical beliefs are not that important compared with other elements of Christianity, such as ethical sensitivity or aesthetic creativity.

Moreover, there are conceptual systems more congruent with Christian interests than the pseudocognitional traditions of Christian history. Suppose, for instance, that the cognitional traditions of the church were never more or other than what we now perceive them to be—expressive symbols rather than assertorial propositions about the objectively real world.

III

I propose now to sort out these theological views of metaphysical beliefs with the following schematism of motives.

(A) *Defense of the faith.* The essential calling of the theologian is to provide reasons for accepting the prime Christian beliefs as true.

(B) *Exposition of the doctrines.* The essential calling of the theologian is to lay open the consciousness of the Christian. Thereafter one must decide what language forms now express most adequately this consciousness. Here the theologian eschews arguments calculated to show that

4

Christian beliefs are true; for how can one consciousness be more right, be said to be more true, than any other? Specifically, if the Christian consciousness has now become secularized, there is nothing to be gained by any theological efforts to regain the lost continent of supernaturalism. The burning question is thus: What Christian beliefs, attitudes, and commitments are most appropriate for life in a secular civilization?

(C) *Rationalization of the Christian vision of the world.* The essential job of the theologian is to delineate the Christian worldview. It is possible that relatively few people adhere to this view at present. That is a sociological issue. The theologian's concern is to show that the Christian outlook is both coherent and pertinent to the human situation, no matter what oddities abound in secularistic interpretations of the situation, and no matter how persuasive those oddities may be.

It is reasonable to expect that the motive that turns out to be dominant in a particular theological performance will be closely related to a particular diagnosis of the situation of religious belief. Would a theologian set out to defend the faith if he believed that the faith was no longer pertinent to the situation of this world? I doubt it. But one might suppose that the mind of the age was sadly darkened by persuasive errors, and one might, therefore, seek to show how Christianity confutes these errors and floods the mind, thus freed, with salvific light.

Such an undertaking could as appropriately come under (C) as under (A). Where precisely it will fall depends on whether a theologian supposes that the persuasive errors of the age are ideological. If they are, the times might yield to a superior ideology.

On the other hand one might suppose that the decisive errors which grip contemporary spirituality are largely failures or corruptions of the imagination. This great faculty of the soul can be redeemed only through a rebirth of images. Accordingly the Christian faith should be set forth and supported as a worldview, as a vision of man's place in the world and his ultimate destiny, as a master metaphor or organon of metaphor. For this purpose the development of a coherent conceptual scheme is at best secondary. It is true that this sort of theological enterprise would have to be defended against the Barthian indictment of all worldviewing as contra Gospel, a view shared by Bultmann. I do not offer that defense here, but it does not strike me as being a superhuman task or one conceived in horrid pride. Perhaps such indictments just have to be endured as reflecting the settled opposition of one type of theological motive to any other.

It is not necessary, and it is probably wrong, to make an irreformable or exclusive commitment to any motive schematized above before we are clear about what making a case for a religious belief amounts to. It has been theologically fashionable for some time to say that an authentic Christian faith is nothing for which a case needs to be made nor can be made; perhaps because such a faith is God's gift, or because cases traffic with objectivity and other spiritual evils. But these considerations are adduced to support either a theory or a belief, and are themselves factors in or of a case. Of course this ought not to count against their being seriously considered. But none of them, and nothing like them, counts against making a case for the Christian faith.

IV

What then is meant by making a case for a Christian belief? Consider (though it is not a uniquely Christian belief): "God is our refuge and strength, a very present help in trouble" (Ps 46:1). This is a Christian belief if Jesus Christ is believed to be the supreme demonstration of God's "very present help."

We must, therefore, specify the context or situation in which making a case for this belief is useful, necessary, or unavoidable. Such a context is not hard to recall or reconstruct. Someone says, "I called in vain upon the Lord."

> O my God, I cry by day but
> thou dost not answer; and by
> night, but find no rest (Ps 22:2).

It may be said that this powerful outburst is itself an expression of faith. The psalmist is obviously firing off one more flare before he goes under.[2] And he is firing it in God's direction. But there is more to his faith than a despairing final salute to the being who is responsible for his predicament:

6

He has not despised or abhorred the affliction of the afflicted; and he has not hid his face from him, but has heard, when he cried to him (Ps 22:24).

God has answered the cries of the faithful. He will do so again; and always. But for the moment God is silent. Therefore, my soul is cast down.

This bit of Old Testament faith is instructive. All around the faithful there are those who say, "Where now is your God?"

My tears have been my food day and night, while men say to me continually, "Where is your God?" (Ps 42:3).

If the psalmists's faith takes these unbelievers into account, the case advanced to aid him must also do so. Indeed the case may, in part, be intended for the unbelievers—or at least for the fainthearted. In any event, what is the case?

(a) Though God is not answering at the moment, I am still calling on the name of the Lord. In more general terms, belief in God, as above manifested, is the beginning of its own case; only selectively affirmative evidence will be permitted to accrue to its accreditation. Only help from God can count as a reason for believing he is the "very present help in time of trouble." But why will not *any* sort of help count? Surely the believer ought to be theologically generous enough, as well as sufficiently hard-pressed, to credit God with whatever gets his faithful servant out of the bind.

(b) No, this will not work. The believer ought to count as evidence only what he can recognize as from God's hand. Otherwise the unbelieving taunter can very properly retort: "You say it is God who restored health, happiness, and prosperity to you. I say it is luck, pure and simple. I see nothing holy, or even anything ennobling, in the recovery of your health, prestige, and bank balance. Certainly you are much better off than you were. You are not for that a better man. Come to think of it, you are rather worse, for now you are more than ever convinced that you are God's darling."

So the epilogue to Job is much sounder than the crude pragmatism the unbeliever so roundly rejects. True, this prose anticlimax to the profound drama of the book would make some people acutely unhappy if they were not convinced that the epilogue was written by some unknown theological hack upon whom the true meaning of the essential book had been wasted. In the epilogue God himself rebukes the theological hounds who have been harassing Job in his fierce struggle to hold on to his faith.

And my servant Job shall pray for you, for I will accept his prayer not to deal with you according to your folly; for you have not spoken of me what is right, as my servant Job has (Job 42:8).

Then, of course,

the Lord restored the fortunes of Job, when he had prayed for his friends" (42:10).[3]

Does this mean that part of the case for Job's belief in God is his readiness to do God's bidding, even if it means asking God to remit to his "friends" the penalty for much bad and tedious theology? This is possible. We might, therefore, profitably ponder the fact that Job's fortunes were restored because he prayed for his erstwhile pious tormentors. Surely that is keeping faith without a vengeance.

(c) It is legitimate to generalize from the Job case in this wise: *The justification of the belief is really the justification of the believer.* This invites the inversion: If the believer's action is a good one, or is actually the only appropriate one, his belief is justified, his case is made.

If this holds, it holds even though the benefactor (Job) and the beneficiaries (the friends) do not agree on the criterion of appropriateness. It holds even though they do not really agree that God legislates that criterion. Superficially, Job and his friends seem to believe in the same God, but what they say, in turn, about God's justice, renders that theological agreement doubtful. Perhaps the divine reproof brought them around. God made his own case: they were prayed for by one truly righteous man though they did not deserve such grace.

This is a shift toward something so formidable that we must look at it carefully. It is simply the believer's conviction that God has given him the clarity and charity to perceive a good for others and the power to do it.

8

But why should we not say forthwith that the believer merely *believes* he has these gifts, this wonderful help, from God? Indeed, a more deadly reproach seems amply warranted: "Hallucinations! You hear God telling you things 'out of the whirlwind' (Job 38:1) when in fact your obsessions were hyperstimulated by that cyclone last week. You see God opening his hand—but since when does your God have hands? It is bad enough to believe the impossible. It is much worse to claim to know what isn't really there."

Now perhaps this imaginary unbeliever needs to be a bit more aware of his own philosophical (metaphysical, indeed) prepossessions. These have induced him to deny the possibility that the believer can make a case on the grounds that the belief at stake is unworthy. It is unworthy for either (i) any reasonable person or for (ii) a really modern person. But in either case the unbeliever would hardly be doing more, in his critique of belief, than expressing a need for a case to be made either for rationality or for modernity. We shall have to look into the possibility of making such cases; and into the very curious belief that a case for either (i) or (ii) is or can be a case for the other. In the meantime there is nothing wrong in allowing the believer to tell the unbeliever what he (the believer) credits as God's help as long as this does not seem to beg a whopping epistemological problem, that of recognizing God in his helping. God is the strong deliverer. What is his deliverance? God is the divine healer. When is health God's gift?

(d) The believer looks to God for a clear perception of good and for strength to pursue that good through thick and thin. For the Christian this means that if it is God who opens his hand to the believer, the good in and of it must be an association with him that comprehends and transforms all good in all things. If God delivers from evil, the evil thus overcome must have been a threat to that divine community rather than merely something that makes life precarious or discomfits the spirit. So also, if God gives health, it must be a normality and fertility of life that enables the believer to move ever farther into the richness of that association with God. "Thy kingdom come . . ." All particular askings presuppose this as their absolute foundation. To say that nothing matters except life in and with God is to say something that falls short of the full biblical affirmation, which is: If the life in and with God fails to matter for a person, for any person, then nothing else can rightly or really matter for that person.

Thus the case the authentic believer is committed to making assumes the form of a personal justification rather than simply the vindication or verification of a truth claim. But this justification is not so much a matter of being proved right in holding to certain beliefs as it is of being warranted in holding to a course of life.

(e) So the case submitted to the unbeliever, or to the fainthearted, is something like a policy: the outline of a course of life. The policy is to look to God for the decisive indications of where association with him is now available. The believer cannot tell *a priori* how this will look to the unbeliever because he does not yet know how inclusive that unbelief, or that faithlessness, is. The unbeliever may be the fool who says in his heart, "There is no God" (Ps 14:1). But he might also be the fool who puts everything into ever bigger granaries to house, as he hopes, ever bigger crops (Lk 12:20). The first fool will not acknowledge anything **as** a good or even plausible case for believing in God. He may even deny that he knows any instances of believing in God. The second fool may very well believe that God somewhere and somehow exists, but he does not believe that God demands anything important or costly of him now, or perhaps ever. So for him faith in God is a matter of a friendly attitude toward conventional religious teachings and practices. It does not occur to him to wonder whether his life is on a collision course with the living God.

If then the two kinds of unbelief are quite different, it is not likely that the believer will find, or ought seriously to look for, one case that would be appropriate for both. Suppose he were to present to the first kind of unbeliever—the philosophic atheist, say—reasons that are presumably clear and cogent whatever the course of life may be. That would be tantamount to demanding that the believer should stand aside from the course of life he believes springs from and leads ever deeper into association with God and enter into an arena in which reason alone is sovereign. How can he do that without betraying his belief? How can he do that without compromising his belief that God alone, rather than reason, is truly sovereign in his mind and spirit as well as in cosmos and history?

V

The air is full of theological protests against this sort of religious self-falsification. But there are also deep suspicions that to refuse this demand is to expose irrational commitments, the curse of which is not mitigated by benign attitudes or by actually being kind to everybody, including fools of all classes.

These suspicions ought not to be treated as though they were hardly more than manifestations of surly and petulant minds. Theologians have sometimes flaunted the irrationality of true faith. Others have argued, or at least asserted, that rationality is there but is discernible only to the eyes of faith.

In the following chapter I shall try to show that reasons for adhering to a worldview (religious or otherwise) are not in themselves viable reasons for preferring one metaphysical system to another. I shall also try to show that the inverse of this proposition is also true. Thus, "proving God" is not necessarily an abandonment of faith. But even a miraculously successful proof for God, such as Anselm confesses he prayed for and found,[4] would not justify a course of life intended to carry one ever deeper into association with him.

Chapter Two

❦

ON SEEING GOD AND PROVING
THAT HE EXISTS

I

I do not understand "seeing God" to be a linguistic fragment of mysticism. Nor do I here suppose that mystical experience is the most vivid moment of religion or the most interesting for philosophical-theological discourse. "Seeing God" is proposed as a shorthand expression for a comprehensive construal of life and the world as belonging entirely to God. Thus "in all things Thee to see" (George Herbert) is to interpret all things as compact of divine purpose. Therefore to praise him is, so to speak, a material inference.[1]

This is not to deny out of hand that there may be persons of preternatural acuity who are able to catch a glimpse of the back of God as he passes by (Ex 33:23), or to whom a more full-bodied vision is granted by supernatural grace. Indeed for the blessed in the world to come there may be direct vision of God through which the enjoyment of his goodness and beauty is raised to perfection indescribable to or in this gross world here below. Nevertheless the Christian life here and now does not rest upon a preternatural acuity; nor is it entirely or predictably sustained by the hope of the beatific vision in the kingdom of glory. The "heavenly vision" (Acts 26:19) in this world has a mundane quality rooted in the being of the human creature. That is, the flat necessity of walking by faith, not only in communion with God but generally in whatever really matters.

Theological principles aside for the moment, this means that seeing God is not an easy human performance nor is it a predictable human achievement. Whether or not seeing God, thus understood, expresses a native need (whether or not this creature is *homo religiosos*), any interesting and powerful expression of such an appetite demands considerable effort. Not that we are looking here to establish as true the proposition that religion is a painfully constructed and precariously sustained enterprise, though that is the case. The matter at hand is simpler than that. Seeing God requires a great deal more than looking out upon the world and back into oneself. One must indeed look very attentively, and long and hard. But that is not because God is likely to slip past in the general confusion. The fact of the matter is that weaving everything together into a concrete interpretation of life and world requires an extraordinary effort of the human spirit. A concrete interpretation cannot be simply excogitated; it is not like a theory or an hypothesis. It is an actual course of life designed and projected to tie life and world together as an offering to God.

II

Seeing God in all things is to think of a worldview, a vision of all things together as they really are, and, as well, of the ultimate state toward which they are all tending.

Here we must brace for heavy seas. It will be objected: (1) This makes faith (understood for the moment as belief) virtually identical with an aesthetic achievement. (2) Worse still, what place is left for God's free word laid upon humanity, or upon some special people, as both a divine command and an authentic knowledge of God?

Certainly there are other protests against what I have proposed. These two are enough for the moment. So to them.

(1) This I do not find to be a fearfully crippling blow. It often reveals a prejudice indiscriminately applied against the aesthetic realm and the truth power of the imagination. Kierkegaard is often summoned as a decisive witness against this double-jointed prejudice because in one version of the "existential dialectic" he seems to have located the aesthetic a goodly distance south of the religious, and, for that matter, below the ethical. But we have a right to protest that in philosophical theology nothing can be decided by appeal to authority. So here one is not permitted to say that Kierkegaard (or Kant or Hegel, Aristotle or Wittgenstein) has proved x. If x is something that can be proved, then one must simply try to prove it. If one cannot do that, or is too busy to do it, or has doubts that x is the sort of thing that can be proved, well and good so far. But if x can be proved, if it is open to proof, then the contract cannot be

farmed out. If it is farmed out, then the best one can say is: If A (or SK) has proved x, then . . .[2]

Hence, Kierkegaard may or may not have scored heavily against the aesthetic mode. That hardly matters here. For we ought not to be too ready to write off the aesthetic enterprise as an amiable or terrifying embellishment of life and the world. Nor should we supinely accept the coaching of others to the effect that imagination is to be viewed as the mother of trivial make-believe. Art can be prostituted; an artist can not only sell himself to the highest bidder, he can make a fortune depicting the mess of pottage for which he relinquished his proper heritage and vocation. And who can seriously doubt that imagination can be divorced from reality? But where are all such somber reflections supposed to lead us? To the temple of science? Science can be harnessed to damnable diabolical evil. Is there then some primordial unspoiled truth and wisdom in common sense? It is hard to believe there is, so easily does it lose its way in the shadows of superstition. As for religion, it can be riveted to mass delusions of grandeur and it can saddle us with unrelievable guilts.

These tragic corruptions of life and spirit do not well argue the abolition of religion or art or science or common sense. Of each it is fair to say: "Don't judge the enterprise itself by the excesses or the deficiencies of particular practitioners."

Another cautionary note is in order. We ought to quarrel with any move to render worldviewing as entirely or essentially aesthetic. The vital center of worldviewing is concern for the good in the great scheme of things entire. That is the singular merit in the disjunctive classification of all worldviews as optimism or pessimism. Looser use of "worldview" makes much of distinctions between idealism and materialism, naturalism and transcendentalism, science and religion. Such distinctions head for metaphysics. Eventually we ought to attend to them, but for the moment the primitive distinction, optimism or pessimism, is fundamental, for in it we try to grasp and express what the world is up to for goodness' sake, and what that has to do with us.

The prime instrument for these purposes is *image*. The world is a kingdom. It is a game of chance. It is a machine. It is an organism. It is a theatre. Each such image expresses a conviction, bathed in hope or despair, about the place now and forever of value realizations, human and other, if other there be.

The Christian faith, then, is a worldview. It is a massive appropriation of a political image: the kingdom. The entire scheme of things is a realm in and over which God reigns, supreme and unchallengeable. And the fate of all value realizations is sealed into his perfection of wisdom, goodness, and power.

(2) But what honest and eminent place is thus left for God's free word laid upon humanity? If Christian faith, so far as it is belief, is a worldview, what becomes of the grand traditional conviction that faith itself is God's free gift? Some of the most powerful theological voices in recent times have reacted with evangelical vigor, perhaps with pious horror, against worldviewing on the grounds that it abandons the absoluteness of revelation in favor of a human creation, all too human, sprung from human need.

The religious motivation perceivable in this protest is worthy of deep respect. The view itself, the doctrine, is logically awkward: it appears to claim for itself a privileged position in relation to any actual or conceivable challenger. I do not mean that it has to be so crude as the flat assertion, "X and only X is true because any and every not-X would make X impossible." Yet the protest can easily lead us to forget that theological methodology is concerned with the humanly describable conditions of theological intelligibility. If, therefore, someone says, "God alone renders his revelation, and perhaps all things else, intelligible," this is *prima facie* a statement about God. It is testimony also to the self-actualizing of God's revelation.[3] Testimonies of that sort are not, and rarely purport to be, statements about the right ordering of theological operations. Indeed I do not see how any instruction for theological operations can be gleaned from such testimony except by divine inspiration. It is surely fitting and proper that theologians should ask God to guide their efforts. But the rationale of their efforts ought to be visible even to the unbeliever. So we ought not to confuse the longing to stand blameless before God with an interest in fashioning a theological position impregnable to philosophic assault.

Moreover, to say that the Christian faith is a worldview does not so far commit one to any particular account of the ultimate authorship of the dominant images thus employed. No logical anomaly is evident in saying that these images are God's gift; they might even be said to be the very substance of revelation.[4] But I should have to say that the import of such claims is not transparently clear. Does it mean that such images ought to be treated with the highest degree of circumspection, as though they were ikons? Or does it mean that the prime images of the faith can be trusted to reorder human life and the world as they ought to be? An affirmative conviction here does not entail a denial that human powers are engaged in the process somehow. But it does not follow, either, that only human powers operate in these great transactions in human experience that carry the force and value of revelation.[5]

The proper conclusion of these reflections is that as methodologist the theologian does not make ontological claims. It is not up to him as methodologist to lay out the structures and powers of being. As methodologist his exhaustive concern is with the structures, rules, and warrants of Christian theological discourse.

Does this mean that as methodologist a theologian is not entitled to convictions and theories about being? Hardly. He may in fact devise a method to show that being is accessible only as this-and-that and not as thus-and-so. But it does not follow even from the most wonderfully successful of such demonstrations that being itself is not or cannot be both this-and-that and thus-and-so. One thinker or another may think ill of being for such lack of discrimination, but others will applaud such grand inclusiveness.

Nonetheless the methodologist must practice some kind of metaphysical-ontological restraint lest he be overpowered by the charge that he has simply defined and structured his enterprise to accord a clear and certain victory for his metaphysical beliefs.

III

A provisional distinction has been drawn between image and concept in the interpretation of the Christian faith. I do not intend here to review the remarkable theological development of image in theologians as different as H. R. Niebuhr (as in *The Meaning of Revelation,* New York: 1941) and Austin Farrar. I propose, rather, to make some more primitive observations about the distinction, image-concept.

The first such observation is that theology as such is a secondary rather than a primary religious language. Thus theology itself is a conceptual enterprise. It does not tell a story or weave a fabric of images under its own license. Rather, theology is a way of reflecting on the story and construing the images of faith. This is not to say that there are no conceptual elements in primary religious language—that of prayer, song, celebration. Such conceptual elements as appear in these activities are largely ordered to the life of the imagination, to its attendant feelings, and to designedly practical dispositions of human energy. Thus in traditional Christian worship much is made of *God*, here italicized precisely to suggest a conceptual element. This does not mean that the Christian at prayer supposes that the direct object of this activity is a mere idea. Someone else, a Freudian psychiatrist, say, or a philosopher sailing under his own colors, might theorize that since there is no God, or at any rate no God who (which) can hear and heed prayers, the pious can only be addressing one of his own ideas; or his own private version of a corporate idea, so to speak.

Here we can hardly help but take notice of the ancient question whether the pious would go on praying if they knew as much as the doubters; that is, if they entertained the metaphysical and/or scientific theories of the doubters. We know that some people continue to talk to deceased friends and relatives. Generally, however, they have little hope or expectation of hearing from the decedents, otherwise they would be posted for therapy; or they might be moved along to the parapsychologists. Moreover, who does not know how slowly various habits die even when their owners admit there is no good reason to preserve them? Yet the dead were once alive, and otiose habits might once have made sense; whereas if God is now a mere idea, or if religion rests on such a metaphysical illusion, then *God* must always have been a mere idea, and the pious must always have been deceived. If the pious were prepared to admit this they would surely abandon the prayer of petition. Meditation, meditational prayer, or contemplation hardly require an attendant or attentive deity.

I realize that I have presumed against that species of radical theology which makes ample provision for a God who has lost his ontological shirt, or his voice, and lives on now either as a mere idea or as an absence. I should think that it would make scant difference to such a being whether he lived thus in the minds of the naïve pious or in the minds of the unbeliever, though as Anselm observed so craftily so long ago, the unbeliever must have *something* in mind when he says, "There is no God."

I return now to the simple main contention: The praying person believes that God is one sort of being rather than another, and this belief is logically anterior to the prayer itself. When one prays, the conceptual factor is probably latent or tacit. But it can be activated by a variety of things. One of these is the skeptical query: "Do you *really* think that God hears your prayers?" The pious do not necessarily construe this critical charge as an occasion for specifying the conceptual-cognitive factor after the manner of, "Our God surely does." But this response is neither atypical nor inappropriate. The skeptic's retort to this, "But how do you know that?" may elicit the response, "That's what we have always been taught." Here a certain type of skeptic will simply give up the game as hopeless, that is as hopelessly lost by his opponent. For us the matter is not so simple or neat. We have to note first that in the affirmations and responses of the pious the conceptual element has not broken into the clear but is moving in that direction. Then, secondly, we must note that it is the business of the theologian to carry this movement of and toward the conceptual the rest of the way.

But to what proper end? The proper end of this conceptual specialization is essentially practical. It is the amplification of the power to see God in all things and thus to participate in the superabundance of his being. There are other objectives, to be sure, such as arming piety against the assaults of unbelief or against the seductions of other faiths. So there is a kind of theology for which the subtitle may well read: How to make the Christian faith triumph over doubt and rival religions.

Surely, though, there is another and far loftier objective of theology. That is to discover and propagate the truth about ultimate reality. This must be the first and highest aim, the divine responsibility of theological thinking.

So it is, of that theology which Aristotle called first philosophy and since then has been called metaphysics. But in dealing with Christian theology we are dealing with a definite and particular religion, as we would be if the enterprise were Jewish theology or Islamic theology. This does not mean that there is a kind of truth rightly called Christian, and another Jewish and another Islamic. What then?

Then a commonplace: Each religion has its own conceptual elements contained in its own cardinal beliefs. And each has its own way of relating the conceptual factors both to religious experience (life in the religious community) and to the generalities of experience (life in the world).

In each case these ways of using the conceptual factors in religions are so many truth-functions, so many routes of inference running from the community of faith to the generalities of experience, the world. Whether any or all of these truth-functions must be responsive to demands, made by one set of believers upon other sets and by unbelievers upon all of them, to appear for trial before the bar of reason as such has again become a lively and perplexing issue. I refrain from pursuing it here for the time being. Here I reiterate that the primary goal of that theology called Christian is to amplify the power to see God in all things and thus to participate in the superabundance of his being.[6]

But how can so prosy and monochromatic a thing as conceptual specialization aspire to serve productively so glorious an end? Within the folds of piety this is not an artificial or academic question. There theology is often charged with dealing altogether in abstractions. I take it that this is a particular form of a pervasive conviction that the intellect, mind as such, has no power to produce or amplify concrete value.

But conceptual specialization ought not to carry the freight of mind as such or the intellect alone. Even if intellect is the Martha in the Christian religious economy, she has her ordained part therein and things go badly without her.[7] Thus theological concentration on the concept *God* is assuredly not calculated to give piety a real object for the first time. The theological task is more modest than that. It begins with pointing out that the concept *God* has a dual function. (1) It exercises—or it ought to—an indispensable coherence effect upon and among the concrete (the lived, the felt) details of the religious life. For seeing God in all things calls for a unique combination of discrimination and recombination of the actual and ideal entities of experience. Of discrimination, because *God* is not a religious-metaphysical name for any finite entity, actual or ideal. Of recombination, because *God* is not a religious-metaphysical name for the ordinary being together of the entities of experience.

(2) A second element of the theological task is to show how the concept *God* exercises—or ought to—the greatest possible congruence effect upon the diverse powers of human agents. The end of the religious life, to participate in the superabundance of God's being, is Christianly formulated as a promise and as a command. A promise: God makes and will make the infinite richness of his life available, which only he can do.[8] A command: Human life is to bring its powers, whatever their present

shaɓe and condition, into congruence with God's righteous, all-inclusive purpose.

Nothing is to be gained by confusing these two functions of the concept *God*. Nothing is to be gained by aggrandizing one at the expense of the other. No task of theology is more important than monitoring the performance of a Christian community as it tries to keep coherence and congruence in healthy interconnection. (Perhaps that might be called the Christian dialectic?) This cannot be done without conceptual specialization.

IV

There is a rather different way of identifying the primary responsibilities of theology. That is, that theologians ought to give top priority to justifying the cognitive claims of the faith. On this view the theologian must above all show what it means to aver: "I *know* in whom (what) I have *believed*." The clear implication of this is that to know God is presumed to be a higher and far more demanding achievement than to believe in God. I propose now to make this presumption the order of the day.

In the first place, this attitude is powerfully reinforced by the great cognitive achievements of the modern mind. From this eminent tutor we have learned that we ought to view with profound doubt, if not with lively hostility, any clinging to *belief* where *knowledge* has been or could be won; this even if an item or piece of that knowledge raises havoc with a cherished value sustainable only by a false belief. So where this tutor *non pareil* presides there is great reluctance to esteem highly any forms of spirituality that are clearly rooted in belief alone, to say nothing of those forms that make a virtue out of unknowing. In the light of the enormous advances of knowledge in the modern world, who can honestly and coherently countenance consigning ultimate issues to mere belief?

Secondly, the presumption that knowledge is, over all, a more honorable estate than belief draws weighty support from current anthropological doctrine. There is, to be sure, a hint of another sort of presumption in calling it a doctrine rather than a (mere) theory. I mean the principle of man's essential unity with nature. For the contemporary version of this doctrine is very largely dominated by scientific-philosophical mechanistic convictions. Which means that *purpose* in human activity must be as much an illusion (indeed the same kind) as the imputation of pur-

20

pose to the spiraling galaxies or to the mathematically patterned dance of the electrons. Indeed this dismissal of the category of purpose is widely held to be beyond cavil, as an item of knowledge.

There is something odd in this situation. The ancient versions of that anthropological doctrine (the unity of man with nature) made rational knowledge, thus knowing-for-certain, an intrinsic element in man's native estate, from which *belief* is therefore a declension. Thus reason itself is divine, that through which alone normative humanity is able to come to perfection in actuality. But the modern version of that anthropological doctrine has no place for this kind of transcendentalism. Reason is now understood to be but a linguistic overlay of intelligence. And intelligence is an instrument for adaptation to the environment, an instrument widely disseminated in nature. But why should the spider's use of intelligence in weaving its web so cunningly—and soundly, by engineering principles—be laden with metaphysical import? And if not in the spider, then why in us?

Now we must ask what the reduction of reason to functional intelligence means in respect to *certain* knowledge, to truth. Should we say that is certain, really certain, which is indispensable for science? But are any of these indispensables, any of these incorrigible convictions, empirical observations or the logical entailments of such? Or should we settle for a softer answer: The real certainties are what most scientists are now largely convinced are true.

These questions are not intended to bring down the proud towers of scientistic presumption from which one can survey the vulgar hordes of mere believers below; which, of course, include the multitudes of those who merely believe that scientists know what they are up to and that what they are up to is good for all of us. The point of such questions is, rather, to discern what is being asked of theologians when they are pressed to show what is *known* about God and his affairs, and not merely what is *believed*. For instance, are theologians supposed to come forward with clear and detailed metaphysical manifests? Or would it be fairer simply to ask them to furnish clear and accurate methodological maps whereon the routes from real belief to putative knowledge are laid out and properly identified? Let us consider these options.

First of all we must remember that until quite recent times overt metaphysical doctrines were regarded as lost causes—well lost, in fact.

They were supposed to wither and die in the pure fierce heat of logical positivism. And for a while it was both high and vulgar fashion in theology to celebrate this demolition of metaphysics. "Thank God!" one heard. "No more of *that* stuff for theology."

Now it appears that the obituaries were published prematurely. Philosophers continue to discourse on "what there is," and without profuse apologies for doing so. Too, metaphysics as a descriptive rather than a speculative enterprise is having its innings. Moreover, metaphysical beliefs—call them dispositions, prepossessions, presumptions, what you will—lived on through the high season of dedicated antimetaphysics. Of these none was or is more ubiquitous or more sturdy than the aforementioned conviction that man is nothing but a complicated chunk of nature, and that the complications are not really man's doings; they are inherent in the complexities of his neural-genetic inheritance.

The times, then, are not entirely unpropitious for Christian theologians to take metaphysical stands right out in the open. I mean theologians besides the Thomists, who until very recent times have never wavered on the central importance of metaphysics for the work of theology.

But now which metaphysics? And how much of it? Is it reasonable to expect theologians to devise metaphysical schemes? When did they ever do that with any notable success? Who besides Aquinas has consciously made significant—that is, for philosophers—alterations in a metaphysical system adopted for theological uses? Not the Hegelianizers in the nineteenth century. Not the Personalists in the twentieth. Not the current Heideggerians. Perhaps this story illustrates one of the limits of St. Paul's principle that the Christian evangelist must be all things to all men.

The vexatious and formidable quality of such questions may have something to do with the attractiveness of the second option mentioned above; namely, for theologians to produce methodological maps, on the assumption that such maps do not, or ought not, conceal metaphysical deposits.

But does this mean that theologians ought not to attack, or even frown upon in public, the antitheistic metaphysical presumptions coursing about the contemporary scene? Should theologians agree that it is professionally unseemly to say to such presumptions as "Come now, reality surely isn't like that at all," simply because the methodological obligation is to map routes of access to reality in order that any assertion about reality, or unreality, can be understood and appraised?

There is something odd and disquieting in that sort of methodological hygiene. For how do we understand something to be a "route of access to reality" if we have no notions about reality itself? To take a humdrum example: Is it at all sensible to speak of a variety of roads to Rome unless one knows (a) there is a Rome, and (b) where it is; and *knows* in a sense stronger and more useful than "at the end of all roads leading to it." Of course we can imagine someone planning or building a road in the hope that it will lead to Rome if there is a Rome and wherever Rome may be. But this is the stuff of fantasy.

On the other hand there is a bewildering and altogether vexatious abundance of notions about reality. Practically speaking, we must say that no one can take them all seriously. Some of them, for instance, are *prima facie* absurd. Whatever is so perceived is ordinarily rejected on the strength of a predisposition to believe that reality, whatever else it may do or be, does not put up with patent absurdities. Or perhaps we reject absurdities because life is too short to invest it in determining what among a vast array of implausibilities and incredibilities might be proved to be both intelligible and true—or, even worse, true but not intelligible.

Here at last is a hint of resolution of the initial hostility between methodology and metaphysics. If methodology is dedicated to devising and testing routes of access to reality, we do not, and indeed we cannot, suspend every metaphysical belief until all the reports are in; provided that, relative to any belief, we are willing to distinguish between our depth of attachment to it and generalizable grounds for holding it or being held by it. Conversely, no matter how deeply entrenched a metaphysical belief may be, nobody is so supernaturally immune to error that the modality of display of such a belief, whatever it may be, cannot be faulted and perhaps corrected by methodological inquiry rightly conducted.

Suppose, then, that one says: "I believe X and cannot do otherwise, so help me God." It is possible to learn that one's statement of X is faulty, but faulty as a language-and-logic performance rather than because reality does not permit access to that X. For example, suppose I say, "I believe God loathes perfidy." Here, it may reasonably be said, *God* (concept or image) functions to reinforce my disapproval of perfidy. But this *God* function is not monistically absolute because I can surely also mean that God is the supreme instance of a perfidy-hater. And I can then say that if God loathes perfidy, I had better look at my own behavior, for it might turn out that God thinks ill of high-sounding talk that is falsified by low-lying action.

Methodologically the denial to *God* of monistic absolute privileges means that the testing of religious beliefs necessarily includes dimensions of existence beyond thought and language. In the religious life the form given to practical activity has vital, indeed central, importance as a route or modality of display of meaning and truth. So my convictions about perfidy hardly prove there is a God who holds all things in full survey. But, believing in such a God, my failure to eschew perfidy as an option for myself creates an unmistakable dissonance in a life presumptively ordered by *God.* We ought, therefore, to suppose that habitual promise-breaking should cast a heavy pall of guilt over a life led by one who says, "I believe God is absolutely faithful," and who yet persists in acting as if faithlessness in promise were an open option for himself. If God is wholly faithful, I do not have a religious option of using *God* as a sanction or justification for treachery.

Perhaps enough has been said to show that neither metaphysics nor methodology can be relieved of the necessity of proving something or other to be true. We have now to deal with the variety of ways we undertake to prove things.

V

Hardly any philosophic cliché has enjoyed greater currency or sanctity in Christian theological circles than this double-barreled one: Trying to prove the existence of God has no place in authentic Christian life; and the God of the philosophers is not the God of Abraham, Moses, and our Lord Jesus Christ.

The principal reason for mentioning this hardy, dull-hued perennial here is that it reflects an important and interesting variety of predispositions, both philosophic and religious. Of these the most important for present purposes is the deeply entrenched belief that proving something to be a conceptual necessity does not fashion any footholds in reality, because life goes one way and logic another. Or in terms somewhat less bromidic, proofs may be *valid* but they can never be true *per se.* Thus, to return to "Start," even if any theistic proofs were valid, there is no way of certifying them (it) as true in and for faith.

Picking quarrels with clichés is not the most rewarding or engrossing business in the world. The stakes here are high enough to encourage us to engage this double cliché because it reveals massive confusions about proof and proving. Perhaps it would be more generous to say that this double-jointed cliché provides an occasion for looking into the phenomenon of proving.

First of all, then, to prove something is to test it for its value (*probus* means "good"). Thus ore is assayed, land titles are "proved up," and Christians are enjoined to "test everything; hold fast what is good" (1 Thess 5:21). The faithful are counseled not to "trust any and every spirit [but] test the spirits to see whether they are from God" (1 Jn 4:1 NEB).

So even in general usage, to prove something means to uncover or establish its true or real nature, be it good or bad, on the assumption that its true or real character is not sufficiently clear or certain on its face. It might be plausible (would it be worth the effort of proving if it weren't?) but it might also be specious; and its deceits might prove very costly.

These common-sense necessities and procedures illustrate another feature of proof and proving: the heavy role of criteria; that is, of tests and measurements the validity and decisiveness of which cannot be intelligently questioned. Thus to the systematic skeptic's assertion (suggestion?) that all assertions can be (ought to be?) doubted, common sense replies that the skeptic himself illustrates a sublime, as well as ostensibly blind, confidence in some instrument (whether of mind or sense matters little) for testing experience and finding it deficient in certainty.

Further on we shall have to look into this ancient and honorable puzzle circling about the status of criteria. I mention it here because preoccupation with methodology can induce one to suppose that methodological certainties neither presuppose nor entail any metaphysical certainties. This appears to be plausible. Might we not be clear and certain about how to test for truth, or even reality, even though all the candidates flunked the examination? But, again, I move to postpone consideration of this possibility, and of the background belief that certainty about methodological principles and procedures does not wait upon or court ontology. For what now demands attention is a sketch of the modalities of proof.

(1) *Demonstration.* Here what is likely to come first to mind is a proof

that sticks; that is, that really and clearly achieves the end set for it. Mathematical models inevitably come to mind, but they do not have sole proprietory rights to demonstration. The proper force of *demonstrate* is to show what is really the case in a way appropriate to what it is that is proposed or claimed to be the case. Thus Descartes' *Discourse on Method* demonstrates something which his *Rules*... does not or could not demonstrate.

(2) *Attestation.* Something may be proved by having a competent person testify that it is the case. It is commonly supposed that proof of this mode falls far short of absolute certainty simply because no human competence is or can be absolute or unchallengeable. To which we generally add: Nor is any human witness (attestor) above corruptions induced or exploited by ignorance, pride, and fear.

The general presumption against the finality of attestation nicely illustrates how good sense and equability can be wrecked by protuberant philosophical prejudice. Why should this sterile specter, "absolute certainty," be allowed to roam without check or challenge over every sector of intelligence, often sending otherwise sensible folk, such as historians, into transports of anxiety over their intellectual status? Surely testimony is sometimes as clear and certain as the interests of a particular context require. True, even there it is not flatly or abstractly wrong to wonder whether the witness might have been mistaken. But we should need to know whether such a doubt were fired by a general conviction, itself incorrigible, about human fallibility or by an uneasy feeling that something in the testimony doesn't quite fit. As we all sometimes say, "There is something odd about the pattern of the testimony," when we cannot in fact, and in some cases have never been able to, fault any particular fact claim in the testimony. We had a feeling that it was all there but it was not all there altogether correctly. Such feelings sometimes turn out to have been irrational but right. They are sometimes rational but wrong. Which means that sometimes we ought to look into the odd matter of saying that any sort of *feeling* is either rational or otherwise.

(3) *Explication.* Something is proved by making fully evident what it is, by "unpacking it," as we are now wont to say.

There is a commonplace difference between explication and demonstration. Explication ordinarily has a conceptual object: I seek to explicate the meaning of a theory or of a belief; I must render explicit something until now tacit or unexpressed. On the other hand, demonstration is as much at home in nonconceptual or low-conceptual matters as it is in conceptual ones. People demonstrate their affections; they demonstrate against war and all manner of evil. But they explicate their notions, beliefs, axioms.

There is another distinction. Explication accommodates a greater range of content than either demonstration or attestation allows. Demonstration is controlled by determinate passions, axioms, and principles. Explication, on the other hand, as a process of disclosure, may involve inference-tracking. To the degree that inferences must be tracked through the actual world they cannot be simply or entirely controlled by antecedent or logically anterior axiom or principle. This means that the contingency factor in explication is more than subjective. If, on the other hand, I am really surprised by the formal implications of my own propositions, I had better stay indoors until I am familiar with my own axioms, theorems, and rules. But as I track inferences through the actual world, I may come upon novelties in the dense interrelationships of things, that is, things not at all clearly sponsored by my anterior principles. Why, for example, do metals behave so strangely in very cold temperatures? A satisfactory scientific answer to that question involves mathematical proofs. These proofs would be cognitively valueless if someone had not followed an inferential route laid down by the data.

So the venerable cliché, "the actual world cannot be deduced" is partly right; but partly, and accidentally, since it overlooks the remarkable range and combination of proofs used to poke at the world.

(4) *Elucidation.* Something is proved by showing that it sheds light on some aspect of experience or of the world on which illumination is generally and deeply needed. Thus, in St. Augustine's thought divine truth illumines the cosmos and the human spirit: God is the one through whom all things are known. But this light is too pure, too overpowering itself in its brightness, to be directly perceived. Accordingly there must be some reason other than direct perception or intuition for accepting the truth of the doctrine that God is light unapproachable, eternal and all-fructifying.

I cite St. Augustine's view because in a fairly large class it enjoys a lofty eminence, at least in terms of historical influence. In recent times we have been hearing more and more about explanatory principles and paradigms that are themselves opaque; or, if not quite that, at least underived, logically primitive.

So it is quite possible that an instrument of elucidation is less clear, both perceptually and conceptually, than what it succeeds in illuminating. If so, we have been carried far from the shores of truth either as correspondence or coherence.

It may be profitable to consider other members of this strange class of things that make sense of the world but are not themselves objects of sense-making operations. Consider here what Collingwood[8a] called the "absolute presuppositions" of a cultural epoch: the concepts and propositions by which a particular order of life is defined and sustained. These are not the fruit of induction, they are not grand summaries of experience, they are grander than that by far. Put in Kantian language they are the bedrock—or transcendental—conditions of intelligibility. As such they cannot but be true, but true in their own way. They are not just valid, for that is a formal virtue. They are true in and for the world, but only true in and for the world they define.

But these sublime taken-for-granted principles have had many misadventures in history. They have moments of terrific incandescence, then they begin to fade. And in fading they become vulnerable to criticism, and finally to rejection. Then they are seen for what they are: yesterday's absolutes, our fathers' gods or those of some other strangers. Which means, of course, that a new sun has risen and dominates the scene, a new god reigns.[9]

Picturesque language sometimes camouflages disquietude and dismay. So here. Can *truth* come and go, ebb and flow? Beliefs, yes, and all manner of values ("time makes ancient good uncouth"). But surely not truth! Why should we set at nought the ancient wisdom: whatever is really true is true forever and ever.

The trouble is, as we all know, that none of the candidates for that supreme distinction seems to qualify. Or they arrive at the summit as truisms with very low candlepower. To paraphrase the New Testament: If light no longer illuminates, how should it be treated?

As a classic theological case in point take God's will. There have been cultural epochs for which God's will was endowed with supreme power of elucidation. Not that mere sinful mortals then presumed to divine God's will from the inside, so to speak, or from up close. Calvin has the great weight of the tradition on his side when he declares that God's eternal decrees are known only by him, though their effects taken together—the whole order of creation, the whole march of redemption—are clearly knowable in and through faith. So even if theologians agreed to pay God metaphysical compliments (to use a phrase of Whitehead's), such as declaring God to be rational through and through, they agreed also that rationality of that magnitude of power and clarity and coherence cannot be apprehended by the likes of us.

On these terms, the concept, *God's will*, is confessedly opaque: there is no way to throw light upon that which throws indispensable and ultimate light on all things else. Yet so far as *God's will* does that, it is true. It has been proved.[10]

But not once and for all. How much elucidatory power does *God's will* have in a spiritual climate, in a cultural epoch, inimical at the top to any kind of teleological explanation of anything whatever?

History warns us against too hasty answers. Thinkers heavily laden with mechanistic principles may yet give a civil salute to *God's will*. But hardly any modern philosopher has drawn so heavily for cosmological-epistemological purposes upon an absolutely arbitrary divine will as that rationalist-mechanist, Descartes. And in popular culture *God's will* has persisted as an instrument of elucidation. To believe that someone's life is divinely ordained, however humble its place in the visible scheme of things, endows it with fixity and surety of value. It is a great thing to believe that all of the great passages in life and history are divinely intended, be they bane or blessing, even though God's reasons are totally beyond us.

For my thoughts are not your thoughts, and your ways are not my ways. This is the very word of the Lord. For as the heavens are higher than the earth, so are my ways higher than your ways and my thoughts than your thoughts (Is. 55:8,9 NEB).

This makes great and good sense so long as people believe God's ways are indeed higher than our ways at their best, rather than brutally different from ours at their worst.

Then a time comes when *God's will* fails to throw any steady or significant light upon the world.[11] When that happens God is no longer perceived as "the true light that enlightens every man" (Jn 1:8), itself so bright that no creature can bear to look directly into it, but rather more as the bottomless dark. Then *God's will* survives as a linguistic tag to be attached or not, as a personal pet or preference, to any item of experience, to any event, cosmic or trivial, though the whole thing seems without rhyme or reason.

This phenomenon—this slipping of an instrument of elucidation from majesty and power in and over an entire society, into an amiable linguistic residue, and thence into a final dead and deadly darkness—all this reads as though it were a recurrent chapter in the life of the human mind itself. Perhaps it is. It might also be supposed that in seeking a principle or a paradigm of elucidation that will ride out every storm of history, the mind works against itself as well as against the "grain of reality." But why is it that we press on to see all things in the light of "the Light of lights" rather than being content to accept provincial paradigms, low-wattage illuminations, as the best we have—and perhaps deserve? Is it that we have to see something absolute that is universal and necessary even in cultural relativity? Must we not suppose that the theory of absolute presuppositions applies to all cultural epochs? Or is Collingwood's theory good only for this moment, this cultural epoch? Could Hegel possibly have been right in declaring that the fate of mind is to live in and through (though not for) self-contradiction until finally it comes to itself in ultimate clarity? But then we ask: Why Hegel rather than St. Augustine: "Our hearts are restless until they find their rest in Thee."

Questions, questions . . . Another one, we hope, will not break the camel's back. Who (or what) is it that presses on for the Light of lights? Many fine thinkers (as well as multitudes of lesser lights) of the present age are content with provincial and provisional paradigms, and with knowing that they are provincial and provisional. Contentment, however, is a psychological matter. Many things can be done to achieve and preserve it, such as refusing the invitation of the absolute and thereafter averring in all seasons that all truths are contingent and corrigible—except *that* truth from which nothing substantial or fructifying flows.

There are other ways of arriving at paradoxical resolutions of the conflict between universality and provinciality in the instruments of elucidation; if, that is, paradox is ever a resolution rather than a hung jury. I forebear considering them here in order to ponder another law of history, another chapter in the strange career of the mind itself.[12] Once an elucidatory paradigm has been left behind by history it cannot be resuscitated. The loss of candlepower is irreversible.[13]

So we ought to know what to make of theological efforts to revive "God talk" when *God* no longer elucidates experience and the world. If the currents of history flow only one way, any effort to reverse them, or to swim upstream, is bound to fail. Why then cannot the church learn something from Constantine's eccentric nephew—and one of Gibbon's heroes—Julian the Apostate, who tried to return Roman culture to the proper service of pagan deities after his great and glorious uncle had committed the empire to Christ? Ah, but Christ had become the irresistibly encroaching sea and Julian a noble but demented Canute. Now secularism is the invincible sea and the church a dismal Canute.

If the revival of "God talk" is thus doomed by the laws of history to fail, it is equally inevitable that we should ask for whom has the light from the Light become dim and doubtful?

Social scientists have been working on that and kindred questions. I wish to take note of a somewhat different mentality, namely, that committed to speaking of cultural epochs, ages, each with its dominant light, none of which is "really real"—the true, perfect, and absolute "Light." Thus ours is the age of secularism. That by which this world, this moment of history, is illuminated is a set of incorrigibly provincial presuppositions that invincibly prevents us from looking beyond or through the perimeters, the horizons, of nature to a greater and more enduring world. Prevents *us:* the forward-looking, the deeply and truly perceptive, the philosophically with-it generation.

It comes to this, then. One either acknowledges the regnant conditions of intelligibility, of sense-making, and commits oneself to them; or one is left farther and farther behind, eventually to move, if movement it is, in dim and brackish eddies far from the creative currents of history.

Truth to tell, the eddying crowd is not perfectly homogeneous. It includes conservative theologians and Fundamentalist preachers. It includes also several species of rationalists. And, of all things, a sprinkling of empiricists for whom scientific method (rightly understood) is the Light of lights—and a plague upon historicism and all its chatter about epochs and ages.

Perhaps the moral of this is that misery loves company, no matter how ill-assorted. But there is another possibility: the demand of truth is a genuine universal, and it will not finally permit a confession of provinciality to stand as a substitute for overcoming it. At least in principle, that is, with (or at least toward) a paradigm of the Light from which all light streams, a principle of elucidation that can be said to be opaque simply because the human mind has and can have no leverage upon it. For that simple and absolute failure there are many explanations, such as original sin, a divine jealousy of divine prerogatives, the ontological situation, or Goedel's theorem. All of these explanations are provincial; every one of them is a provincial explanation of a universal condition. There is no cure for that condition short of heaven. It may be that heaven does not design to cure that either.

So we do not need to quarrel with socioscientific generalizations about the elites and the multitudes who profess now to be unilluminated by "God talk." There is little reason to suppose that God's will has gone dead because the mind of the age looks elsewhere for fundamental and ultimate illumination. The chances are that that mind is simply an empirical generalization parading as a provincial absolute.

Why then has, if it has, the light from the Light dimmed so remarkably? It is possible that *God* is not being properly construed in "God talk." There may be a systematic, or at least general, conceptual miscueing in contemporary Christian teaching. People may be looking to God for things inappropriate to *God.* They may be confusing gods with God. They may, in St. Paul's sufficiently vivid phrase, be making gods of their bellies—their gonads, their orgasms, their take-home pay.

There is, then, something instructive in the problematical slogan, "Let God be God!" The slogan is problematical because if God truly exists, nothing has or could prevent him from being himself or from doing entirely and purely as he pleases. But of course this means: if *God* is adequate to that reality which is truly and absolutely God.

Hence it is appropriate to ask anew whether there is a route by which *God* can be restored—in defiance of history, if you will—to elucidatory power. As a Christian I cheerfully confess that this cannot and will not happen unless God so wills. But humanly regarded, the necessary condition for learning what God wills is a readiness to act for the realization of a human good. Indeed, a persistent readiness, a disposition—very likely a predisposition.

Thus another modality of proving God heaves into sight.

VI

(5) *Confirmation.* In the hard sciences nowadays confirmation is the best thing, in the truth line, that can happen to a scientific hypothesis. No longer, in those quarters, is the air filled with heady talk of proof.

This development might induce Christian theologians to say to the scientists, "We are well ahead of you fellows in dropping *proof* from the truth business. Proof is the business of mathematicians (and of distillers). Where the great interests of life are involved, the routes to reality are fundamentally different. They cannot be reduced to pure conceptual clarity or to abstract logical precision. For what do mathematicians have to do with reality?"

But of course the people in the hard sciences, in making the linguistic turn to *confirmation,* do not see themselves as jettisoning either logical rigor or empiricist methods. So they may have some reservations about accepting the inference that they, too, properly belong to the club of thinkers who have learned that the real world does not submit to proof.

On the other hand there is surely something to the conviction that beliefs of the profoundest existential import must submit to appropriate testing procedures, precisely because of the magnitude of the stakes. There is no *prima facie* reason, once we have seen through appeals to the mind of the age, for trying to adopt the canons and procedures of the sciences for these purposes. Yet the range and weight of the interests involved in religion demand more, surely not less, of rigor and integrity in "testing all things" in order steadfastly to adhere to goodness and truth.

Confirmation in the religious life is a kind of testing for those high ends. It is a mode of proof comprised of four functions.

        (i)   Counting-for

        (ii)   Vindication

        (iii)   Reinforcement

        (iv)   Justification

These all bear on that kind or element of religious belief identified as worldviewing. Worldviews contain conceptual elements. They may include theories, both cosmological and anthropological. But concept and theory are there for existential purposes. For the great functions of worldviews are to illuminate the context of life-choices, to reinforce fundamental and ultimate commitments, to justify life-policies, and to rectify the course of life when that is necessary and possible.

This is a crude summary of the existential purposes impacted in worldviews. Great as these are, and imperious as their pressure is, there is another sort of interest in or about worldviews: What leads us to accept one of them as true? For no matter how salutary may be the effects of adopting a given worldview, history teaches us, or at least warns us, that illusions may be benign and practiced deceits, amiable for the time being.

(i) So one of the functions of confirmation is to determine what counts for an outlook—counting-for. What in the experienced world bears out that viewpoint? Thus, making a case for the Christian outlook means seeing whether the experienced world can be Christianly construed without effacing the lineaments of the world or distorting experience. So suppose we say, for example, "God is love"; and then proceed to say that "God is love" entails for the Christian "Love is the only way to live." Or: "I must be rightly loving to all kinds of people in all circumstances and situations." This does not mean that the latter proposition, that practical inference, that eduction of a life policy, is *the* meaning of the first one. In imputing a quality or an attribute to God I may or may not be engaged in establishing either a directive or a warrant for acting along that line myself. Some action or some disposition may indeed be entailed, but not necessarily the same or even an analogous one as the attribute specifies in God. Thus in saying that God is wise beyond all description I (properly) intend that he should be worshiped, not (directly) that I should be as wise as possible. To be really wise is surely to worship the all-wise God. But that intention is not *the* meaning of "God is all wise."

Then is there any strong and clear sense in saying that when I learn (come to believe) that "love is the only way to live," the Christian outlook is so far confirmed? Does my intention to live lovingly (as that is specified by the New Testament, say) count for the outlook, Christian, which includes "God is love"?

That depends on what we take counting-for to be. If we take it to be a social rather than a subjective test, counting-for will include recommendations, endorsements, and, very likely, prescriptions. Consider a general (nonreligious) situation: A asks B why love is better than hate. To give his question some high muzzle velocity, A cites testimony from the Nazi concentration camps that a deep and pure hatred for the oppressor seemed as sustaining as forgiving love. To this B replies: (a) Life at large ought not to be construed with the metaphor of the Nazi concentration camps; and (b) a firm policy of hate puts one at odds with the nature of things and with the divine intention. To this, in turn, A rejoins that such noble sentiments, such high falutin' ideas, are simply B's beliefs. No, B replies to that, not just *my* beliefs, nor just *beliefs* if you take *belief* to signify something like a hunch or supposition. For "God is love" is something that can be tested. A funny kind of test, no doubt, because it requires the construction or the discovery of a set of interpersonal relationships best described as loving, or at least not at all like hate and hating. So our readiness to relate to others in love and as loving counts for the truth of "God is love." It goes to show that the Christian outlook, that part of it anyway, is true.

Here A says: All right, *but only true for you.* To which B answers: True for me, yes, but that means *true for persons.* In all the things that matter most truth must be personal.

This suggests that persons, the really human world, rather than propositions or beliefs, are the chief objective of religious proofs.

(ii) Vindication makes this even clearer. The tests of experience are calculated to determine whether the believer, and not merely his outlook, can be vindicated.

Vindication injects the element of vicissitude into confirmation. More particularly, vicissitude as personal trial; existential anguish, we should probably now call it. One form of this: the mind of the believer may be harrowed by the possibility that his most cherished beliefs are simply and entirely wrong. There is another form of vicissitude, a deeper and fiercer anguish, that attends being harassed, scorned, hated, and rejected by a world so far lost in sin and error that it calumniates God as well as persecutes his people, and all with impunity for the time being. The psalmist is taunted by the unbelievers who say, "Where is your God?" So he says:

How deep I am sunk in misery, groaning in my distress:

And what is his existential resolution?

yet I will wait for God; I will praise him continually, my deliverer, my God (Ps 42:11 NEB).

What would constitute a vindication of this impassioned and embattled believer? Perhaps a stupendous cosmic event would do it—the heavens opening and hordes of wrathful angels descending upon the wicked, unbelieving and oppressing world. But cosmic events can be indiscriminately violent. Abraham bartered the Lord God into allowing a righteous cell to escape the otherwise total destruction of those monuments of urban iniquity, Sodom and Gomorrah. The righteous have not always been so potent an advocate of the innocent in the cataclysms of nature and the terrible vicissitudes of history.

The psalmist has a different answer to the question about his vindication. His answer makes very modest demands upon the Lord God to administer the forces of nature and the energies of history for his immediate and dramatic advantage. He will continue to praise God, his deliverer. He will go on waiting, faithfully.

Does this mean that the believer is vindicated by his perseverance in vicissitude? That depends on what he believes and, in believing, is committed to. If he believes that God is "the rock of his salvation" in a dry and thirsty land, he ought not to be daunted by the deserts of life. Whether or not they are created and positioned to test the faithful, when they trap him on all sides, he is confirmed by continuing to praise the Lord, the rock of his salvation. This desert does not make him believe that the world is altogether a desert; nor does it persuade him that "God" is but a name for his terrible thirst.

But suppose that the desert kills this pilgrim, he dies of thirst. What more radical disconfirmation of his belief could there be? How could we mercifully or conscientiously say that God was his deliverer when in fact the poor wretch was delivered to such racking torment ere he died, and to a death satisfying only to the vultures? If this pilgrim persisted in his beliefs to the end despite the overwhelming evidence—pitiless sun, trackless sand, merciless delusions of oases—must this perseverance not be counted as a fatal flaw of character? Not so fast, not so ready with such a conclusion. The desert killed him, not his character, not his beliefs. And since all men die, and most suffer betimes, how shall we say that death, and vicissitude short of death, *counts for* any worldview except pessimism? How shall we say, for that matter, that the varied and relentless evils of the world count against any affirmative worldview? The native drive of life, of being itself, is to persist; though of course the pessimist thinks ill of such a habit. The native drive of spirit is not just to persist but to make the best of life; though the pessimist may think that the best thing to do is make an exit. These native thrusts of being and self-being put it to us so to construe all things together, good and evil, that life may abound and spirit may rejoice all the day long.

So before we pass any summary judgment upon the desert-struck pilgrim (who is Everyman in some season of the soul), we ought to be sure that this forlorn wayfarer believed that God would surely spare him that particular death. No doubt he so hoped. But beliefs are not always liquidated when cognate hopes are frustrated. Why would we say that nonetheless they ought to be?

So perhaps our thirst-racked desert wanderer acknowledges that he is to die in that desert. Yet he believes that God will continue to take care of him, dying and dead. All things are in God's hands, a falling sparrow, a dying man, a cooling universe.

But in what way is this relentless believer vindicated? Do we not wonder whether there would have been far more of intellectual honesty in a gesture of defiance, however feeble the gesture, against his cruel fate? Perhaps some final obscenities or blasphemies scrawled in the sand and soon to be obliterated by the indifferent winds and the tracks of the vultures. Would we at least not be better served if he had used that last breath of life, that last wisp of consciousness, to confess that his beliefs had been as fantastic as the mirages which shimmered so cruelly before him?

Such wonderments and speculative concerns share a spectrum with more traditional views; they define one band of it. For the tradition, the ultimate vindication of this paradigmatic pilgrim lies at the end. Not his end but the end of it all. In the great beyond, at the last judgment, in heaven: then, and not until then, will Standfast be vindicated. In the meantime (which often seems to be an eternity), Standfast must learn to

37

be patient under the vile abuses of natural circumstance and the contumely of unbelievers.

Here again we are on the verge of confusing believing and hoping, this time from the affirmative rather than the negative end of the spectrum. But a shift of sympathy does not entail or warrant, of itself, a shift of logic. So far, then, as believing is taking something to be true and entrusting oneself to it because it is true, a believer is vindicated if he does indeed stand fast no matter what. That is, no matter through what thickets, swamps, and deserts that route runs. "He kept the faith to the bitter end" does not guarantee that the faith, abstractly defined, was worth the candle, to say nothing of the auto-da-fé. We need, we always need, to know what else Standfast was committed to by faith, what besides holding on to the very end.

Now perhaps Standfast, our desert wanderer, has a question or two for his theological critics. Suppose he asks: "Why do you always suppose that only yea-sayers are particularly vulnerable to the destructive vicissitudes of the world? Why do you skeptics and nay-sayers think that you fare better than I in the selfsame world? You skeptics don't want to make any philosophically inexcusable gestures of generosity toward the make-up of the world. What are *you* afraid of? As skeptics you surely don't believe that reality is lying in wait to expose and humiliate any such generosity of gesture. What then? What other, and in your record more serious, reason do you have for keeping your beliefs, your outlook, so closely hauled to what you call fact? Perhaps your eyes are fixed immovably upon the signals of your philosophic soulmates. But is it legitimate for free thinkers to be so incorrigibly other-directed?

"O yes," Standfast continues, "I hear you go on and on about the vital importance of lopping off superfluous beliefs. That used to strike me as being splendidly businesslike, tidy, and tough-minded. But I asked you once what rendered a *religious* belief, or any other combination of vision and disposition, superfluous. And you said, 'Well, the fact is I just don't *need* the beliefs you entertain, that's all.' So it came home to me that though you called yourself a skeptic you hadn't, in fact—to use one of your favorite phrases—moved all belief into suspension. All along you have been operating with a view of yourself as ego, as human, probably as modern man—with some kind of an omnicompetent belief. You trust absolutely in your ability to manage, no matter what. So it isn't just that you don't need God. You believe you don't need God even if there should be a God.

"Now for you nay-sayers: What positive beliefs animate your rejection of religious belief? What behavior of the world confirms your beliefs and vindicates your existential self-investments? You say there is no God because *God* is meaningless. And you construe this denial to entail that the only value agent in the cosmos is man; if indeed values have any 'reality.' What sort of commitment to human values is entailed by that? What kind of experience would vindicate that existential investment? What kind of experience would vindicate a refusal of that engagement? How is it that so irresolute, frail, and fickle a creature as man is to be greatly loved and trusted? Or is he? Surely you don't mean to say, 'Well, if not man, then what?' That would strongly argue that one must, simply must, love and trust something. From there it is a short leap to 'Believe what you must in order to make sense of your life policies and loyalty packages.'"

The intent of the foregoing is not to encourage the Christian believer to suppose that he has no unique and vexatious problems in proving his case. The point is, rather, that a time comes when any steady or deliberately continuous life-performance must submit to the question: Why this life-performance rather than that? The general form of any serious and responsible answer to that question is: Because that is the way I saw and assayed the world and thus set this course through it.

VII

In whose sight does one seek vindication, whose other than God's? These seem to be the leading candidates for that high position:

(a) An ideal (not necessarily) divine observer; such as (a1) one's ideal self; or (a2) an ideal other.

(b) The "beloved community," the ultimate (in finite terms) peer group.

(c) Any reasonable and well-informed person who has similar value commitments.

I believe that (c) is the heir apparent and presumptive. When one seeks self-vindication the "beloved community" is presupposed but it is not intended, because one of the things requiring vindication is one's participation in the life of that community. Thus the dialectic runs something like this: Granted that believer and unbeliever share certain fundamental values, the unbeliever wants to know how Christian beliefs bear on those common value concerns. The believer ought to reply that the Christian community is held to the pursuit of those value aims by a particular structure of beliefs. True, one can esteem justice and resolutely pursue it without giving a thought to God and his righteous will. But the question is not whether believing in God is a necessary condition for esteeming justice and seeking to realize it in the actual world. That question requires empirical data, though perhaps not a simple empirical adjudication. The question, rather, is whether vindication for believing "God is just altogether" is not forthcoming until (unless) it can be shown that a practical dedication to the cause of justice is congruent with the "way things actually are." This is fundamentally different than saying that the believer is vindicated so far as he acts or is disposed to act on belief in God's justice.

So once again the methodological fat seems to be headed for the metaphysical fire, for what is the route of access to "the way things actually are"? Particularly, how can one speak with any reasonable assurance of justice, not only as the direction in which the human world ought to move but as the course it is actually pursuing, even in seasons when numberless multitudes of the oppressed cry in vain for succor, divine or human? It is only in and by faith that one can reasonably and resolutely take the stronger line here, because it necessarily involves an envisagement of the future. For the Christian this envisagement necessarily is a concrete adumbration of that future in life-policies and commitments resolutely adhered to here and now. So to "walk by faith" means to move one's flesh and blood toward justice. It is anything but filling the air, the long-suffering air, with pious surmises about the glories of heaven while one stumbles heedlessly over the bodies of the wretched of the earth.

VIII

(iii) *Reinforcement.* Belief is tested for truth by discovering whether a large and central purpose is reinforced by it. If a belief fails this test for confirmation, there is no point in saying that it may be true in and for some other world.

The supreme purpose of the Christian is the imitation of Christ. That is the decisive clue to the concrete adumbration of the future. That is what it means to so glorify the kingdom of God that the vicissitudes of life and spirit in the kingdom of man become intelligible and endurable.

Reinforcement, as a religious test of truth, involves Christian community more heavily than vindication because the stake is clearly being sustained in the faith of that community. The objective is no longer the esteem of that reasonable person for whom one tries to make the case for Christian faith. Not that his esteem has become a negligible interest. It matters deeply, but now as a condition of communication rather than as a medal of achievement in the arena of philosophic contest. What now matters far more is whether the Christian community will so sustain one's commitment to Christ that "growth in grace" becomes a reality rather than a linguistic tag generously distributed as a good conduct medal or a merit badge. Beliefs that do in fact provide that sustenance, that reinforcement, have passed a particular test of truth. By itself it is not paramount. It is one link in the chain of proof.

IX

(iv) *Justification.* This is the ultimate stage of confirmation.

In the traditional (Pauline) sense, to be justified means to be incorporated into Jesus Christ: the believer is taken up into that divine being, power, and righteousness. Moreover the person is incorporated just as that person exists; which is to say as finite, mortal, and sinful. So to be justified is to be unconditionally affirmed by God. One is justified by that One for whom all things are possible.

Thus the vital core of confirmation is what St. Paul calls being conformed to the mind of Christ. This condition transcends infinitely, so to speak, the natural human desire to be proved right in some high contention and to be found acceptable by those whose acceptance matters most in the quotidian world. Now justification means being wholly caught up in the only game that finally and absolutely matters.

But note that it is no longer important at this stage to prove that this is, in fact, the only game that finally and absolutely matters. That incontestably human interest has also been transcended; not forgotten but transcended. The imitation of Christ, which is a commitment to adumbrate here and now, in the quotidian world, the ultimate community, the kingdom of God, the commonwealth of divine love; this becomes all-engrossing. Only thus is it possible to prove that the unlovely and unlovable are nonetheless actually loved; that is, by loving them, by seeking with them a common and ultimate good. To identify oneself with "harlots and publicans" for other reasons, such as showing that we are all human after all, imposes one's company upon people who have not asked for it and who may not be able to profit from it because it carries the virus of self-righteousness.

Therefore, the commandments to visit the sick, to minister to the dying, to feed the poor, to be in the midst of alienation in its infinite variety—these good works are done for sweet mercy's sake, to be sure. But they are to be done above all because justification restores one to the body of generic humanity in the only way that finally and absolutely matters: in creative love.

X

One of the most poignant illusions of the philosophic life is the belief that somewhere there is a perfect proof for (or against) something of immense significance, an absolutely cogent and convincing demonstration that X is (or is not) the case. Theologians are not immune to the sting of this will-o'-the-wisp; St. Anselm, for example.

There is a related phenomenon of equal, probably greater, poignancy. That is the disposition to submit not only one's beliefs but one's life to tests one is bound to fail. I do not know whether the framer of that famous injunction, "Test all things . . ." was sufficiently aware of the immense threat it presents to the tester: that, in the ultimate affairs of the spirit, the tests are all trained on persons rather than on propositions and concepts, on the believer rather than on beliefs. Gripped hard and fast by the vicissitudes of being in the world, and discomfited by the philosophical exploiters and advocates of those vicissitudes, belief and believer may not measure up even to the minimum standards of dialogical fair play. True, these are often the failures of the believer rather than fatal defects in his beliefs. But surely there is a real possibility there, too. Surely it must sometimes occur to even the most devout and reflective believer that the Christian worldview itself is wrong.

This is a real possibility if it means that someone might sincerely find that the Christian reading of life and world is false. In what way false? Decisively, for having evoked and encouraged expectations that were not fulfilled, rather than for having supplied the mind with the wrong set of photographs of reality.

So religious untruth emerges as the noncongruence of expectation and aspiration with the form and movement of life in the world.

Untruth of this sort is much too serious a threat to be dismissed with the skeptic's glib "Who knows anything for sure about the real form and movement of life in the actual world?" Metaphysical propositions as such are not on trial here. The target is the certain power of religious belief to mislead expectation and foil aspiration.

I do not find a fair expression of these malfunctions in such transcendental beliefs as immortality. What show of evidence can be mustered on the strength of which such beliefs are to be pronounced simply wrong? Assume that all such doctrines are wrong—that is, are metaphysical errors—and you have a mighty grievance against a society and a church that use such beliefs to obscure or reroute efforts to achieve justice on earth. But such assumptions are not self-evidently true.

A much more telling case is the promptness and thoroughness with which belief in justice as the ordained goal of the human world can be foiled and soured by the multitudinous injustices of history. We ought not to turn this belief into something purely transcendental. But we also ought not to turn the question of a cosmic commitment to justice entirely into an issue decidable by weighing the evidence on some nonpersonal if not nonhuman scale.

The problem, in other words, is the profoundly vexatious one of determining when, or whether, the ethical dysfunctions of human experience ought to invalidate one's belief that justice is a divine prepotent intention of the entire scheme, and thereafter ground one's existential commitment to justice in despair rather than in hope. In respect to such commanding concerns, the validation of the moral agent counts far more than the verification of his claims for the truths of his beliefs.

Thus the falsification of religious beliefs is not something that happens in a spiritual vacuum. It is not the result of an operation conducted by philosophic thinkers whose instruments have been stripped of all metaphysical commitments. Falsification here is a failure to find one's religious outlook confirmed concretely by one's own life-performance. Compared to the gravity of this falsification, the failure of the world to behave characteristically as a soul-making enterprise can reasonably be set down as a second-rate failure.

Why should one want to deny that these falsifications occur? Or that their possibility is one of the vicissitudes the person of faith is summoned to endure? God is surely not properly praised by trying to render human insight inerrant, human loyalty incorruptible, human courage steadfast. The Christian has no stake in denying that his belief in God might be wrong. He seeks justification for his commitments to living persons, the final and absolute commitment of love. So how can he be sure that it is right and good to die for others, when to take steps to preserve his own life would falsify his avowals of love for them no matter what?

Well, a question for a question: What kind of certainty ought one to seek, let alone claim, as the rational underpinning of such a commitment? Should we propose a variety of reality tests, such as an inspection of one's motives or a determination of the worth of the intended beneficiaries of one's death? Should we invent a calculus of benefits to be conferred by one's death, the question of the worth or merit of the beneficiaries being waived?

The questions are appropriate. No answer contains a greater certainty than the tests of coherence and congruity rightly applied. The question, "Is it right for me voluntarily to die for others?" is a coherence test if I believe that I ought to love others even to the bitter end. If I really believe that such love is divinely ordained and commanded, and so is much more than an admirable thing in the few who do it, then if I refuse the bitter cup I am surely self-falsified, not just inconsistent, not just guilty of too much slippage of principle under dire vicissitude. These, yes; but also and decisively self-falsified.

Finally, then, certainty about the proposition "God exists" is different from certainty whether I ought to act out love for others to the bitter end. For "God exists" is a shorthand expression of a global outlook. The chief functions of such outlooks are to place human history and personal existence in the cosmic scene, and to throw off hints and clues for existential decisions. In the end, nothing but a consistent readiness to accept all of the personal risks ordained by it, proves such an outlook, such a faith.

Chapter Three

❧

CHRISTIAN FAITH
AND CONCEPTUAL SCHEMES

I

Is the development and use of a systematic conceptual scheme irreconcilable with authentic Christian faith?

This seems to be part of the ground contested by dogmaticians on the one side and systematic theologians on the other. It is said, for instance, that systematic theology, in using a systematic conceptual scheme, inevitably gives that scheme priority over the entire subject matter of faith, including revelation. It is almost as though some human conceptual contraption had been substituted for God himself; though, of course, the systematic theologian has at least a chapter, perhaps a whole volume, devoted to *God*.

On the other hand, dogmatics is surely more than a set of pastoral homilies and private ruminations sponsored more or less by the lectionary.

So if the systematic theologian operates with a privileged conceptual scheme, which he has either devised or borrowed, the dogmatician operates with a fixed hermeneutical method designed to extract from scriptural texts the real, if not the ultimately real, meaning of Scripture as word of God.

Here the impartial observer may ask whether either party supposes that its basic working stock, be it conceptual scheme or a hermeneutics, has any sort of divine authority or sponsorship, since it appears to him that each party has in hand something that displays as many earmarks of human contrivance as the other. "I hear," says he, "that the theology of revelation is not itself a direct bequest of the Almighty. And I might add that the little I know about any sort of theology strikes me as being pretty small beer to be claiming the imperial seal."

45

This naïve chap has a point; alas, it is a pretty obvious one! Neither side in this dispute claims a clear divine warrant for its methodological stance. What then is the heart of the quarrel? It is which side is prepared to let Scripture speak for itself, on the assumption, shared by each party, that Scripture plays a unique and somehow decisive role in revelation. Moreover, each party also confesses that revelation is preeminently God's business and the minds of mortal and sinful persons ought therefore not to lay grubby hands on it recklessly.

Furthermore, it is not a question, in this loud if not always fertile argument, whether one party operates in total freedom of conceptual factors. One has but to riffle through any text in hermeneutics[1] to find conceptual factors galore. The nub of the issue is whether conceptual elements can or should be developed into a coherent schematism with a view to metaphysical business.

If we take Barth to be the chief of the dogmaticians in this century, we have a wonderfully unequivocal answer to this question: a categorical No! Not that Barth has the slightest doubts about the reality drafts of revelation. But in his view conceptual systems cannot break through the crust of the phenomenal world into reality. Nor can such systems transcend the man-referencing of natural reason in all of its cognitional activities. The fact that the church in history has sometimes baptized such a system only shows how far afield the theological leadership of the church can wander from its proper tasks.

If we take Tillich to be the chief of the tribe of systematic theologians, we shall find a remarkably complex Yes in answer to our question; not that he is reluctant to devise a conceptual scheme and deploy it across the spectrum of Christian theological topics. In his view, that is the business of orderly Christian thought whether or not "systematics" is the right name for it. But what is the cash value of the conceptual scheme? For Tillich the schematism does not lay bare or exemplify the very structure of reality. But just as surely he does not intend to restrict the schematism to extracting insights and imperatives from Holy Writ. What then is the third option?

The third option, in the employment of a conceptual scheme, is what Tillich calls ontological: the schematism bears on, perhaps exhibits, the structures of being.[2] But for Tillich's purposes we must say ontological rather than metaphysical, we must say "ontological" rather than *ontologi-*

cal because being is a symbol and not a proper concept; it is "being" and not *being*. So what is grasped by "being"? That question must be rephrased as: What of the human situation in the world is expressed by "being"?

So the Tillichian conceptual scheme has an intuitional-expressive function rather than a descriptive-argumentative one. Dialectic does not move the mind closer to "what is," but it might throw some light on what is in a particular mind in a particular situation: a kind of theological psychoanalysis.

So for both Tillich and Barth the conceptual elements in faith are not valid for metaphysical transactions in the classic modalities. Nevertheless, for Tillich and not for Barth the systematic development of those factors is the preeminently valid route for properly exhibiting the eternal truths embedded in the Christian faith. But these truths are not assertorial propositions, they are not really conceptual. They are symbols.

I do not intend in this connection to travel further into the Tillichian realm of symbol. The thing of greater importance is the ongoing argument over the reality value, not the mere presence, of systematized concepts in Christian faith and life.

Let us suppose, therefore, that there is no significant or interesting argument over whether or not conceptual factors are important for Christian theology, since theology itself is some kind of conceptualistic game. The heavy firing begins with the question, "What or how much is a conceptual scheme good for? More specifically, what is it good for in relation to the Christian faith?"

This puts us up against an antecedent question, namely, how we are to understand *faith* as in "Christian faith." It is much too easy to legislate a fast answer to the question about conceptual schemes by simply saying that faith, the authentic article, cannot tolerate endowing conceptual systems with any proof functions or any other cognitive value.

What then are we to understand by "faith"?

(1) Faith denotes the content of belief. Content of belief denotes statements of various kinds, such as dogmas (propositions a church declares to be altogether true and authoritative), reports of historical events and their interpretation, guides for right moral conduct, guides for the life of prayer. Faith in this first sense may also contain elements of cosmological and anthropological doctrines. For instance, for many Christians crea-

tion, as a teaching concerning the origin of the cosmos, is accepted as a binding truth, that is, as a dogma. But the dogma by itself does not specify what sort of show the world actually is, how large it is, when it came to be, what its laws are, or how many kinds of creatures it contains. Instruction on such matters comes in from secular sources, though theologians may monitor it or even try to control it. Here a very important theological task comes into view, that of showing how the definitive core of Christian beliefs is able to survive in health, clarity, and power the impact of secular knowledge. For example, can a theologian make creation meaningful given the scientific teaching that the physical universe has been around in one state or another for billions of years? That God created the whole thing does not seem logically affected as a proposition by the discovery that the whole thing is incomparably larger and more complex than anybody even imagined before the age of science.

We haven't been hearing a great deal about creation from theologians lately. This might mean that they have been intimidated by the scientific cosmologists. But it might also mean that theologians are not convinced that creation belongs to the core of Christian belief.

Likelihood swarms around a rather different possibility. Perhaps faith is not to be construed as belief or as the content of belief. Perhaps it is nothing importantly conceptual, discussable, and arguable in terms of ordinary experience or the generalities of experience. Perhaps faith denotes an event, an experience, a happening, the presentation of something not even knowable in the ordinary frames and vectors of human knowledge. If it were legitimate to speak of faith having an object, perhaps we should have to say that its object is intuitively grasped and imaginally rather than conceptually expressed.

These "perhaps" statements are not intended as speculative, as though they were so many abstract possibilities advertising for tenants. On the contrary, they sketch where much of Protestant theology is actually living. We then have to take seriously another view of faith.

(2) Faith is, or is something emerging from, a life- and world-transforming experience. In the recent Protestant theological past the standard word for this experience was "encounter." In its theological incarnation this concept retains something of the sense of a confrontation in which a response rather than a reaction is demanded; thus a personal engagement. So "encounter" means being personally addressed or summoned

by God. God reveals himself decisively in these personal transactions. Descriptions of such events will, perforce, be in human words and sentences. The Lord on Mt. Sinai does not make it one of the commandments that he is to be called He-Who-Is-Encountered.[3] But descriptions, explanations, and reflections of the revelatory event are not the direct object of faith, they are not the content of faith. Human words about the event are the medium of interpretation. God speaking is the event itself. It would seem to follow that, faithfully understood, any philosophical-theological worry about the truth-value of *God*, the concept, is entirely beside the point. Only God himself can make anything existentially important out of *God*. This holds for any other conceptual factor in Christian experience.

"Christian experience" in encounter theology, is not to be given a subjectivistic value. But an objectivistic turn is also to be avoided. This is to say that the philosophical (and commonsensical) dichotomy, subject-object, is transcended by encounter. To be personally addressed by God is a transcendently real event. Therefore, it cannot be categorized as other events and entities are. Concepts, as well as every other aspect or element of human existence, must be rendered obedient to God's all-commanding word.

So faith as encounter, as man's role in revelatory transactions,[4] is not a cognitive affair, at least not in any ordinary sense, since for the modern mind a cognitive transaction involves the mind moving around on the "inside" and somehow making authentic contact with an entity or power moving around on the "outside."

It is worth noting again that the theologians of encounter do not say that there are no conceptual factors in the interpretation of revelation-faith. There is, of course, a concept of God *(God)*. Christians do not have the same *God* as Muslims or Rotarians. Moreover, some propositions are truer than others; for example, "God is the transcendently real subject" is truer than "God is an object among other objects."

Very well. But does "truer than" mean (a) better conforms to reality, to "what is"; or (b) is a more accurate report, description, or interpretation of the encounter event? The theologians of encounter surely did not intend that *God* is simply an organizing concept applied to the data of experience. Nor did they propose that "God" is a name applied conventionally and projectively to the best qualities of human subjects or the sublimest moments of experience. To the contrary, the supreme and ultimate Being is himself the criterion by which the truth of all statements about him, both descriptions and confessions, are judged. Taken with one sort of low-flying literalness, this would entail the supposition that God says something like, "Now see here! Once and for all do not ever call me an object because I am always and only *the* subject." This makes God sound remarkably like a theology professor.

Happily a more sober reading is at hand. The grandeur and the misery both of "God" and of *God* are rightly apprehended only in dealing with God. He is the absolute master of all such transactions.

So now we must ask whether the content of faith consists of reports of experiences of God; ground familiar to both mystics and pietists. Or put it this way: Is faith humanly transmissible? And yet another question: If it be so that divine revelation is deep calling unto deep, if it be an encounter that shakes the soul to its foundations, are there any clear criteria that facilitate and warrant a movement from reports of experience to assertions about "what is"? Behind these questions lurks the anxiety that "God" is being used as a name for something that mightily stirs us, and *God* as the concept denoting the class of such agencies.

An important fringe benefit is available if the content of faith, as far as it is transmissible, consists of reports of existential encounters: it protects faith against cognitional falsification. For if, in saying "God has spoken!" I really mean "I am all shook up but in a wonderfully creative way," the cognitive question of truth has become the moral question of sincerity, consistency, and the impact on others of that creativity. And if "I know that my redeemer liveth!" really means "I am in better shape than I used to be, and I hope to be in better shape still," it can be falsified partly by asking others what shape I used to be in. This would be only a partial falsification, or perhaps none at all. I may have intended to report only the shape of my interior life.

Such exemptions from the levies of truth are costly. Part of the cost is the obliteration of a transsubjective reality that engages the faithful in encounter. Moreover, if encounter is to carry the transsubjective traffic intended for it, the linguistic and conceptual factors in it demand some kind of systemization. Otherwise its truth function would be random rather than patterned, it would be psychological rather than ontological, it would be episodic rather than time-inclusive.

I conclude that *encounter* as a category of Christian reflection makes, and must make, solid and affirmative connection with faith (1). Part of the content of faith is a conceptual structure, a pattern or system of beliefs.

Moreover, the situation of the believer cannot be described intelligibly in encounter-revelational terms alone. The situation of the believer is that of standing before God in absolute assurance that it is indeed God and his truth by whom the believer is confronted. But he is also standing in a world that has a unique history, as the believer has also a unique history. These interlocking histories must be assayed by the Gospel, but they are not describable entirely in Gospel categories and images. I may say that nothing of those histories really matters now that God in Christ has claimed me for his own. That does not mean that those histories have become null and void. To be divinely delivered from bondage to the past does not mean that the past has been metaphysically obliterated. I might wish it were so, but the wish is bootless, perhaps sinful as well.

I conclude, then, that the paradigms and conceptualities of faith are designed to relate the believer authentically and efficaciously to his actual situation in the real world. They are therefore more than components of reports of experience. So, in the imitation of Christ, Jesus is the paradigmatic person who probes the depths of creatureliness and exemplifies God's love; not love as a natural capability of human life inflated or extrapolated to infinity, but the love of God, He Who Is.

Thus, the paradigm is the pattern of perfect obedience to the summons and command of God the Father. Accordingly, what God reveals in encounter is something to be enacted. Faith is response to that summons, it is obedience to that command. So we have moved to another interpretation of faith.

(3) The essence of faith is obedience. Better still, it is obedience joined to trust. God is to be obeyed because he can be trusted to keep his promises and his threats. From God come the ultimate life and the final death.

Looked at commonsensically, obedience is something yielded and trust is something bestowed in one's relations to others. I obey because I must; I trust because I will. Transferred to the Christian life this becomes: When God commands, who can refuse to obey (that is, and live to tell it)? But though he slay me I may yet refuse to trust him. So in obeying God we may yield what is due him; but we may do this reluctantly, perhaps churlishly. "I know you to be a harsh master" is the excuse proffered by the unworthy servant in the parable.[5]

Even the theologians who make the most of obedience as the essence of faith must recognize how harshly the concept rings in the ears of strictly modern people. It drags behind it powerful intimations of authoritarianism. These are hardly offset by even the most eloquent assurance that obeying God is nothing like obeying earthly lords and masters. Such assurances fail to reckon with a modern metaphysical sensibility: human life subjected to cosmic principalities and dominations is the wrong, the fatally wrong, image. Is this not an integral part of the secularist bequest? If man is alone, that is, as value agent, as person, in the cosmos, he does not need to grovel before imaginary cosmic tyrannies, be they benign or malignant. If a person persists in doing so, there must be something out of kilter in his psyche.

This does not mean that obedience as a prudential policy in intrahuman affairs is about to vanish from the scene. In fact there may be now a growing disposition to feel that obedience to the law is the first condition of civilized existence. There is a good deal of ambiguity in this. The most vocal exponents of law and order are often the people who have gained the most from the current legal systems and from the manipulation of the rhetoric of obedience; or at least they are the ones who feel, for whatever reasons, most threatened by challenges to the established order.

But this is not the only ambiguity surrounding the concept of obedience. In many of us an intuitive sense survives that the whole creation obeys laws imposed upon it rather than extracted from it. The laws of science are theoretic impositions upon what to the naked, untutored eye is a bewildering mass of disparate data. Yet the spinning molecule and the spiraling galaxy do not obey the scientist. They honor constraints imposed by being: "the law in their members" is not arrived at by consensus of the components. Modern science is marvelously ingenious in cooking up mathematical schematisms for these cosmic constraints. This achievement has been known to lure a scientist here and there into conceiving God as the supreme mathematician—a theological development not anticipated in the Book of Numbers.

Theological appropriations of this sense of built-in constraints, under or with which all things behave, define a very broad spectrum. Of the historical (human) world alone we may well wonder whether obedience properly includes things so diverse as dumbly baring one's neck to the knife of fate and being sensitive to the demands of a self-imposed and self-vindicating moral law. In each case people are likely to say they did what they had to; only the attitude was adjustable. So one dies when the moment comes, though one may choose to "Rage, rage against the dying of the light." But no matter how one then carries on, the light remorselessly fades. So also for the demands of duty. In respect to these, we do not ordinarily try to create the impression that we simply could not have done otherwise. "I had to do it" generally means, in respect to duty, "I couldn't have lived with myself if I hadn't done it." Thus moral constraint is as real as the harsh demands of fate. Granted that they are different kinds of reality, they are alike in exacting obedience.

The great Christian theological masters agree that obeying God is different both from bowing the neck to the axe of fate and heeding the adjurations of duty. It is a poet who sings:

> "Stern Daughter of the Voice of God!
> O Duty . . ."

Many modern theologians endorse the sentiment and so far tend to discover the full content of the divine command in the moral law. This is a significant break with the tradition. There, to obey God includes trust, loyalty, love, and reverence. These are dispositional factors held to be truly personal at both poles, as an expression of the self and an acknowledgement of God's personhood, the proper object of worship. To have faith in that God is to obey him to whom we look in love and awe. In infinite wisdom, he orders the law of the soul of mortal man as well as the immense cosmos.

In this account of faith (3) as obedience there are clearly elements of faith (1) as belief. If, for example, I ought to obey God, I must have in hand some reason for doing so, such as a conviction that God has power of disposal over both body and soul. Obviously I ought to respect the prerogatives and wishes of such a being. Or I may believe that God knows what is best and is everywhere and always to be counted on to bring the best to be. Different from each other as such reasons are, they are both manifestly conditioned by beliefs about God's existence and his nature.

53

On the other hand faith (3) also makes a bid for some of the ground on which faith (2) stands. For if I am to obey God, I must have some actual dealings with him. Otherwise "God" might simply designate some great and perfectible (or at least improvable) value in mankind itself rather than in a being of unimaginable splendor and shattering power beyond the boundaries of human existence and possibility. If "God" and *God* do designate and apprehend transhuman reality, then some appeal to experience is necessary. That experience ought to be something that epitomizes the human condition as well as the situation of the believer: an event, a transaction that is momentous rather than merely memorable.

So also for faith (3). If I am to obey God, I must already have been involved in transactions of such a nature that now I can say I know whom I am obeying. But these transactions are not necessarily extremely dramatic world-shaking events. This is to say that in the Christian context revelation is neither an epiphanic nor a theophanic concept. There may be ecstasies in which God speaks, but these all presuppose an anterior knowledge of God. Thus whatever we want to make of the experience of Moses on Sinai for historical purposes, in the story itself God has had generations upon generations of dealing with Israel. Moses professes not to know whom he has encountered, or at least not to know how properly to name him, which is not quite the same problem. In other words, in the story Moses knows that he is not trying to fill in the blank external cause of an ecstatic experience. He also knows that he is not dealing with some provincial "godlet" into whose bailiwick he has inadvertently wandered. To speak irreverently for the moment, Moses knows he is up against Number One. He has not stumbled over some Baal. Nor has he had a "mountain-top experience" to be enshrined in memory forever thereafter as the moment when he got real religion. He who now commands Moses will not even let himself be properly named. "God" is thus dismissed; but not necessarily *God*. Moses has other things he has to attend to, things other than pausing to mark the difference between a name and a concept. It is a distinction of some importance for theological work.

II

The visibility and specific gravity of the conceptual factor vary from one view of faith to another. It does not follow from the indispensability of this factor that it must be given a schematic character in any view of faith. Nevertheless this may be true. Several things suggest it.

One, if words are used consistently, that is, to denote or express the same things, a schematism so far obtains: a language, or language game, thus appears. Words are not used randomly, they are subject to rules; more properly, their users are subject to rules. Whether or not these rules were originally excogitated by one person on a set occasion does not bear in any way on the systematic character of a language. Its schematisms may strike one as quite irrational ("O those irregular verbs!") but the world abounds with irrational schematisms; some of them penalize us heavily if we presume to ignore them either from rational principle or from mere eccentricity.

Secondly, significant answers to the question, "How much (or what) is a conceptual scheme good for?" do not presuppose some kind of faith or some kind of experience devoid of any conceptual schematism. Each view of faith assigns a different weight to such schematisms, but the series does not begin at zero. For instance, the most ambitious conceptual schemes have been fashioned to open up and vindicate faith (1), beliefs. Sailing under the splendid banner of "Faith seeking Understanding" St. Anselm pushes the frail bark of human reason into the ultimate mystery of God's being and of his redemptive act. Perhaps no one before Barth really understood that Anselm was not all that ambitious, metaphysically speaking. But the most powerful minds of the Middle Ages thought he was; and devoted a lot of energy to furling the sails, trimming the ship, and scanning the horizons for ports of entry somewhat nearer home. But even for those purposes they resorted to conceptual schemes—Plotinian, Aristotelian, or what not—none of which can be said to be extrusions of pure biblical ore. Indeed, even the most drastic curtailment of theology's metaphysical thrust had itself to be defended by appeal to an extraordinarily sophisticated conceptual scheme rather than by appeal to the sturdy instincts of simple piety.

Now, again in our own time, the metaphysical value of the conceptual schemes of theology has been so successfully challenged that "the God of the philosophers" has only a light scattering of friends left above ground. And once again the rationale for putting the metaphysical *God* on permanent leave very rarely consists of appeals to the self-sufficiency of simple devout belief or to the usages of piety more generally. And, of course, very few of the antimetaphysical theologians testify that the true God has told them directly—as they were kneeling in the Prayer of Humble Access, for instance—that Pascal and/or Kierkegaard are right and that Descartes and/or Whitehead are wrong. No, the theologians who celebrate the passing of the *God* of theism have filled their victim with arrows from philosophical quivers. Perhaps this is just another case of God, the providential spirit, turning the wrath of the unbeliever to divine account. Nonetheless, there is a surface oddity in the spectacle of theologians looking to worldly philosophers for decisive instruction on how to do the proper domestic work of theology.

Assume, then, that the metaphysical weight of the conceptual factor in faith (1) has been severely reduced, if not destroyed. Assume, secondly, that this radical reduction in metaphysical value does not produce a comparable reduction in the systematic character of the conceptual factor. What, then, is the new or the residual value to be assigned to conceptual schematism? The protagonists of faith (2) have an answer: Concepts are to be understood as heuristic devices to interpret true piety.

I think it follows that the interpretational schemes of theology, so understood, have no cognitive value in themselves; they cannot be said to be either true or false. Thus the immense weight given to self-understanding in these quarters.

The defenders of faith (2), along these lines, may have views of true piety that do not perfectly accord with grass-roots Christianity. These people are not likely to know offhand what to dance when the theologians pipe existential authenticity. But then they may not have been any less uncertain when they were taught that God is *ens realissimum et perfectissimum* or *actus purus*.

For faith (2) the conceptual schemes of theology are not supposed to apply to transhuman reality. Granted that one does not *encounter* oneself. Nevertheless what one encounters, in the divine-human engagement, falls within the horizons of consciousness. Man's language must therefore discharge a vital function in rendering intelligible the meaning of that encounter.

So theological-philosophical concepts properly interpreted—which is to say, rightly organized and delimited—illuminate human reality.

To be sure, human beings come to be and pass away in a world they never made. We are thrown into this world and we are snatched out of it. In the interval between coming and going, itself the only real time, some people are able to hack out a clearing of meaningfulness. In fact to be authentic one must sense that one is summoned to do just this. But this word of summons does not break the encompassing silence. Rather, the silence is rendered pregnant—for faith. This does not mean that the person of faith knows anything not known to the nonfaithful, if any. Rather, in faith one rises to a new level of self-understanding and, one hopes, of self-acceptance. But why not of self-hatred, self-alienation, or self-despair? Because the Christian takes his stand on love; there he posits himself. He does not know whether in the end—the end of history, the end of the cosmos in its present shape—the winner's crown goes to love. Such metaphysical concerns falsify the legitimate role of eschatological concepts, which is to supply, or interpret, clues for the faithful appropriation of one's own death.

This restricted applicability of conceptual schematisms urged by protagonists of faith (2) will reflect ethical elements. These are sometimes fashioned into antimetaphysical warheads. Suppose, for example, we were convinced that the greatest challenge at the moment to people of goodwill is to participate in the suffering of the world. For here we are: the old world, its gods and all, is dying, or is already dead but not decently buried, and a new world is struggling to emerge. Is this a time to indulge in metaphysical dreaming? Is it a time to debate solemnly whether goodness has any friends beyond this earth and our history? No! A thousand times no! And let each time display an increment of moral fervor, of will to be for goodness' sweet sake. For the time may be brief, not because unknown gods are displeased but because man has come of age. He has at last become too wise to look to an Other, who does not exist anyway, to do for him what he must do for himself. But he is also wise enough to aim the gun where it will do maximum, indeed total, damage. *Man come of age:* we are now able to liquidate the human enterprise. Earlier ages of necessity looked to God or chance for this dread consummation. So one might contrive a new proof for the nonexistence of God: If God existed he would already have liquidated man. But man has not yet been liquidated. Therefore, God does not exist. But this, of course, is a shameless travesty. To be is to love, it is to care for others as for self. That is authenticity. God cannot exist, therefore, because man has power, thanks to having come of age, to liquidate himself. If God really existed he would not permit such a thing, he would not permit such a possibility to materialize.

Thus faith (2) is vulnerable to invasion by apocalyptic spirits, as any faith is likely to be in this age. Serious and enduring religions have always recommended that people should remember that they are mortal. But only now has it become possible for human beings to inflict death on a planetary scale as a matter of policy. So the "last man" paradigm, Everyman eschatologically collapsed, makes terribly real sense. This means that part of the stock-in-trade of traditional religion has been severely compromised, namely, that death is simply part of the eternally fixed structure of the cosmos. For now the death of mankind can be engineered. It is one thing to believe that there is a time to die for each person and that time is somehow a cosmic determination, since "natural causes" are all governed by putatively universal laws. It is a very different thing for mankind to die, not from natural causes but from the total failure of moral vision, from a lethal corruption of virtue. What, in such a world, does existential authenticity mean?

A very different question is also to be asked of faith (2). What sort and range of confidence in cognitive-noncognitive conceptual schemes does it suggest? Where did the protagonists of faith (2), as essentially attitudinal, learn that the conceptual schematisms of theology, of any theology, had very little or no metaphysical cash value? Where is real knowledge of "what is," since it dwelleth not in the tents of theology? Does it cohabit with science? If so which is the lucky one in that kingdom of many chateaux and baronies?

Here we may need to be reminded that one ought not to make demands on others that one would be very reluctant to levy upon oneself. Is it at all reasonable to ask theologians, not only to identify their philosophic tutors but to argue the proposition that what they have learned is really so? Is it proper to ask Bultmann to make the case for Heideggerian ontology as well as show how that schematism properly elucidates Christian existence? Are we not in principle all relativists, however sturdy some of our denials of it may be, so that, as theologians in an antimetaphysical historical moment, we must learn to interpret the faith as though it in no way competes with the lords and masters in the kingdom of knowledge?

I put these questions as rhetorical only in part. They touch upon matters to be explored elsewhere. For the time being, I register a conviction that in the case of faith (2) we have a clear case of determining what the conceptual schematizing of the Christian faith is good for—that is, how far it can be extended and what kind of truth it provides—by applying a philosophic scheme, the truth of which is simply assumed. The essential program for the interpreter of faith (2) is to use the appropriate schematism to interpret the viable elements of Christian teaching.

So two questions are now before us. One: What renders a conceptual scheme appropriate? Two: What renders an element of Christian teaching viable?

In regard to the first question it may be useful to keep in mind that appropriateness is not truth in disguise, since according to faith (2) the conceptual factor has heuristic value only. Hence, the appropriate schematism is simply the one that best fits the historical situation of the church and the believer. "Best fits" is obviously a matter of judgment bound to fall so far short of apodictic certainty that such an aim does not even apply. This is then something like the reality principle in psychotherapeutic usage. In neither case is reality anything metaphysical, it is not what really is. Rather, reality is the content of standardized perceptions; it is what people perceive to be the actual world. So one is well advised not to fly consistently in the face of social conventions and expectations, not, however, because those expectations are demonstrably right and good. They are simply *there* as a fabric of human relationships, indeed as a human world. There are other worlds, to be sure, but each of them is also a dense fabric of arbitrary conventions and expectations.

Thus theologians of the faith (2) persuasion have a heavy investment in discerning (diagnosing) the actualities of the historical situation. Here the options are sparse: (a) intuition and (b) social-scientific schematisms. In respect to either and both of these options we must ask Whose? Thus (a): my own; or those of people I judge to be generally superior in perceptual and expressive powers, such as artists. And in respect to (b): What method and school of social science?

It is true, of course, that any faithful presentation of the Christian message requires some awareness of the actualities. "To serve the present age/My calling to fulfill," as the hymnist puts it, certainly demands reasonably clear perceptions of the lineaments of the present age. But faith (1) surely, and faith (2) presumably, may well be pursued by the question whether human nature has a metaphysical definiteness imparted to it by its creator. So even if the present age is a demonic congeries of novel temptations (or in more neutral tones, of largely unique sociocultural developments), there is still that immortal soul—"A never-dying soul to save/and fit it for the sky."

One reason for the prominence of faith (2) is the loss of any kind of metaphysical definiteness in the scientific reading of man. Another reason is the immense influence of historicistic philosophies according to which to be human is to be historical. That has come to mean man is not a *substance*, he is a *subject*.[6]

Thus faith (2) multiplies theological investments in conceptual schematisms. It adds those of social-scientific use to those of philosophy.

The load seems to be lighter on the intuitional (a) front. But unique problems loom there, too. Why, for instance, should others be instructed as well as impressed by my intuitive readings of the present situation? Why do I think Faulkner has it right? Or Camus? Or Picasso? Or Bergman? "Here," I say, "is the present predicament of man. This is the state of the human spirit." "Not so," says my neighbor, "it is certainly not the state of *my* spirit. And I would like to know why my preacher spends so much time reading dirty books and going to dirty movies." Obviously my neighbor is a Philistine. Is it so clear that I am a David?

How then is a theologian supposed to determine what the viable elements in the Christian tradition are? Does this call for the application of an arbitrary conceptual scheme? Or is there a minimal bedrock mentality —an outlook, an angle of vision, call it what you will—that is already acting as the filter through which all postulants for truth and other kinds of value must pass to be worthy even of conscious reflective testing by one imbued with the modern spirit? Are the boundaries of general credibility already firmly in place, the preconditions of perception and preference? If such were the case, then to fail to acknowledge their reality would be to fall straightway into mires of fantasy. For instance, what does "never-dying soul" mean in the contemporary world? It may emit a dim unearthly glow, but what larger and richer life does it have? Or put it in this-worldly terms: How much of the contemporary world represents any kind of persistent concern for, or commitment to, the individual person as the carrier of an ultimate reality?

A question for such questions: What does it mean to say that here is a belief that has lost its viability? This might mean (i) a lot of people in fact do not accept it as true. But it might mean (ii) that even the people who profess it ought to admit that such a belief doesn't make much sense in the sort of world in which we now live. But does this mean (iii) that there is now decisive cognitive evidence—such as neurological data and theory—against that old piece of metaphysical baggage, the immortal soul? Or soes it mean (iv) that the historical (sociocultural) situation makes such a belief very hard to support; which is to say, that one's passage through this world is not predictably illumined, corrected, or in any way improved by believing in a never-dying soul?

This seems to be as good a spot as any to file a caveat against any easy conjunction or merging of cognitive viability with its attitudinal counterpart. Truth claims in science lose viability when alternative and superior (in respect to clarity, simplicity, and coherence) ways of comprehending the "facts" appear, or when a theoretic advance—which originally may not seem to make much sense—generates new data or is part of a data-generating movement. Viewed one way, then, it is a patent absurdity to say "There came a time when the Ptolemaic astronomy simply and totally lost its viability." That old schematism survives in the meteorological section of the mass media and in all ordinary communication about the rotation of day and night. In the "real" knowledge of nature, however, it has long been defunct.

But when we descend from the infinity of the heavens to man, and ascend to him from the infinitesimals of molecular structure, what are the comparable revolutions in "real" knowledge? Suppose we say, "Now we know how the brain functions." Does this mean that until now man hasn't really known what knowledge itself is? A wonderful possibility! Except that in this case this new knowledge, never before seen on land or sea, must be entirely self-referencing and self-englobed. Like divine election, you either have it or you don't. If you have it, you cease knowing what not having it is. If you don't have it, there is no possibility of really knowing what you are missing.

Which is to say that many, if not all, cognitive revolutions are, insofar as they come off, successful efforts to put mind and world together in new perspectives. But this means that some element or kind of continuity is presupposed in every such revolution. It means that some mind is able to stand simultaneously in two worlds; and either is or sees a connection between them.

Attitudinal changes, on the other hand, may be absolute; that is, they may exhibit sharp discontinuity. Such changes have histories, including autobiographies. But there is not one fundamental attitude that embraces both worlds, the old Adam and the new. Of course one may posit a metaphysical continuity, but both Adams may deny that that affects either of them.

So when we hear that this or that element of Christian teaching is no longer viable, and the church had better reduce its theological budget accordingly, we ought to ask whether this problem has been generated by cognitive transformations or whether it represents severe attitudinal dislocations that may or may not have direct relationships to scientific revolutions.

Secularism is a case in point. There is quite a variety of theological attitudes and assessments of this phenomenon. Identification of the phenomenon is a more immediate objective. So let us say that "secularism" surely denotes an attitude, a precondition of perception. But this phenomenon also contains elements of belief. Secular man simply does not believe some Christian principles are true and good. Some of those traditional elements are rejected because he thinks that science shows us that the real world just isn't like that. That is, secular man is a creature science has outfitted with world-pictures aeons removed from those of biblical and traditional faith. Moreover, the scientific worldview encourages, perhaps inspires and justifies, attitudes toward human nature and conduct that cannot be reconciled with Scripture and tradition. Why then should not a new man emerge in the new world disclosed by modern science?

So it is easy enough, and true to boot, to say that this new creature, secular man, cannot accept the ancient picture of the cosmos as a three-storied affair. Our secular age has poked its nose deep into the empyrean and behold! not a trace of an angel, not so much as an unidentifiable feather floating everlastingly in its own mysterious orbit. As for God, deep heaven whispers not his name; if it does there is no decoding such a signal.

The theological difficulty over which secular man stumbles is much less whimsical, rather less dramatic, and considerably more poignant than his troubles with biblical world-pictures. How shall we believe that caring is the heart of the cosmic enterprise? That is the theological crux. It has nothing much to do with the triumphs of astrophysics and rocketry. Angels belong partly to the picturebooks of archaic religion and partly to the metaphysical theology of the Middle Ages. Secular man had closed both of those books long before the age of the astronauts dawned. The *God* of absolute transcendence had lost most of its credentials long before $E=MC^2$ broke free from the mathematician's brain.

So again the core theological problem has a sting very different from the pathos of childish religious toys broken beyond repair. For now we have to ask what it would take to believe that caring is the heart of the cosmic enterprise. Cosmic it must be because our history has been sufficiently tortured by tribal gods. Caring must be either a human-mammal mutation produced by a random throw of the genetic dice, or it is the primary business of the whole show. But what would it take to believe so brazen a piece of metaphysics?

Well, for one thing, one would have to believe that caring gets things done in the near and familiar world, that is in the things in which human well-being are found. Not in the cosmos to start with but in this society, our neighborhood, the family, the state: anything and everything of human doing. This is, of course, easily managed as a sentiment used to embellish, or thinly disguise, the realities of callous, even brutal, indifference to the sufferings of people near at hand, to say nothing of our invincible ignorance of the plight of untold millions far away. But really to believe that caring is the way the grain of reality runs, well, that is a tall order. What about those very persuasive images of man the predator, the "naked ape"?

But the plot thickens unconscionably. For, secondly, one would have to believe that caring gets things done, gets them done as nothing else does. Nothing else gets things done so effectively, so appropriately, so joyfully, as caring does; better than self-interest or any other form of the profit motive, better than fear or guilt, better than duty.

Perhaps the worst is yet to come. Thirdly, one would have to believe that even if noncaring entities exist (there is at least a *prima facie* case for so believing), they can be made to sit up and take notice by caring. If I say that I want some of my money to be used to feed starving people in Bangladesh, then my caring can constrain nerve and muscle to write a check, mail a letter; and caring can make ships to sail, and bankers to make transactions, and trains to run, and grain to be distributed. And if a metaphysician, wearing whatever hat, tells this Simple Simon, "Cells and electrical charges, positive and negative—a wonderfully complex electronic system—did it all," I shall thank him for thus telling me that electrons and their kin all care, too. An unexpected dividend. But perhaps the metaphysician may only have in mind to tell me that there is a biochemical basis for all human actions no matter how sublime their ethical qualities. This is a much more modest lesson. It is about as breath-taking as discovering that Alexander's Bucephalus could not have performed his prodigies without oats. But the heroics of the horse are not ways of describing the behavior of oats.

The theological friends of secularism ought to show us how the spirit of modernity makes it easier for us to believe these things. The theological foes of secularism ought to show us that the pace, achievements, and direction of contemporary culture make these things about caring virtually impossible—that is, flatly unreasonable—to believe. From neither camp ought we to uncritically accept testimony suborned from astrophysics, neurology, animal psychology, or the latest wrinkle in the seamless (seemless) robe of philosophy. What we have a right to ask is a conceptual scheme that comprehends man and cosmos; a scheme that does not make our caring an inexplicable freak of nature, a brief and pointless flash of light in a dark and cold cosmos. To stop short of this is to use secularism as a device for selecting and vindicating only those elements of the Christian outlook which offer the least offense to the spirit of the age. But what if this spirit itself is an aberration, a fugitive from righteousness, an enemy of human well-being? Earlier in this century theologians could invoke the principle of progress to exorcise such morbid musings. But progress was a casualty of the guns of August 1914, and its earthly remains went into the ovens of Belsen. The ghost of inevitability dwells with the Marxian dogmaticians. Their cakewalks around the brutal tactics of Communist totalitarianism ought to scandalize the spirit of the age if it had any clear and commanding ethical sensitivities left.

Faith (3) offers some possibilities for the deployment of a conceptual scheme beyond the human situation. This view of faith makes much of man's relatedness to ranges of being beyond himself. Obedience, trust, loyalty, these are supposed to denote relationships rather than states or term-qualities. To be sure, one who trusts has a trusting nature; but does this mean that his nature is a metaphysical substance to which trust mysteriously adheres? Hardly. So also, one who obeys, obeys something or somebody. He accepts a relationship before he performs a duty or executes a command. If I am ordered to do something, I have a right to ask of him who orders it, "Who are you?" The proper answer to this question is one that discloses a relationship. Commonsensically, it will also disclose a being—I am your father, I am the Captain, I am the Dean, I am the Lord God.

Yet common sense will not take us as far as we need to go, and it is likely to be a fuzzy-headed guide even for the short stretch. It will not help us to answer the question about the being of the one who commands or the one who solicits our trust or the one who arouses our affections. Commonsensically, we are sure that the being which relates to us as father has more to him than fatherhood, noble in principle as fatherhood is. But what more do we need to know? In fact what more can we know about the being who commands than the actuality of the relationship disclosed by his commandment? In trying to get behind that actuality into the mysterious depths of beinghood, one may lose one's grip upon the actuality. We can, of course, *believe* that the one who commands is incomparably rich in being, is endowed with so many and such great perfections that the whole course of time would not suffice to display or enumerate them; hence eternity. But we must not permit that overbelief to obscure or diminish the actuality of the relationship, for that is what we do comprehend. Perhaps this would hold even if the one who commands should turn out to be the self itself, man legislating for this person, the real and ultimate self dictating to the empirical self—that makeshift, jerry-built, happenchance, commonsensical person who smirks at me from the mirror. That chap is certainly on the receiving end. He is the one who is so puzzled about who is sending along all these commands.

Shall we not say then that faith (3) calls for a conceptual scheme in which relations with transcendent being are at least allowed for if not clearly demanded? Is it not the case that one who hears a word is already out in the world, if "word" signifies an intelligible utterance, an actual communication? The hearer of such a word is already out in the human world of intersubjectivity, he is already participating in that kind of being called sociality. In this world he may be grossly deceived if he supposes that there is some way of tracking the speaker of that word into a mysterious metaphysical lair and there finding the real being who has spoken that word.

A fortiori, then, if the word is not only intelligible but is existentially decisive, if it is the word calling the hearer into being, that is, into a self-relating but not self-referential activity, into "answering" where that stands for finding authentic existence. The more decisive the word, the more penetrating and inclusive the command, the more alluring and persuasive the solicitation, the less reason or excuse there is available for attempting any metaphysical tracking. Put it axiomatically: The richer my commerce with reality becomes the thinner become excuses for trying to discover who or what "out there" is egging me on. The richer the human community becomes, the more it is steeped in goodness and beauty, the less cause we have for asking reality to put on a particular face.

In such a high and holy moment it might well seem improper to press the inverse rule; to ask, that is, whether our excuse for metaphysical tracking increases in plausibility as human existence thins out and begins to break up. Or should we write such ventures off as bad faith, as systematically wrought bad excuses for not taking at face and desperate value whatever there is to be trusted and obeyed, if not loved?

It is not perverse to call for that odd and disquieting inverse rule. It is not adequate to dismiss it as bad faith. For if I am intelligent, I ought to trust only what is trustworthy in the long and hard pull, and I ought to obey only those who demonstrate a right to command. So far this does not elevate intelligence to divinity. So far it goes only to make us truly human. So if somebody tells me that I have no right to question God or conscience or the state or majority opinion or whatever is ticketed as unchallengeable, I am entitled to ask such a commander for his credentials; and if he rails in high dudgeon at my impertinence, I am entitled to request that he desist from acting as though he were divine and absolute. And to this it is a very poor answer to say "But you *must* trust something or somebody, you know." No one denies that. What is at stake is the contention that to be truly human, and not simply to cross the street or buy a hen, I need to trust unconditionally, unreservedly—and perhaps cheerfully as well.

Such is the logic of faith (3). To make its claim good it is not enough to make a few psychological and sociological excursions in order to report that, in fact, a lot of people do so trust and, in their own view, are the better for it. The only way the claim of faith (3) can be made good is to correlate it rightly with faith (1). The Christian believes that God is wholly to be trusted, devoutly and cheerfully to be obeyed. Moreover, the Christian believes that God has put him in that definitive relationship. He believes that God is caring, that, in fact, God is the pure case of caring and the invincible master of it. So, conceiving of himself as standing in that wholly unique and decisive relationship, the Christian believes that an account can be given of all that exists. The account will be rough, sketchy, incomplete. But it will be true as well as faithful.

III

A conceptual scheme is necessarily involved in any interpretation of Christian faith, whether this be understood as faith (1), (2), or (3), or as some compound of belief, encounter, and obedience. No matter how acutely and devoutly attuned to Scripture a theologian may be he cannot limit his interpretation of the Christian message to biblical language. An age that has lost on so massive a scale as our own any profound or acute sensitivity to biblical authority simply makes this theological fact the more compelling. Nor can theologians limit themselves to the language of popular piety. An age of rapidly declining church membership makes this theological fact more compelling than it has been for centuries.

It hardly follows from a proper acknowledgement of these facts that theologians ought to take on board a systematic philosophic conceptual schematism. Would it not be more correct to say that theologians need to use a conceptual scheme that is clear, internally consistent, and congenial both to the essential Christian message and to the mind of the age at its best?

These specifications have the ring of a counsel of perfection. It is more likely that they would be read as a recipe for theological schizophrenia. Congenial *both* to the essential Christian message and to the mind of the age at its best? Much of liberal theology attests to the fact that it is possible to make each of these two things mean the other. But on the other hand it is very hard to make a clear and convincing case for whatever language one takes to be the mind of the age at its best.

Moreover, it is possible to have too exalted a notion of what the mind of the age can deliver. Perhaps we should do well to think of it as a set of intuitions, of things taken largely for granted, rather than as a global metaphysics or as a largely coherent world-picture. Perhaps the mind of the age is rather more like a set of preconditions governing standard perceptions of reality than like a range of perceptions.

If there be a set of such primordial intuitions at the base of contemporary culture, theologians would poorly serve the Christian cause by ignoring it or by adopting a negative attitude toward it—or by placing the imprimatur of truth pure and undefiled upon it. Colossians 2:8 warns the faithful against "philosophy and empty deceits." But St. Paul (whether or not he wrote Colossians) did not reject Roman culture *totaliter.* He incorporates part of its conceptual heritage into his theology.

I do not intend here to discuss the complexities of St. Paul's views of the relationships of Gospel, the wisdom of God, to the wisdom of the world. It is easy to call his view of this dialectical, but then we ought to unpack dialectical. I do not propose to go any further into that than to remark that any relating of Gospel (the central Christian affirmations) to a concrete historical situation involves one kind or another of relativity. "Relativity" is not just another way of spelling "relationship." Theological relativity is a way of designating how the primordial intuitions of contemporary culture are to be acknowledged in the interpretation of the Christian faith. Not just that the mind of the age is to be recognized for what it is, but how its meaningfulness is to be acknowledged.

It appears, then, that some kind of relativizing of the Christian message is an essential part of the theological vocation. It is the part which exhibits the theologian's role as a critic of the church's actual representation of the Gospel. It is first of all the preacher who must try to speak in the church at least one clear word, one intelligible thing, whether or not he has the tongue of angels besides. This word ought to be intended to take hold of its hearers where they really live.

In some ages nothing could have seemed easier than finding the natural habitat of the nonbeliever, that is, his real historical situation. It was an abomination surely to be repented of, perhaps reformed, but if incorrigible, then fled. Indigenous gods were vanities, if not howling obscenities. To be a pagan was to be an idol worshiper, by definition.

A very different theological stance *apropos* gods and their worshipers is suggested by St. Paul's avowal:

For although there may be so-called gods in heaven or on earth—as indeed there are many "gods" and many "lords"—yet for us there is one God . . . and one Lord (1 Cor. 8:5,6).

This is an astonishing acknowledgement from a Jew, that conjectural allowance "there may be so-called gods . . ." Where is that "radical monotheism" which was, and is, the glory of Judaism? It is there. It comes to light in "Yet for us . . ." But it has an earlier and more subtle expression as well: "there are many 'gods' and many 'lords' "! Put into the schematism employed here, "gods" and "lords" are so many linguistic cultural symbols of value elements—both affirmative and negative, constructive and destructive—in the general culture. In H. Richard Niebuhr's terms, they are objects of loyalty and dreaded powers. They do not have transcendental status; little do they need it. Their only lodgement in being is in the minds and hearts of humans. As such, they absorb love but they cannot give it. They live in our light, not we in theirs. But they are vain things, hollow illusions, only insofar as the religious veneration of anything simply natural and human is ultimately foolish. In the meantime, in the infinitely variegated here-and-now of history, it is not foolish, it is anything but a monstrous aberration, to cherish, love, honor, and obey the finite goods time allows. And it is not merely foolish to dream fondly of such goods when the seas of misfortune close around us.

Yet, as Paul avers, there is a very different way of relating the Gospel to the situation of its hearers and to their world, which is to place them, to place the human enterprise, the human community, in the caring which alone and altogether is divine and is thus worthy of all love and obedience. This presupposes revelation: It is God who calls, ordains, and gathers up. But theological demonstration of this placement presupposes a conceptual schematism that does not bear the imprimatur of revelation. Revelation is of God and from God. Its theological construal is human, all too human, a poor thank-offering indeed, but not so poor as a blanket refusal to think on Christian existence and leave it all to the Spirit: a mess of poor leavings.

So, of course, theology is a conceptual enterprise. It rests on the inescapable assumption that the conceptual factor cannot be alienated from the Christian message.

There is another assumption hardly less significant. The other elements in Christianity, even those clearly noncognitive, require interpretation through a conceptual scheme, no matter how remote from the immediacies of experience that scheme may seem.

Finally, it is reasonable to assume that part of the argument among the protagonists of faiths (1), (2), and (3) has to do with the kind of authority to be vested in a conceptual scheme. Granted that the authority and right of investiture are human rather than divine, we need again to ask what criteria are appropriate for assaying the scheme adopted by any given theologian.

The responses that come first to mind inevitably turn out to be relevancy. For instance, that theology ought to relate sensibly and sensitively to the present scene. This is as infertile as it is true.

Or take consistency: theological schematisms ought to be self-consistent. Again true but largely uninstructive; certainly not decisive. Even a paradox specialist, unless he is a rhetorical exhibitionist, intends to say the same things rather than contradictory ones about the nature and importance of the paradox—say the Incarnation. Reality may come at us as (and not merely in) paradox. But there are paradoxes and paradoxes. So the principle for determining the authentic paradox is not itself a paradox. Furthermore, consistency as a criterion for testing assertorial propositions ought not to be confused with consistency in the use of a categoreal scheme.

Congruency is another obvious candidate. Theological schematisms ought to fit the actualities of Christian experience and Christian history. True, but what does it actually mean? Suppose we agree that no sensible Christian would begin a prayer with:

> O Thou in Whom Existence
> And Essence are identical:
> *Actus Purus* be Thy Name.

But who has legislated that theological schematisms are supposed to be grafted into the routines of piety? Or that the high calling of theology is to reform piety rather than to interpret, elucidate, and justify it?

Certainly theologians ought not to adopt schematisms that, properly understood, attack the main nerves of Christian experience and thus put piety out of business. Very few Christian thinkers have done that on purpose, to be sure. But just as surely it is possible for a theologian not to realize how poorly his scheme relates to the actualities of the faith. So, in urging the metaphysical merits of Thomism, a theologian might convert some people from true Christianity to Thomism. And a Hegelian theologian might convert others from true Christianity to Hegelianism. Such things have happened. They suggest a way of reading the history of Christian thought.

But again there is the familiar obtrusive difficulty. What is the criterion by which a clear and competent judgment—"This, rather than that, is true Christianity"—is rendered? Probably without exception great philosophical captivities of the Gospel have been devised by theologians who earnestly believed that there had to be a conceptual route into the heartland of faith. If we ask, "By whom or what have the redemptions from such captivities been executed?" and we are not satisfied with the response of piety—"By God. And let him be thanked, therefore!"—what is a proper answer?

Answers come in from every quarter. Every one of them, except those of unreflective piety, has some kind of metaphysical agenda, tacit or avowed. The most tacit agenda belongs to those who say that the real business of theology is just to render explicit "the grammer of faith," not to defend it before a mythical bar of rationality.

The tacit agenda of this view is systematically antimetaphysical. That is, *beliefs* about reality are probably inevitable, in religion and outside of it. But there is no way any of these beliefs can be shown (known?) to be true. This is a claim, if ever there was one, about "what is."

I am not concerned here with appraising the various metaphysical agenda of contemporary theologians, important as that task is. The more important question is the antecedent one: What criteria are available for appraising any particular theological schematism? The last candidate I intend to review here is *fertility*.

Like all the others (and perhaps like all criteria judgments) fertility has its own question-begging features. It asks whether a theological conceptual scheme enables church and Christian to get further on with the main business. Does a schematism potentialize a creative advance? One of the assumptions embedded in this criterion is that theological thinking, like any thought directly concerned with experience and the actual world, is supposed to make a practical difference, not just a subjective modification but a situation modification.

Another assumption bears more directly on Christianity as a religion. The main Christian business is to show the world the world-creating, situation-transforming power of caring. The chief demonstration of this truth is, of course, itself practical: by caring. A New Testament writer says:

If anyone says, "I love God," and hates his brother, he is a liar; for he who does not love his brother whom he has seen, cannot love God whom he has not seen (1 John 4:20).

Thus the proposition "God is love," is a kind of warrant and justification for caring as the inclusive life-policy. Historically this has not licensed the philosophical inversion: "God" and *God* are simply word and concept signifying the seriousness and sincerity with which some people, those called Christian, take the business of caring. The theological rhyme and reason go exactly the other way. Since caring is the main cosmic business intended by God, mankind either tunes in on it properly or else . . .

Fertility is the criterion which brings the others together into a concreteness and specificity they lack otherwise. So armed and provisioned, a theologian need not be unduly frightened or embarrassed when asked why this scheme rather than that. In respect to philosophical masters, why Whitehead rather than Aristotle? It is not to the theological point to respond that Whitehead is more modern. The ovens of Dachau were also modern, and so is creeping electronic surveillance of the general public, and foodstuffs robbed of natural nutrients and jazzed up with vitamin supplements.

An equally ready answer is at least as hazardous. That is to say that Whitehead, or Aristotle or Plato or Heidegger, is the system with the greatest aesthetic appeal. None of these answers is true, but perhaps there is one that best expresses the pathos of the human condition. Nor is it necessary to contend that this scheme rather than that, or any other, is an indispensable condition of intelligibility for the proper interpretation of the Gospel.

I suspect that in such views the differences between *scheme* and *system* may be overlooked. A system is a body of propositions. A system is a good one if and only if these propositions hang together; that is a minimal requirement of a system. On the other hand, a conceptual scheme is a set of categories, each of which is set forth as an axiom. So a conceptual scheme as such makes no assertions about "what is." A system is engaged with such assertions; systems are devised to grapple with all things actual and possible. Systems require conceptual schemes; conceptual schemes are not necessarily put to metaphysical work. Systematic thinkers sometimes create the impression that they have—or they will have if they live long enough and all the ink in the world does not disappear—deduced the whole world from the scheme. It is now high philosophic style to regard this as a bizarre aberration from philosophic sense and legitimate aspiration. Banished from the realm of reality, the deductive ideal of system has found a home in appearances rendered mathematically systematic, that is, in science.

This does not quite mean that there the systematic deductive principle is safe and secure from all alarms. For it seems that we are now entitled to some doubt that either scheme or system as such bestows intelligibility upon fact or report of fact; unless facts and reports of facts are defined as needing concept and system in order to file any serious claims at all. If a report of an empirical item is not understood when it is made, it is either poorly made, or the reportee was not paying attention or was deficient in powers of comprehension. These fundamental defects in reporter and reportee are not predictably amended either by schematism or by system as reflective rational enterprises.

So, where the preaching of the Gospel is not understood, where its central point is simply missed, it is reasonable to infer a defect either in the preacher or in the hearer. Neither defect can be remedied by the adoption of a scheme or a system. Not by a scheme, because schemes as such make no assertions. Not by a system, because systems as such make no reports.[7]

What then is the proper role of the theologian relative to the facts and reports of facts which constitute the empirical factor in the Christian faith? He ought not to say that his conceptual scheme is the only route of access to the actualities of the faith, to say nothing of claiming that there is a system that is the only route to deity. On the other hand it is proper for the theologian to protest when these actualities are misrepresented by the conduct of church and Christian. Given that the absolute actuality of Christian faith is the experience and expression of caring, moves—conscious or unconscious—to make or let something else, anything else, count for more are the only really lethal heresies; for example, accepting and recommending the credo of the business community that economic profit is the chief business of man. But when a theologian claims that the *real* Gospel is not generally understood by the good and faithful people of the church, he runs beyond his license; if, that is, he wants to be understood to be a Christian theologian. It is a different matter if a person is a religious thinker who happens to believe that Christian history and experience contain some items the proper value of which cannot be realized unless they are extracted, refined, and mounted in an appropriate (philosophic, scientific, art-aesthetic) way. In that case we are entitled to ask: What is the heavy working capital of that extractive and revisionary view?

There are two responses to this sort of question that are theologically interesting. One is to come forward with an alternative worldview, a vision of human life in the world that cannot be squared with the Christian actualities. The other is to propose a system in which caring is subject to exhaustive causal explanation; and in the end it turns out to be not more reality-instructive than gastric juices or gonads.

Various questions of Christian theological strategy and tactics in relation to these alternative worldviews, conceptual schemes, and philosophical systems come to mind. What, for example, is at stake in "refutations of refutations" of Christian metaphysical beliefs? The defense of Christian actualities? The intellectual respectability of Christianity or of some version of it? Various answers to various questions. I do not propose to consider them here. Rather, I conclude this chapter with another sort of question: Have we not, for much too long, postponed drawing the proper distinction between worldview and vision?

IV

A rudimentary distinction is at hand. A vision is an intuition of reality expressed generally in pictorial or metaphorical language. Socrates says that the true philosopher seeks a "vision of all time and existence." What he sees may take a lifetime (or several: an odd argument for reincarnation) to express discursively-conceptually. But the first medium of its communication is a metaphor, such as mind, machine, soul, life, or organism. In the right metaphor the germ, essence, drift, and culmination of "what is" is uncovered.

In the hands of conceptualizing and dialectical geniuses, metaphor is expanded into system. And the truth of a system is arguable quite independently of the presence or absence of the vision. The vision is an actuality (fact). It takes a good deal of going about to show that its full and proper import is reality. So long as the vision endures in its primordial purity nothing else is so important; it then defines importance. But it does not persist in that state. So its relation to all other actualities and possibilities has to be made out. For these purposes it is necessary "to walk by faith," in one or another conceptual pattern, in a language with cash counters in the everyday world.

So there is a Platonic vision of the world and a Plotinian one and a Hegelian one. But there is also a Plotinian system, and a Hegelian one —perhaps not a Platonic one. The system is a propositional expansion to the outermost limit of the vision and its metaphor. There is, accordingly, something curious about a metaphysical system. It is a body of conceptual propositional indicatives designed to make cosmic sense of a metaphor; but again, the arguments (proofs) of a system do not stand or fall with the success or failure of the metaphor to grasp the imagination. Metaphors claim nothing but attention. The systematic articulations of a metaphysical thinker may have an austere power that commands respect even when imagination is unillumined. One can argue *from* metaphors. What kind of arguments can we have *about* them?

An outlook or worldview may begin life as a vision. Once an outlook is on its own it does not presuppose a vision, because an outlook is a conviction, or a cluster of convictions, about the fortunes of human values or, more generally, of the good, at the hands of "what is." An outlook is a way of "viewing" things. Yes, but the viewing is as much a treating as a seeing. Thus an optimistic outlook is hardly a simple unitary perception of all things cohering for goodness' sake. Such an outlook is much more a matter of looking for the good in all things and in every situation in the conviction that good will surely triumph in the end.

So an outlook entails, and may potentialize, a material-existential inference, a moral commitment. No doubt worldviews involve pictures or images of the total scheme of things. They are quite as much general policy convictions. Which is to say that looking for the good is not a stationary and inert gazing about to see whether there is anything interesting or important going on anywhere. "Looking for" is at least "looking after," that is, tending, shepherding, providing for, seeing to. Indeed the connection between outlook and fundamental life-policies is such that one might plausibly invert the relationship and claim that outlooks are generated by life-policies and moral commitments, their function being to justify and sanction those policies and commitments.

There is no clear or urgent reason for deciding what account of these connections is generally correct. Perhaps there are born optimists and born pessimists; as ancient medicine had it, there are persons of sanguine humor and others of melancholic humor. Such notions may encourage us to distinguish sentiments from convictions, and inclinations from dispositions. Worldviews no doubt include, or at least touch, sentiments. Sentiments are an important part of the verbal gestures in which worldviews are expressed. The heart of a worldview is a recommendation that a particular disposition—the "set" of the self to act one way rather than another—is a more potent sense-maker than any other. Thus the ancient stoic preached resignation as the right disposition by which concretely to relate the self to the ultimate reason of the cosmos. And the Christian Gospel prescribes caring as the only route of access to life abundant and eternal. Each of these dramatically contrasting life-policies can be reduced to largely inane and infertile sentiments. Such sentiments may be widely endorsed as insights into what life is all about. This is a fundamental category mistake. On the one hand, sentiments are the residue of insight, and on the other, they are part of the veneer with which worldviews are all eventually equipped.

Outlooks do not acquire their vitality, their convictional-dispositional potency, from sentiments. Nor do they depend for their vitality either upon conceptual schemes or systems. A way of construing the world and a disposition to be in the world in a particular way for particular purposes—a worldview, that is—may acquire conceptual structure. It may indeed emerge as a philosophical-theological system purporting to make ultimate sense of "what is." The history of metaphysics is to a considerable extent the story of the rise and fall of such empires. The fortunes of the great visions and their respective root metaphors have not been tied to that remarkable rhythm. Neither have the worldviews which have reigned in the heart and mind of Western man. Their alternations seem to have had little to do with the ebb and flow of philosophical-theological systems.

More particularly, the Christian outlook as such does not derive its vitality from lordly theological systems. That is not to cast aspersions on systematic theology nor to deprecate the influence of powerful theological minds. The question, rather, is whether the theologian can throw clear and useful light on how the Christian viewing of "what is," is to be properly related to life-policies that are the decisive expression of Christian conviction.

A satisfactory answer to this question is not likely to be forthcoming until we take another look at dogmatic theology.

V

Dogmatics is a conceptualization of the Christian outlook. The objective of dogmatics, so understood, is to clarify conviction and commitment when they need it; when, that is, the behavior of church and Christian suggests confusion, ignorance, ambiguity, failure of courage, or perversity. Accordingly the dogmatic theologian does not offer a freehand sketch of what is. He functions as a member of a Christian community in which what is shared in the first place is a conviction that caring is an ultimate reality, and that Jesus Christ is the ultimate paradigm of that.

Ostensibly stronger claims could be made for dogmatics. (a) One could claim that the content of dogmatics is revelation rather than outlook. (b) One could claim that dogmatics is the religious equivalent of systematic metaphysics, aspiring, that is, to cover everything in heaven and earth.

In respect to (a), I observe that to speak seriously and faithfully of revelation as the content of dogmatics is to avow that there is an outlook that is sponsored, and perhaps produced, by God himself. Whence it follows that faith is not merely a function of moral commitments or an effect of psychic-social tensions. Well and good. But we need also to distinguish confessing that God is the cause of my outlook from making an appeal to a divine warrant for the vindication of my convictions and commitments in the eyes of other human beings. Dogma is a human device. I do staunchly believe that some Christian dogmas are about the decisive encounter of God and man. But the proximate objective of dogmatic formulations is to clarify, consolidate, and, as far as possible, potentialize the adherents to the Christian outlook.

As for (b), dogmatics is bound to canvass heaven and earth only as far as convictions and commitments oblige one to picture and conceive oneself and humanity in relation to all that is. The systematic metaphysician may indeed spring the system from a root metaphor, an analogy that he proposes to stretch or otherwise adjust to fit all there is. To do this he fashions theories; he speculates. In these things his objective is to round up everything "in principle." So he rounds out a conceptual system. A dogmatician may also be endowed with speculative gifts—Augustine, for instance. But dogmatics does not demand their exploitation, as metaphysics in the grand style does.

It is a mistake, however, for the dogmatician to try to make the strongest possible case against systematic metaphysics as though that were a dedicated enemy of faith and divine revelation. Moreover, to defend revelation, as distinguished from *revelation,* is to be presumptuous. Theologians concerned with the problem of evil sometimes venture to say a good word or two in God's behalf. Such ventures would be more plausible and grace-full were they limited to some commendations of *God,* that is, to the concept embedded in Christian faith. Given God, he neither needs nor could profit notably from human commendation or reproof. If God does not exist, the propriety of *God* and "God" would have to be adjudicated by considerations of mental hygiene, broadly understood.

I do not mean to suggest that a defense of *God* and/or "God" is theologically absurd or impious. But the appropriate Christian theological enterprise relative to the actuality of evil is to trace the vital connection between outlook and those life-policies in which the principled reduction of suffering is a necessary demonstration of caring.

Yet we may still wonder why the dogmatic suspicion of metaphysics retains as much potency as it does. What would lead a dogmatician to suppose that his business is enhanced by the disqualification of metaphysics? I make out two quite different answers to this question; perhaps one ought rather to say two quite different motives. (1) A need to establish philosophical credibility; (2) a desire to protect theology, and perhaps belief itself, from destructive philosophical raids.

A characteristic expression of (1) would run: Hardly anybody of eminence in philosophy is doing systematic metaphysics. Perhaps all this means is that a lot of philosophers have simply lost interest in metaphysics. Perhaps it means that it is widely believed that some philosopher has demonstrated, rather than merely asserted, that the case for metaphysics is hopeless, as far as truth is concerned. In any case where (1) prevails there is a lively conviction that dogmatics cannot afford to be associated, even vaguely, with a philosophical lost cause.

It is unreasonable to expect theologians to demonstrate the truth and wisdom of their philosophic predilections and commitments; that is, to the satisfaction of the philosophers. In the modern world few theologians have even aspired to do that. Those eighteenth-century figures, Berkeley and Butler, were philosophers in clericals rather than dogmaticians. Nevertheless, when a theologian proceeds on the assumption that a philosopher has disposed of something, say metaphysics, it is reasonable to ask him how he thinks that demolition works, why he credits the case. How good are those arguments of Ayer, anyway? This is not quite to ask theologians to plunge into philosophical wars on their own, and all for the greater glory of Christ and his kingdom. But it is surely appropriate to warn them that at present any consensus in philosophy may be regional rather than rational.

Moreover we may well ask why an antimetaphysical consensus, if such there be, better serves the interests of true faith and serious reflection on it than systematic metaphysics does or can.

Such questions move us to (2) above as a theological motive for seconding the motion that systematic metaphysics be adjourned *sine die;* but also *sine Dei.*

(2) Systematic metaphysicians have always had something to say about God. Whatever they have said on this topic as philosophers they have said because they judged that the rational construal of the general features of experience demanded it. It is not true that all systematic metaphysicians have rejected as subrational any appeal to special or unique experiences. It is true that metaphysicians ancient and modern tend to refract all testimony about such experiences through the prism of reason, presumptively universal and constant, or at least through rational processes not professedly provincial or *ex parte.* Whence arises a profound theological suspicion that the real God of metaphysics, including systematic atheism, is reason—human reason at that—no matter what protestations of traditional piety a particular metaphysician, such as Descartes, may have

made. So the charge is that metaphysics converts the human mind into an idol and this idol takes the place of God himself. And perhaps the protest that such an idol is at any rate a nobler one than Mammon or the belly or sex, only proves how provincial metaphysics is, after all, and not only provincial but prideful to boot. The systematic metaphysician does not recognize that everything human, reason and all, is under divine judgment; and nothing more so, more rightly and decisively so, than every human pretension to know God and have God independently of his own free and absolute revelation. Thus metaphysics occupies the penthouse on the roof of Babel's proud blasphemous tower.

But since the judgment of God upon all creaturely pretension is so wonderfully inclusive, why should the metaphysician be singled out for such particular judgment, apparently conveyed from heaven to earth by prophets of the Lord disguised as dogmaticians. Is the metaphysican to be convicted, on the basis of a proper spread of evidence, of being a perverter of truth and morals? Has he wrought great mischief for piety? Is he the fiercest wolf ravening at the door of the church? Or is he the deadliest termite silently consuming the foundations of true piety?

Not many contemporary dogmaticians go on in this vein, to be sure. Until recently, theologians could plausibly assume that systematic metaphysics was not that much of a threat to the persistence of faith or to the dignity of theology as an academic discipline. There were the Whiteheadians, yes, and the Thomists. But the one crowd was heavily committed to a vocabulary, a categoreal spread, that nobody else in Babel's penthouse could understand. The Thomists were mostly Roman Catholics whose allegiance to the church was so complete that their metaphysics was a house organ. Now metaphysics is showing some signs of life. Its speculative wings have been clipped. But that does does not at all mean that the philosophers flying at the low altitudes of descriptive metaphysics are any more prepared to bow and scrape before the claims of faith than were the grand masters of the craft in ages past.

What then is the proper moral of this odd tale? Shall we conclude that the dogmatician scents a real enemy of the faith in metaphysics, ancient or modern? Or is the metaphysical philosopher an academic rival, perhaps an academic threat of some sort? If he is an enemy of divine truth, God can be trusted to dispose of him—the theologian ought to have at least that much faith. On the other hand, if the metaphysical philosopher is an academic rival, let the dogmatician either show the metaphysician that they are not in the same game or try to best him in the one they share.

Yet there is a more excellent way. The argument can move in another direction. The proper business of the dogmatician is with dogma. Dogma is a conceptual specification of faith grasped and expressed as outlook. Thus, whether the business is called dogmatics or systematic theology, it has some kinship with metaphysics as a propositional expansion of a metaphor (or of a vision). In both cases the end in view, the controlling purpose, is to show how "what is" must be construed if the truth of it is to come home to the human mind. Dogmatics has a stake in being and truth no smaller for all its differences of stance from systematic metaphysics. For it is not enough simply to lay out in high and seemly order what the church has taught. That order ought clearly to sketch the route of access to a truth that illumines as well as embraces all of the risks and all of the certainties of human existence.

VI

Finally two related considerations require attention. One is the question whether the dogmatician must resort to using philosophical language no matter how deep his suspicions of, and vivid his polemics against, metaphysics may be. The other question is whether in the "age of analysis" metaphysics has found an asylum if not a home in the land of theology.

As to the first of these issues I ask what is meant by "a philosophical language"? It might mean (a) a conceptual scheme generated for cosmological business, such as Aristotle's, Kant's, Hegel's, Whitehead's. (b) But there are also conceptual schemes devised for phenomenological business —and hang the cosmos; such as Heidegger's and Jaspers's. (c) There are also conceptual schemes invented for epistemological business, such as Locke's or Kant's or Ayer's. (d) And let us not overlook conceptual schemes developed for ethical business, such as those of Aristotle, Kant, Butler, Mills, Rawls, to name a few. If we assume that a conceptual scheme can be worked loose from any of the decisions and commitments for which it was originally designed—either as a clarification of common language or as a systematic convention—and employed, then a theologian has a right to convert it for the service of faith, whether his special interests are theological versions of cosmology, epistemology, phenomenology, or ethics. Surely it is absurd to contend that if I wish to use *substance*, I must stand by either to repel boarders from the spectral ships of Aristotelianism, or float their flag. Nor do I need to worry greatly about being charged with borrowing language from, say, Aristotle. He did not invent "substance," he does not have a monopoly on *substance*. If there are substances, they do not owe their being to Aristotle. Of course, if I do not have the wit and wisdom to use "substance" and *substance* intelligibly and consistently, that is a different problem.

There is still another sense in which one may speak of "philosophical language," namely, when the term stands for the general character of a philosophic policy and program—philosophy pursued as analysis of the linguistic-logical structure of other "languages," such as science, art, and religion, to name only an ancient trinity.

Obviously a theological adoption of this does not involve adapting a philosophical lexicon for religious purposes. On this basis theology can be done by using standard concepts for special purposes according to rules unique to the religious life. This does not mean that all of the concepts of faith are draftees from common sense; *God*, for instance. It does mean that the conceptual scheme adopted for construing the connection of belief to life-policy may indifferently use draftees from common-sense discourse and from technical vocabularies.

So the Christian theologian does not need to seek an exemption from current language, philosophical or otherwise. He ought to show how human discourse is presupposed by revelation but is not eviscerated by it. Indeed the more a theologian insists on the "worldliness" of the revealing word, the less inclined he ought to feel that he needs to look for a special vocabulary in which to deploy either its propositional or its existential import.

We do not, therefore, properly look for a way of liberating dogmatics from conceptual schemata. In its own way dogmatics is supposed to give an account of "what is." Thereafter, it should make recommendations concerning the appropriate disposition to be expressed thereunto. Dogmatics is more than an outline of what authentic Christians believe; that is catechism. Dogmatics is responsive to conceptual aims and conceptual criteria that go beyond the requirements of catechism. The urgency here is practical. The world in which Christian life must go forward is full of competing outlooks, some of which have marked religious overtones, and some of which have metaphysical outworks. In this situation the Christian calling includes more than the command, "Be good!" It is first and foremost, "Obey God!" For access to the good is through God. So we must know who God is and who we are. Know, not simply believe or suppose or hope.

Does this really mean (2) that dogmatic theology inherits some of the burden of metaphysics when philosophy deserts her or unnaturally restricts her activities and range? Probably, but the prospects are sobering. In the explicitly Christian theological context metaphysics may have to live on short rations. That is, dogmatics makes large metaphysical claims, but the case for the claims is unlikely to satisfy rationalistic appetites. For the grounds on which the dogmatic theologian submits the Christian outlook for acceptation and embodiment are not identical with the grounds generally submitted in systematic metaphysics. Dogmatic claims are not less inclusive, but the arguments are different. Dogmatic claims, for all their inclusiveness, do not have the generality of systematic metaphysical claims. The generality of the latter is required, paradoxically, by the singularity of the vision of the world which the system develops propositionally and dialectically. The singularity of dogmatic claims is dictated by the inclusiveness of the revelation with which the dogmatician begins. Thus dogma begins metaphysically with creation. There the primordially decisive and inclusive action of God is expressed. It follows that creation is neither a general principle nor a general description of the cosmic situation. The intention of the dogma of creation is certainly cosmic: God is "the Creator of the heavens and the earth." Creation, then, has no other instantiations. Whether there are remote analogies of it is a nice problem for philosophical theology. But, to repeat it, creation as dogma does not contain or entail a description of the cosmos.

So Christian dogma begins metaphysically with creation. But historically, Christian dogma begins with Jesus Christ, the actual historical being in whom beginning and end are shown forth.

There is a real and momentous tension between these two points of commencement of Christian dogmatic theology. Elaboration and justification of this tension lie beyond the perimeters of this essay.

Chapter Four

CONCERNING FAITH AND HOPE

I

Hardly anything better illustrates the internal circularities and external relations of outlooks, commitments, and patterns of action than theological discoveries of hope. In the contemporary scene this repristinizing of hope is tied in with a reappraisal of the reality of time. Traditional Christian thought immunized *God* from temporality: He who created time cannot be supposed to be in any manner or degree tinctured by it. Here the powerful influence of a Greek metaphysical bias against time is unmistakable. The traditional Christian view is that time is real after a fashion; it is certainly not a mere illusion, but neither is it an ultimate. The theology of hope[1] moves against metaphysical bias by asserting that both God and man are oriented toward the future. Apparently this does not mean that God has a future in the sense in which man does—or hopes now he has. Rather, God *is* the future; the future is altogether within his command who is life everlasting rather than static eternal substance.

Such propositions are represented in the theology of hope as expressions of faith and not as deliverances of metaphysics. Yet their import is clearly metaphysical in that they bear on what is and what is to be. But the case for these expressions of faith is not to be confused with the case-making of systematic metaphysics. Thus a methodological issue emerges: What in the Christian context is the proper relation of faith and hope to each other? So be it noted that we are indebted to the theology of hope for calling attention to the importance hope ought to enjoy in Christian experience and reflection. Very likely it is true that hope in the modern world has been overshadowed in the triad of supernatural virtues by faith and love. Or is it the virtue rendered most tenuous, least plausible, in our civilization? I intend here to treat the methodological issues raised in the theology of hope rather than substantive views on the metaphysical issues of time and eternity or on the reality of the resurrection of Jesus Christ.

So again we have to press for clarity about methodological issues. What more is there to methodology than determining the possibility of a kind of discourse independently of employing that discourse? That is, the use of that "language" is presupposed by any "meta" enquiry into its "possibility." The philosopher of science does not create physics or geology. The philosopher of religion does not create religion—there are philosophers who would like to put religion out of business, but that is a different matter. So the methodological theologian does not create the Gospel; though since early Christian times there have been theologians who believed it was up to them to re-create it.

It appears then that methodology is not a course of instruction in how to use a language. But perhaps its real business is at once more ambitious and more abstract than that; if, that is, the primary focus of methodology is on the conditions of intelligibility for a given kind of discourse or language. Very well, but what does this rotund phrase, "the conditions of intelligibility" mean?

The most obvious answer to this question is also the most useful one in this context. The conditions of intelligibility signify that which renders a language understandable. But the primary function of any primary language is not itself to be understood. It is, rather, to make sense out of a kind or range of experience. A primary language is an instrument of understanding rather than an object of understanding.

Whether or not there are universal and constant conditions of intelligibility depends on whether there is one kind of discourse somehow empowered and licensed to monitor all other kinds and to adjudicate all disputes over meaning and truth arising in and among them. On the methodological side, this is the grandest claim in and for philosophy. But what about the conditions of intelligibility of philosophy itself? Does it have a language of its own? Or does it elevate some other language to be the paradigm of sense-making and rational order over all the others?

I do not promise serious consideration of such questions. But there is an anterior issue that must be addressed. That is the question of the chief components to be identified as the logical conditions of intelligibility, whether or not any of these components can be legitimately universalized in anything but abstract form.

There are at least two such components: (1) axiomatic principles and (2) routes and rules of inference. These are the main instruments by which discourse is rendered intelligible. This is to say that if there are profound failures at either of these points, that part of experience and the world within the jurisdiction of a language will be darkened and confused. And surely the profoundest failures of all would be the falsification of the axioms of a language and the arrival of all its routes of inference at dead ends.

But what does it mean to ask whether an axiom is or might be false? For what is an axiom but a primary definition, a conceptual decision, so to speak? Axioms assert nothing; but only of assertions can we ask: True or false? On the other hand the axioms of the "thick" languages, those in which, for good or evil, the great business with the world is done, can hardly be arbitrary stipulations. Such axioms are propositional reductions of intuitions, of primordial apprehensions of "what is." If as such they have a truth-rendering capability, why should we hesitate to call them true? Can we really believe that the source of light is itself dark? The situation, therefore, is quite unlike that in which we say that sound nourishment is a necessary condition of health, and health is an important condition of sound thought. It little matters to the results of my thinking whether I eat bologna or bullheads. But the relation of axiom to discourse surely does not display a similar indifference.

So it would seem. But to be thoroughly at home in the spirit of the age is to have a powerful sense of the adventitious and contingent character of all axioms; especially in the thick languages. The provenance of such axioms is mysterious; perhaps some kind of science, itself not axiom-free, might clear it up. But we are not supposed to have any serious doubts about the irredeemably provincial character of all axiom-derived systems. Hence the skeptical question: Where is the principle worthy of all acceptation? Such a "truth" must be as vacuous as it is putatively sublime. So the legitimate children of modernity sense nothing odd in holding the principle of historical-cultural relativity to be axiomatic, which means that the axiom cannot be known to hold for any but this age. Individualized, this means that "Nothing is good or bad but thinking makes it so" is true only for those who think it so. And that "Man is the measure of all things" is true only for Protagoras.

It must be the case, then, that a person who believes that there are some genuinely universal principles, some axioms of universal import, is living in the wrong world. Which goes to show that when a view cannot be refuted, the next best thing is to give it a sociological classification and hope the difference will be overlooked.

To give the Devil his due, however, it is only fair to say that the intention of the relativists is not to confuse the question of the intelligibility of a conceptual system with the question of the persuasiveness of a worldview. The intelligibility of a conceptual system derives in part from axioms that are clear and are consistently employed. Whether an axiom or a set of axioms stipulates or expresses something that the spirit of the age will have difficulty digesting is an empirical question. So it is up to the church to figure out what to do when worldly wisdom (now appropriately identified as "conventional") is light years away from the Gospel and is moving steadily farther out. This would be a fine chore for practical theology.

II

(2) Routes and rules of inference.

It is customary in modern logic to distinguish inference from implication. Something of the sense of the distinction is suggested in the following dialogue:

P: In something you said yesterday you implied that Smithfield is a crook.

Q: I did not *imply* that. You *inferred* it. What I said was that Smithfield's behavior would bear looking into. That does not imply "Smithfield is a crook."

P: Well, perhaps not strictly. But what you left out just now was the *way* you said yesterday, "Smithfield's behavior would bear looking into."

Q: O come now! What do you mean by the *way* I said it yesterday?

P: I mean the sardonic raising of that left eyebrow and the dropping of the corner of your mouth.

Q: I see. So now you're trying to hang me for the way my facial muscles work.

P: Aha! Now who is confusing inference with implication? You infer that I think saying "Smithfield is a crook" is a terrible thing to say. I did not imply that.

Q: Damnation! I did *not* say "Smithfield is a crook"!

P: Not in so many words. But you meant it all along.

Q: How can you be so sure about what I meant since I didn't say it?

P: That's easy. I've had lots of experience in dealing with you.

The main force of P's summation is that he is an old hand at putting various items of experience together in such a way that the resultant pattern is valid for reality. That pattern is not so tight as a mathematical proof, obviously, but it is—or it aims to be—empirically instructive in a way that purely formal proofs dealing only in implication cannot possibly be. The business of weaving such patterns is what is intended by "routes of inference." So understood, inference is a rational method for establishing or exhibiting connections among different kinds of realities. It is not the route of formal deduction, because the conclusions of an act of inferring are not contained in the premises; the result, in fact, is richer than any of the premises. That is, the result is richer than any one of the items or strands of evidence woven into it. Thus, how can P rationally proceed from (i) raised eybrow, (ii) dropped mouth-corner, (iii) tone of voice to: "Q thinks, or Q wants us to think, 'Smithfield is a crook' "? What is P's proper answer? You have to *learn* how to put such fugitive items together to constitute Q in this situation; and then infer, "Smithfield is a crook." And, P should add, learning something like that is nothing like learning a mathematical-logical true-false table.

So P is not "leaping to a conclusion." He has walked to a conclusion over an inferential bridge. No doubt there are intuitive elements in the process, but the process itself is not intuitional.

How does this compare with the connections of which the poet is a master? Here is Jahweh speaking through Hosea:

> So now I will be like a panther to them,
> I will prowl like a leopard by
>   the wayside;
> I will meet them like a she-bear
>   robbed of her cubs
> and tear their ribs apart,

like a lioness I will devour them
   on the spot,
I will rip them up like a wild beast (Hos 13:7,8 NEB).

On the surface the mighty poet-prophet has simply used metaphor to make a daring connection of disparate realms: the animal kingdom and the Lord God of Israel. There is more to it than that, however. This becomes apparent when we ask what the poet intends to achieve through his conjunctive metaphor. Surely his objective is not just to represent God's righteous indignation as vividly as possible. His use of the terrible images exposes a double inferential route: (a) moving from an antecedent anticipation of being blessed to a present certainty of being cursed; (b) moving from an antecedent historical situation ("I cared for you in the wilderness, in a land of burning heat, as if you were in a pasture") to a present dire situation ("I have destroyed you, O Israel; who is there to help you?").

Moreover the two sets—(a) psychological and (b) historical-situational —are conjoined by the prophet, though neither (a) nor (b) can properly be said to imply the other. In other words, (a) might be unrealistic, perhaps quite neurotically so. And (b) might occur independently of (a). In fact we are likely to suppose that historical situations are not altered significantly by personal dispositions. (This is a vulgar and profoundly misleading supposition; I address it further on.)

So Hosea establishes an inferential route between (a) and (b) that is worlds away from any formal: If x then y. But this does not mean that the inferential route is less rational. For the route is not (a) If Israel is fearful enough, then (b) the predicted situation will not materialize. What Hosea proposes is (a) If Israel, being fearful of the Lord, truly repents (turns again), then (b) an otherwise certain doom will be averted by God's mercy ("I will not turn round and destroy Ephraim; for I am God and not a man.").

The prophet has made a bold inferential venture. It is a vexatious one for many Christian theologians. He does not argue that the sinner's gestures of contrition induce a change in God provided that they spring from a heart sufficiently wounded. He does argue that God's disposition to be merciful to the sin-wounded creature is reinforced by a voluntary and agonized exposure of the wounds.

Of course it can be supposed that Hosea works with the model of a long-suffering, benign human father who is sorely tempted to become the father alienated once and for all from his son by the latter's unrelenting mischief. This supposition begs most of the really interesting and important questions. Why do we so readily suppose that Hosea is trying to render belief in God intelligible to a people battered ferociously by the tides of history? Perhaps because we are reminded of the plight of the church in the modern world. Old-style oppressors of the People of God said, "Where now is your God?" Nowadays, theologians are harassed by "What! You are still fiddling with 'God talk' at this point in philosophic history?" Hosea is playing a much bigger game: how to bring Israel to lay hold *faithfully* on her historical situation. In his view this is what God himself is doing through the visions and parables of his prophets (Hos 12:10).

Hosea, then, stakes out an inferential route. He moves from an antecedent grasp of realities to a consequent grasp of other realities. This antecedent-consequent pattern comes to light in a fertile metaphor connecting anterior and subsequent historical situations.

Metaphor, yes; but why fertile? Because it enables us to see that God is the supreme historical agent. Supreme, but neither absolute nor solitary. God's power and wisdom are adequate in any and every situation. But God is not the sole active power in any situation—except creation, if that can be called a situation. Too, the metaphor is fertile because it enables a faithful person to make evil times yield good. Good is more than holding fast to one's beliefs and intrachurch functions despite soul-shattering adversity. The good which God demands through the prophet includes mending one's ways ("refrain from doing evil"), and thereafter being just, loving kindness, and walking humbly with God. ". . . to do justice, and to love kindness, and to walk humbly with your God" (Mic 6:8).

This is a lot of traffic for so delicate a bridge of metaphor. There are routes of inference that do not specialize in metaphor. There is none that reaches home with apodictic certainty. From the axiom of God's everlasting and all-provident caring, peace and prosperity here and now cannot be deduced. That is, or should be, obvious. From the magnitude of the suffering of this present hour, God's everlasting and all-provident caring cannot be deduced. That is part of the suffering of the faithful. If yet the faithful persist in the life policies which God ordains, though they see him not, what—besides sheer doggedness, personal and institutional—accounts for this? Surely there is some kind of patterned connection between divine promise and earthly vicissitude, a connection that is both rational and existential. In the language of piety, there is always a road leading from any situation, no matter how terrible, to God. There is no certainty that multitudes will find it and take it, especially when they realize that it does not detour around "the valley of the shadow of death."

It is part of the conventional distinction between implication and inference to assign some degree of probability to inference and to reserve certainty, rational-logical, to implication. From this we often are led to infer that probability is a weak second best for which the thick practical concerns of life must wistfully settle while the noble craft of truth floats overhead in the beautiful unattainable empyrean of certainty. Moral certainty is not thus best understood and coveted. It is rather a firm and clear grasp of routes of access to realities that gratify the hunger for the good.

Therefore, the prime function of axioms in the density of actuality is to adumbrate that situation in which the appetite for good is both satisfied and stimulated. It is up to practical reason to devise or to apprehend, whichever is necessary, the routes of access to that situation.

III

Consideration of the conditions of intelligibility does not exhaust the agenda of theological methodology. Somewhere along the line theologians ought to show that the axioms and inferences of faith are plausible as well as intelligible. Thereby theologians are ushered into the misty realm of contemporary sensibilities, religious and other.

I intend to canvass only a small sector of that vast intriguing realm: the sector of hope, hope as defined and restricted by the reigning lords of sensibility.[2]

One of the signal achievements of these lords is the confusing of plausibility and intelligibility at a crucial point: hope as transcendently eschatological. Thus the very distinction between immanent and transcendent modes of hope is jeopardized. The distinction is an important one whatever the theological or metaphysical outcome may be; whether or not, that is, one believes there are sufficient grounds for holding to a transcendent hope.

The immanental mode is hope for good in and from the visible world, the structures and powers of the here-and-now. One hopes that the stock market will rally. One hopes for health when ill or anxious. One hopes that the nation will be secure and prosperous. In all such cases we ordinarily look to easily identifiable but largely unpredictable powers. In respect to the economic order, for example, we look to such things as buying power, industrial and agricultural production, favorable trade balances. But in all these things the margins of unpredictability are considerable. Economics is an exact science only in its retrodictive modes.

Since all the powers of this world are largely unpredictable, our actual situation is commonly cloaked with obscurity—obscurity but not mystery. There is little or no sense of mystery about the situations in which immanental hopes arise and to which they are addressed, or about the powers to which we look with such hopes. For the goods at stake I need not look beyond this world, this actual scene.[3]

Transcendental hope relates a good of surpassing value to structures and powers behind or beyond the visible world. Thus we hope for eternal life and for the perfection of human community.

Such hopes may well assume conceptual specificity. In Christianity, for example, eternal life is the concept of a good that surpasses any and all of the goods of the actual world. But this is true also in very different worldviews. It is true for the unalloyed and interminable pleasure of the hedonist. It is true for the world-consuming ecstatic union of the mystic with the Ultimate One. And of course it is true for the unending "length of days" of popular piety. But whatever content is given to eternal life as the world-surpassing good, an overweening passion for it is a potent threat to the goods of the here-and-now world. Such a passion can convert the standardized "good citizen" into a monocular pilgrim relentlessly seeking a home far removed from the tinsel, trammel, and turpitude of Everyday—that world that is "too much with us."

So it is fair to say that hope for eternal life is likely to display at least one other transcendental dimension: It banks on powers behind or beyond the present constitution of the actual world to alter radically that world. In fact such a hope may itself be a power making for alienation from the actual scene.[4] But this is not the whole story by any means. In the hope for eternal life there is sustenance to make the spirit strong and resolute in all of the vicissitudes of the mortal and corrupt world. We may call these sustaining powers psychological or sociological. That merely identifies the beneficiary—the psyche, the *socius*—not the benefactor, the effect, not the cause. What then, or who, sustains the faithful pilgrim when he traverses a dry and thirsty land? Surely not just a sense of his own rectitude; one can starve to death on that. Nor is it just the objective lure of a fertile ideal. The pilgrim is sustained by a sense of walking an appointed route in a company essentially divine. A "cloud of witnesses" accompanies him, discernible only to the eyes of faith, and by saints disguised as rejects and reprobates.

We cannot say less of the perfected human community, the ordained and ultimate home of the human spirit. As a transcendental hope this is a good that the actual world does not give and cannot take away. And again this is a hope that may well alienate one from the here-and-now, because "the beloved community" rebukes the arrogant and mordant exclusions of Everyday, this world in which we are bound and deter-mined to love only "like" and reject "unlike." And again, this beyond-world of transcendent beauty and richness we can have now only in and as hope. We can live everlastingly toward it; we cannot now live within it. The powers making for that kingdom cannot be domesticated in Ev-eryday. Judged by worldly standards, thus, this hope is wildly impracti-cal. Yes, but even without that hope we often wonder why we ever dreamed that this practical world would or could work for the blessing of humankind.

So the beloved community, as well as the pilgrims sustained in its hope, belong to powers that transcend the actual scene. Nonetheless, these powers can be tracked into as well as beyond Everyday. They are vector forces arising in the mysterious depths of being and flashing through Everyday in "majestic instancy," then bearing off toward a global future, all the while knowing exactly where and when all things creaturely will finally arise and converge. In the meantime, authentically spiritual crea-tures are able through faith to discern that trajectory and, in hope, to envision that glory.

IV

On the murky miasmal flats of contemporary sensibility, immanental and transcendental modes of hope are profoundly confused. An obscure but prepotent sense of immense cognitional achievement dictates the criteria of eschatological intelligibility. This is a terrible triumph of plausibility.

The triumph is terrible because it is so inclusive. It embraces at once the situation, the objective, and the power of hope. The situation of hope is exhaustively described in immanental terms. It is assumed that man is the only self-propelled and self-critical being in the realm of sentience; for what scientific assurance do we have of a caring other than our own? None, says worldly wisdom. Accordingly, the spirit of Everyday, for which there is no distinction between plausibility and truth, must proceed to reduce the objectives of hope to a suitably realistic, which is to say practical, shape and level.

So also for the power of hope. From what quarter should we look in good faith for power to lift human life into its fulfillment? Only to man himself, only to his own powers. But, says worldly wisdom, these powers are the benefactions—a mixed lot—of chance throws of the genetic dice, randomly coded by an uncaring, witless cosmos.

Thus the situation, objective, and power of hope are all profoundly affected by worldviews. In fact they express the tilt of worldview toward the cosmic future and human destiny. This does not mean that hope is deprived of transcendental dimensions simply because the great achievements of scientific knowledge so legislate. What in those cognitional gains informs us that the transcendental objectives of hope will never be forthcoming? What assured finding of science implies or warrants the inference that "what we see is what we get" and nothing more? The Everyday appropriation of scientific lore is much nearer the heart of such mischief; more particularly, the acceptance of a worldview called scientific, since science *per se* is not in the worldviewing business. So on the strength of a worldview putatively scientific it is said: If you do not accept this outlook you are out of touch with reality. That is a terrific price to pay for holding on to ancient creed and passé metaphysics.

But what are the benefits of a life thoroughly imbued with the spirit of the age presumptively instructed by science? A sanforized hope, for one thing—hope systematically preshrunk in the interest of being re-spectably realistic. Thanks to science, it is realistic to hope that ere long cancer in all its forms will go the way of diphtheria. With what wonder-ful—why not simply say miraculous?—rapidity is science reducing the weaponry of that Horseman of the Apocalypse named Pestilence! The spirit of the age is having somewhat smaller success with that Horseman named War; he has enjoyed his greatest triumphs in this century.

On the other hand it is unrealistic, perhaps superstitious, to hope for an old-style miracle to cure a metastasized inoperable cancer. Strange things in the line of healing happen occasionally, no doubt of that, but these ostensibly mysterious salvagings of the body are to be understood as challenges to science and not as paradigms of transcendental caring.

And how does it fare with the hope for life beyond death? The spirit of the age permits us to hope for something immanently manageable, not for something transcendently desirable. So it is plausible to hope for a humanization of death. This includes dying made personally manage-able, a process and culmination accepted with dignity and allowing suit-able expressions of caring from those who are not yet to die. The humani-zation of death also means that it would be denied access to social policy: we hope for the elimination of war, capital punishment, and genocide. On the other hand, it is not creditable to hope for a real and blessed life of one's own beyond one's own death. This traditional transcendental hope is discredited by the alogical convergence of two read-outs of sci-ence: (i) Consciousness (and therefore the self?) is entirely dependent upon the brain construed as a bioelectronic system. (ii) Unrecognized and unslaked ego-needs dictate the hope for immortality. So if the real needs of the ego can be gratified immanently, the hope for personal immortality will wither away. And given (i) a human self would need a body in order to enjoy immortality. Contemporary sensibility is worlds away from finding plausibility or any other spiritual comfort in that ancient and hybrid piece of metaphysics, the resurrection of the body.

If now we pause to ask why hope should be modified by any form of the concept *real,* except the most obvious one—"Do you *really* hope for that?"—we shall probably discover that hopes are said to be realistic just so far as they are in accord with the environing social actuality. That is, "realistic" is not supposed to put us into metaphysical overdrive, it is not an appeal or route to "what is." Quite to the contrary, "realistic" is intended to put one in touch with a dominant worldview by which attitudes and sentiments are supposed to be structured, and with social expectations by which life in Everyday is supposed to be guided and appraised.

"Realistic," accordingly, presupposes that possibility is purely a function of actuality, and actuality embraces both "then and now." So understood, possibility, human possibility, is not affected by powers of being that range at will across time and the cosmos. The possible is what the faceless lords and masters of Everyday would approve or—O precious thought!—applaud.

It is true that "realistic" artists sometimes posture as prophetic spirits whose powers of perception and intensity of passion have enabled them to break through the crust of conventionality and grasp the harsh realities of the human condition. So an artist is realistic if in his story chamberpots are used entirely for their original, and therefore real, purpose rather than to house geraniums. And if he claims that that archaic vessel, and its original contents, are really the ultimately meaningful symbols of the human condition, critics will rate him philosophical as well as prophetic.

Somewhat more seriously: Why should hope not do its best to catch and be caught by the stride and rhythm of the truly ultimate powers? Why should it fall back from the boundaries of Everyday with moans of contrition for daring, if but in prayer and dream, to pass beyond them?

Everyday, of course, has plausible answers to such outrageous questions. "What's the good in all that?" "Where's the pay-off?"

V

A proper respect for the realities of hope obliges us to distinguish the credible from the creditable. *Credible* is what one is prepared to believe, that is, to accept as being the case. *Creditable* awards an honor-point for believing and/or doing the right thing. Suppose, then, that I am prepared to believe the resurrection stories in the New Testament, but I am depressed to learn that the *cognoscenti*, my intellectual peer group, will not give me any honor-points for that. In fact what I profess as credible threatens the validity of my candidacy for membership in that group.

Now what does this common but curious phrase, "I am prepared to believe," mean? I suggest that it illustrates the distinction between credible and creditable. In the example of the resurrection, I have access to the reports and claims of New Testament writers, to say nothing of theological interpretations and arguments down the ages since New Testament times. Very well. Suppose I say to myself, "Those stories are true, I believe them," rather than, "I think there is some kind of truth somewhere in those reports and claims; the problem is how to get at it." Nonetheless, in reporting my discovery (which at that moment I am not at all inclined to conceive of as a self-discovery, as a discovery of my own existence, authentic or otherwise) I do in fact say, "I am prepared to believe." Does not this suggest that sometimes one must put considerable effort into believing something, as though the matter believed in were pretty hard to acquire and sustain in its truth-candidacy? So it surely seems.

But what sort of things so complicate believing? A considerable variety. For example—familiar enough by now—the ethos of one's world or of that sector of Everyday in which one lives and moves and has one's quasi-being. To believe against the running tide is costly and chancy. Social scientists have recently proved what we have known all along, namely, that very few of us will buy the risks of a truth that is likely to alienate us from the particular herd whose approval is our light by night and our sedative by day.

Another kind of consideration is more respectable, it flatters an image of self as more persistently rational than the person who worries about his status in a peer group or about being thoroughly *au courant.* That is, it is very hard really to believe something for which there is little or no clearly supporting evidence. We **are** entitled to wonder whether the gross weight of this belief-inhibitor is not much greater than it has ever been in Western civilization. For the imperialism of methodology is such that *evidence* is presupposed to mean data specifiable and quantifiable at the going rates in science. So it is only in the most grossly retarded or regressive religious contexts that we should expect to hear such things as, "I know God is real because I feel him in my heart" and similar appeals to the ineffabilities of personal experience.

It might, therefore, occur to us to discover in William James a remarkably prescient thinker. It is not extremely difficult to find holes in his account of the relation of willing to believing, but that is not the heart of the matter. James saw that modern man must draw deeply and heavily upon the wells of resolution in order to embrace the outlook which alone can illumine, reinforce, and justify the richest moral life. So he summons us to *create* the vital connection between perception and action. The decisive evidence counting for that outlook has to be generated by the agent-self, it cannot be read off the face of the putatively objective world.

This is a far cry from make-believe; surely that is James's earnest hope. Is it a hope well-grounded? Only if his worldview is right. But that judgment is suspiciously akin to the proposition that one must believe there is a true account of the situation of the believer, that is, of the metaphysical-ontological situation. What sort of evidence counts for *that* belief?

I do not suppose that that question lights up an impasse. But I waive it for the moment in order to address and perhaps resolve a rather different question. Have we not been confusing believing with professing what one believes? As we commonly think of it, believing is an interior mental act. To profess the content of that act is to express it in and to some sort of public. Thus "I am prepared to believe *x*" may be the equivalent of "I venture to tell you that I believe *x.*"

Is it so clear, however, that professing one's beliefs presupposes and in part replicates an interior mental act? And is it so clear that that interior mental act (believing) is much harder to make go in this unbelieving age when its objective (content) is some item of traditional religious teaching?

It is not hard to construct a situation in which one says, "I am prepared to believe." without intending to call attention to an interior mental act, arduous or otherwise. Think of a society that advertises the likemindedness of its important constituents as one of its most attractive features: Let that mind be in you which is also and preeminently the spirit of the age. So, in order to display the right tribal features, I say, "I am prepared to believe what the peer society believes." That ought to satisfy the keepers of the gate; they are not likely to press on into my interior mind so long as they are sure that I do, or intend to do, the right things as well make the right professions. But if subsequently I make trouble, or am significantly ambiguous about other troublemakers, truth technicians can use a polygraph on me. Thereby they obtain data as objective as those of meteorology, and they infer my salvation or damnation from pointer readings. Let us thank God for machines and their humanoid partners who care not one fig for interior mental acts! (How does the world appear to those for whom "truth" stands for a flattened line? Do they hold high converse with the watchers in intensive care for whom a flattened line means death?)

Consider a rather different case: I am convinced that x—"Caring is the name of the cosmic game"—is true. So I say that I believe it with all my heart. But the weight of contemporary sensibility lies against x as anything more than a cloistered privatized sentiment. To the extent that I really believe x with all my heart, I hold in this belief a warrant, and perhaps also a sketch, for life-policies that go against the grain of a world some of whose benefits I greatly want to enjoy. If I also accept as a divine paradigm of such a life a being who radiates threats against Everyday ("I have come with a sword rather than with peace") I place myself even farther beyond the pale of plausibility-intelligibility. In such situations I do indeed have to make some preparation to confess x.

What is that preparation? It is not likely to be a repetition of that interior mental act which brought me to x, or, more accurately, brought x to me. True, I may have to ask myself, under the pressure of new evidence or of new light on old evidence: "Do you really think x is true, is really the case?" There is no automatic yea or nay to such questions.

There is a different sense in which I may have to make preparation for believing. That is when I try to count the cost of professing x in a situation laced with threats of various sorts against the credibility—if not the prosperity, liberty, and life—of anyone who professes x. Comfortable Americans find it hard to picture themselves in situations so grave. What century do they think they are living in? There are situations galore— historical, imaginable—when "I am prepared to believe x" is virtually identical with "I am prepared if need be to die for x." There are heroes, saints, and avatars of faith only if x is worth the cost; only if x is true.

So one should hope and pray to be able to meet the price of such an x. One should pray for forbearance, courage, patience, and, if necessary, for oblivion in order to prevent betrayal of others. In such dire situatons it is not likely that one would hope for a transcendental demonstration that x is true, so that the visible cloud of witnesses would see one's vindication. But perhaps an increment of resolution wherewith to keep faith to the bitter end would be a kind of demonstration. Not *more geometrico*, but who really believes that a demonstration of that order has any bearing on, offers any sustenance for, our native hunger for being-in-truth?

VI

Nothing so far adduced or inferred requires us to jettison the notion that believing is an interior mental act, if "interior" is understood to reinforce "mental" rather than to specify a place where such an act occurs. This is not, so far, to move against the application of the distinction interior-exterior to the life of the mind.

Then what is going on when one believes something? Believing is an inward preparation or disposition of the self to enact something bodily, that is, in the external world. So when I say, "I believe x is true" I am intending whatever x is; but I am thereby also disposing myself to enact it, to solidify and objectify it, to realize its meaning. Indeed as far as x does not tug, however weakly or dimly, at my powers of self-activation, x is (intends) a pure aesthetic object: something that conjures feelings of such high intrinsic value that the self as a mind-body system is content to set the clutch at "Idle" for all other conscious business for the time being. So, about x in that mode, I do not properly say "I believe it" but rather "I enjoy it." Accordingly, the pietist is not necessarily making a metaphysical truth-claim when he says, "Christ is in my heart." He may mean that he is enjoying, or is remembering how he enjoyed, certain feelings of peace, communion, and freedom, of which he posits Christ as the true (real) cause.

On the other hand, pietist or not, when I say "I really believe x," I do mean to claim that x has activated my life-system. Not that the words as so many inwardly sounding vocables have that agency—they are but a medium—but that the inner springs of self-existence thus tap into the power of "what is"; or are drawn by it, lured from latency into act.

The meaning of x is therefore a disposition to enact the clues, to fill in the sketch x provides. It would be legitimate up to a point to say that x implies a life-policy, a pattern of commitments and enactments. Thus, "Caring is the name of the cosmic game" implies "I ought to care." But the legitimate appropriation of this formal implicational connection can be overdrawn. The heavy traffic ought to flow through a material-inferential connection. This comes to light in so commonplace a charge as "If you *really* believed x you would do thus-and-so. Your failure or refusal to do thus-and-so is weighty evidence that you do not really believe x. You merely *say* you do—probably for ulterior reasons."

What should one say in response to that charge if one really does believe *x?* Surely not: "O yes I do, but you have to take my word for it because you do not have access to my interior mental acts." That is true enough. The crippling difficulty in it is that it blocks the professed believer's own access to the material inferential route by which one's bid for vindication as a believer can be attained. The false move to interiority reduces *x* to an aesthetic object. When I do that I can therefore have *x* but I cannot enact it. It also means that the evidence of my having *x* will be systematically ambiguous. My pulse is racing, my nostrils are dilating, my cheeks are flushed. But it could be that I have emphysema rather than faith. I may say "In my heart I know I am right," but the world does not know from that how right my heart is. ("The heart has its reasons . . ." Yes, Blaise, but if minds can be crooked, hearts can be corrupt.)

Or suppose someone says, "I appeal to God to vindicate my claim that I really believe despite my ambiguous conduct." Then it is proper to ask such a person about that God; specifically whether that God is related to the being who says, "Why do you call me 'Lord, Lord,' and not do what I tell you?" (Lk 6:46).

"Aesthetic object" is used in this connection to call attention to the affective factor in believing. Ordinary language often renders believing equivalent to feeling. For example: "I feel that it is going to rain." We have to learn from the context whether "feel" is intended cognitively ("the signs certainly indicate rain") or affectively ("whenever I feel depressed the weather takes a turn for the worse"). The ordinary cognitive "feel" refers to things you can see for yourself. On the other hand, you have to take my word for it that I am depressed. Indeed it is conceivable that you may simply have to take my word for it, because I may rigorously eschew hangdog facial expressions in favor of an unrelentingly cheerful countenance, and as carefully avoid quoting pessimistic poets. For, you see, I do not want pity, I want only for the sun to shine soon.

The affectivities of Christian belief are supposed to modify the public self rather than the interior one. This means that the situation of the authentic Christian believer is very strange indeed. He is faithful only insofar as he admits a public norm into the nuances of his interior life. He must not only act as a believer, he must also feel as a believer ought to feel. His whole being has been interiorized by the Christ who belongs to God. So the true believer ought to feel the peace and joy which are the affective components of the new metaphysical situation, "being in Christ."

Is this really different from claiming that a Christian ought to *say* that his inner life is flooded with peace and joy? Is this not on all fours with your having to accept my testimony about my depression? What more than a verbal performance can be asked of us creatures in whom feeling is the element least susceptible to normative allocations and assessments?

The two situations are not the same. When St. Paul says that the person of true faith ought to feel a supernatural peace and joy, he is calling attention to an inverse material inference, to wit: If you really see the riches of the life in Christ, you are bound to feel its peace and joy. Thus the existential connection is made from the objective side. It derives from "what is," not from subjectivity.

So Paul's counsel is not that one ought to make a heroic effort to feel peace and joy, come hell or high water. The proper affective features of the life in Christ are not available through private effort. On the other hand they are not passions, that is, subjective effects of external causes. The appropriate affects, "peace and joy," are the emotive concomitants of the expression, the enactment of faith-as-belief. So however majestic doctrines about the absolute priority of Grace in faith may be, the existential appropriation of belief ("*x* is true") is a profoundly personal act. It manifests the agent-self laying hands on its own situation to effectuate its own destiny.

"Profoundly personal" does not mean a solo, purely self-originative performance. A social context is presupposed, a community in which the self comes into its own as a full-fledged participant in a common destiny, but not as a product of social forces that relentlessly spell out one's fate.

Peace and joy, then, as normative in their own way as moral precepts, are affective concomitants of being related authentically to the beloved community. I cannot feel the peace of God unless I am at peace with my brothers and sisters in the faith. I cannot feel the highest joy unless I rejoice in the being of others. I must learn to rejoice in their being, not merely in their achievements. So to consent to the being of others pertains to the chateaux of divine love.

So the norms of feeling are most intimately related to objective-situational realities. Being at peace and expressions of joy are public facts rather than ineffable qualities of a private self; as public as barograph and polygraph spider tracks signifying, to the trained eye and properly programmed mind, a change in the weather and truth-or-lie. But if I am a mischief-worker, a dynamo of hostility effects, these too are as much observable facts as the rising and setting of the sun. If I cast a pall of gloom over the lives of others, thereby lowering their vitality and thus diminishing their appetite for being, that is as much a public fact as the impact of billiard ball A on billiard ball B.

The affective demands of the Gospel, in St. Paul's view, are a Christian version of a phenomenon virtually universal in religion. Some religions accept postponement of the highest and purest peace and joy until another world, a world whose perfections reduce the scene here below to the status of a diseased and ephemeral fantasy. Other religions maximize human resources for the best peace and joy this world affords under the metaphysical conviction that there is no other living world.

The religions of the world can be arranged in a rather different spectrum, that of community in relation to self-perfection. And those that place an accent on community form a subspectrum on the issue of the voluntaristic principle. Does the route to salvation—the highest and most enduring peace and joy—require the self to create its own place in the ultimate community? Or is that place defined and ordained from eternity?

Traditional Christianity occupies a position well toward the latter end of this subspectrum. This is a notorious feature of it, in the eyes of contemporary sensibility. It is an integral part of that melancholy outlook and social system identified as Calvinism. It is unfortunate that we are so commonly unaware of the extent to which that outlook and system live on in a society intellectually hostile to it. Our world has immense confidence in scientific ways of determining what niche in it people ought to occupy. These secular forms of foreordination are accompanied by a very weak doctrine of salvation. Filling one's niche, faithfully discharging the duties of one's role: these qualify one for a Useful Citizen Award—often a watch with which to keep track of the empty time of retirement, that is, of uselessness. But whether one ever attains, in this here-and-now, real peace and triumphant joy is generally regarded as a personal—private—problem. Nonetheless the mass media are busy non-stop assuring us that there are all sorts of fun and games to be had in exchange for our inheritance: pottage highly spiced and devoid of nutriment. Esau got a better deal.

It is possible, and here it is useful, to use *foreordination* without taking on board metaphysical stowaways or degenerate sociocultural residues. The concept can be used, that is, to signify the sense (the "feel") of being at last and truly in one's rightful place in the human enterprise, the awareness of being now and really at home. Traditional theology adds: insofar as God intends that for the faithful in time and the creaturely fallen world. In the traditional view the true church is the community in which "the foretaste of glory divine" is an objective, not a private, actuality. So though the homeland of the pilgrim is not the fallen world, he is given a goodly company with which to traverse the wilderness.

Traditional theology itself exhibits a significant subspectrum on the issue of the boundaries of alienation from the everyday world. In general, the theologians who do not acknowledge any legitimate and significant civil managerial functions for church and believer are the ones who press world-alienation to its outermost and innermost limits. But the traditionalist theologian cannot drive alienation all the way without falling into Manicheanism—the view that actuality is the ultimate (or, more correctly, primordial) metaphysical catastrophe.

The sense of being in one's divinely appointed place requires both an interior and a public confirmation. The public confirmation is being accepted by a Christian community as a lover and maker of peace, and thus as a faithful child of God ("Blessed are the peacemakers, for they shall be called sons of God" Mt 5:9) and as a bringer of joy to others. The interior confirmation is peace and joy as normative affects of God's approval.

Confirmation of that peculiar and powerful sense of being foreordained elicits (infers) an equally powerful sense of being able to live at last as much from the outside as from the inside. That is to say, the surety of the Christian life is grounded in the perception of objective callings, summonses, solicitations, and provocations clear enough, and potent withal, to restructure infertile or unhealthy situations. The aim is not to make that part of the world conform to one's ego-needs but, rather, to maximize in it the options and resources for human growth. All of this, moreover, in the faith that such is the manifest and perfect will of God.

That is the only sure and authentic hope of glory.

So the justification of the believer is entirely different than having a seal of approval stamped upon the interior self. "Justification by faith alone" signifies that the interior self is at last reconciled with the public self, the word and the act are at last living with each other in peace, power, and joy. The present indicative is intentional; up to a point it is legitimate to say both "ought to be" and "shall be," but that means that there are logical-existential tensions here very similar to those of moral experience. "I am doing what I ought" does not mean "I am doing it correctly and thoroughly." But it is also the case that "I am doing what I ought" does not simply mean "I am *trying* to do what I ought." For the *ought* names (indicates) an activity and not the objective or end-state of that activity. So justification names a way of intending-acting. The faith by which one walks is not perfectly enacted in anything one does ("I do not perfectly obey God"). But at the same time intending so to walk is an enactment and not just a case of citing a motive or looking in loving despair at a paradigm of perfection.

VII

Hope, in the Christian outlook, is transcendental. This does not mean that a great virtue is to be made of discontinuity between a vision of the great divine future and the actual here-and-now world, as though the kingdom of God and the kingdom of man were mutually repellant substances. Undue stress on that discontinuity is a symptom of a false sense of transcendence. Christian hope is properly transcendental when one apprehends in faith the end toward which the whole of creation is being moved as the very thing in which one's own being is to be, is being, perfected. Christian hope thereby relates the actualities of self, society, and cosmos to an unseen reality. Unseen but present for that reality is the mysterious, infinitely potent, life of God within the world. But this is the same world shared with every variety of unbeliever, the world in which "hopes deceive and fears annoy." So we can hardly fail to ask what assurance there is that this transcendental hope does not deceive. Let the faithful person act on the conviction that he must not be conformed to this world and its righteousness. How can he be sure that the higher principle to which he professes allegiance, the righteousness of God's kingdom, is truly transcendental rather than the forward throw of his own ego-needs? Might it not be the summons of that dimension of self-existence writ large in Freudian theology as Superego?

This is but one reminder among many that there are many situations in which we have to decide between an intuitive certainty and a certainty available only at the end of an inferential route. The testing of hope's surety is such a situation. For instance, an appropriate expression of Christian hope is, "I believe that the souls of the faithful live forever in the presence of God." For the faithful in the land of the living here-and-now it is intuitively certain that nothing can happen in this world to disconfirm or even to cast a shadow upon that glorious vision. The abstract ground for this is very simple: Hope looks always to a future that cannot disappoint or deceive. According to that, whatever deceives and disappoints is local, finite, mortal, incomplete, imperfect, and is exposed as such by the vision of glory.

But the believer is under orders he takes to be divine to test all visions. He must, that is, track them to see what comes of them in the actual world. For only those visions are of God and from God which draw the self-as-ego up into a public self foreordained to bespeak peace and bring joy. So it is true that the proper hope of the Christian is surely to participate in the glories of the eternal kingdom, to "see God and enjoy him forever." But hope is also ordained to relate the faithful perspicuously to the life of God now and everlastingly committed to the transformation of fallen worlds.

Therefore, hope has an active as well as a passive modality. One must wait for the ultimate transformation, the creation of "the new heavens and the new earth." So to wait, so to hope, is to hold resolutely to an envisagement of self- and world-perfection. But that envisagement is not a pure aesthetic perception. Rather, it is the forward throw of a life-policy for here-and-now oriented upon the peace of God and boundless joy.

VIII

One of the prime functions of faith is to grasp and formulate the grounds of hope. From faith come the axioms which charter particular routes of inference, at the conclusion of which, if they are properly run, lies practical certainty. "If Christ has risen from the dead, then . . ." The central problem of the Christian life, and therefore of Christian reflection, is not to devise some all-winning way to obviate or defang that "If."

Indeed, preoccupation with anterior and interior certainty can be profoundly mischievous. Moreover, that "If . . ." is not intended to launch an hypothesis or a pious surmise. Its purpose is to open up (in that sense to demonstrate) the connection between the ground of hope and the superstructure of Christian existence: a life-policy.

How then are we to reconcile the inescapable looseness of inferential routes with the divine demand for radical obedience? The theological task thus disclosed is to track down the appropriate material inferences from, for example, "If Christ has risen from the dead . . ." In St. Paul's terms, what does it mean to care about Christ's dying and rising again to God for us sinners?

Much experience and many voices testify that the believer must wait and listen for divine instruction about that. There is much to ponder and something to accept in that counsel, but not everything. The Christian life is a resolute pursuit of ways in which to glorify God. For that, faith furnishes clues—not, certainly not, a detailed map. Intuitive certainty is properly lodged in that moment of faith in which one says, "I know that I must start from x." Thereby, the projectile called Christian existence is aimed and launched. But its trajectory is not predetermined. The determination of that is a function of a complex series of contingent choices.

In faith, therefore, one takes bearings by looking back to the starting point. Through hope one takes another reckoning: from the envisaged end and longed-for arrival. Love holds the antecedent and interior self to the foreordained public self.

The divine concert of these virtues—faith, hope, and love—comes to light when the public self becomes the substance rather than the adumbration of things hoped for. Then the interior self—that old Adam, the ego—will have blissfully surrendered the last vestige of its pseudohegemony. Then indeed, as St. Paul says, all things will have become new.

Chapter Five

⚜

SOLA SCRIPTURA:
PROBLEMS ABOUT AUTHORITY

I

Theologians rarely deny that Christianity is a religion of the book. For modern theologians "the book" is a congeries of intellectual problems; this is the source of a special anxiety called hermeneutics. We have the book, yes; but it is either silent or hopelessly mystifying in respect to existential concerns, as these are voiced by contemporary sensibility, unless the book is properly interpreted. The Bible speaks, but its utterances must be translated into signs, symbols, and concepts that make sense within the parameters of modernity.

There are other dimensions of the problem of authority in modern theology, but the bible occupies a unique place in that complex; perhaps still a commanding place. At any rate, it is the focus of this disquisition because both the practical Christian and the theologian appeal to the bible either as the principal inspiration of their several and, one hopes, common interests, or as a warrant for their convictions. Both the practical Christian and the theologian assume that from Scripture emanates indispensable light on and for the understanding and guidance of human life.

So we have at once two problems:

(1) How is the real and essential teaching of the bible to be distinguished and separated from its useless information, its archaic cosmology, and its nonrelevant prescriptions?

(2) Since the bible does not contain all that we know and need to know about human reality, how should the truth of Scripture be related to truth otherwise ascertained and already absorbed into the fabric of life in Everyday?

Sola Scriptura: Problems about Authority

Assumptions lurk behind these questions. They ought to be considered before we take the plunge into the questions themselves.

II

Why does (1) seem to be as difficult as it is important? A very important part of the faith of the practical Christian has been the assumption that the bible really means what it says and all that it says. On the witness stand in the courts of law the Christian is expected to swear on the Bible that his testimony is the truth, the whole truth, and nothing but the truth. Why should he expect less from the book by which so mighty an oath is exacted from him? Yet has any Christian in almost two thousand years tried to execute all the requirements of the Old Testament law? Do many of the pious now claim to be profoundly illuminated, edified, or instructed by the Book of Numbers? Does it pertain to the living mind and heart of the Gospel to believe that the wonderful and terrible moral density of human existence all descends from the oddly felonious behavior of a primitive human pair in a Mesopotamian valley irrecoverably divine?

These are not purely rhetorical questions; in almost any congregation some affirmative responses to them would be forthcoming. But for the time being I shall treat that fact as evidence of a deep and anxiety-tinctured desire to hold some authority in faith to be exempt from erosion. There is little or no evidence that even the earliest Christian community, or the most primitive since then, ever felt bound to obey the Levitical law stipulating that a woman who grabs the genitals of her husband's antagonist when he and another man are fighting must suffer the amputation of the offending member, her hand. The church in history has in fact produced a splendid variety of explanations and justifications for a selective reading of Old Testament law, and of Old Testament history as well.

Does this mean that theology, as far as it evinces a sense of responsibility to and for the Bible, continues to be, promises to be, a series of strategic retreats from any view of Scripture as a global truth, an inclusive and decisively important "world"? Evidence for this interpretation of theology can be marshaled in the following way:

(i) A considerable part of the Bible is historical narrative. What does that history have to do with us, religiously? Why is it more important

109

than the history of the Hittites or the Mayans?

Here we are sure to hear a flourish of theological trumpets on the salvation history theme. But we have to be sure that behind that fanfare there is more than a way of extracting from ordinary history an extraordinary import, or of imposing such import upon ordinary history. Later on we shall have to ask whether the proponents of salvation history mean to say that there is a series of real events—as real as anything that happened to the Hittites or the Mayans—that nonetheless really happened only to and for the faithful; a series concurrent with ordinary events but neither contained in them nor implied by them.

(ii) An important part of the Bible is liturgical. What sorts of theological presumption underlie the conviction that some, but not all, of the liturgical precepts and structures of Scripture are still and forever normative?

(iii) Ritualistic rules are a prominent element of the Old Testament. There are ethical elements in this legalistic mass. As already noted, Christian theologians have long practiced extracting these ethical elements from that mass; often enough they have encouraged legalistic attitudes to grow luxuriantly around the ethical. Moreover, the extracts are presumed to have as much authority for Christians as the "whole Bible."

(iv) The Bible is a seedbed of once powerful symbols portraying the human situation. Are those symbols still vivid and potent? If so, is not *that* the real authority of the Bible? But if this be allowed, then whatever grips and structures the imagination with comparable power has comparable authority, whether it is Shakespeare or Salinger. Moreover, what would "authority" then mean? Something that commands obedience, such as a law or a magistrate? Or that which pertains to the commands of God transcendent?

(v) Even a cursory reading of the Bible makes it abundantly plain that there are many cosmological outcroppings in it that now can speak only to antiquarian interests. Why then should we suppose that the Bible is full of instruction for us on the weighty theme of human life in the cosmic scheme, the latter being infinitely more complex than ancient cosmologists dreamed? Theologians old and new reply that man is not saved by adherence to cosmological theories, old or new. But modern theologians cannot easily forget that modern cosmologies render man an unaccountably intelligent upstart in a cosmos too vast and complex to be understood—except by the cosmologists.

These are hints of the racking vicissitudes scriptural authority is having to endure in the modern world. Through all of them, theologians have persisted in asking the question identified as (1) above: How is the real and essential teaching of the Bible to be distinguished and separated from its useless and wrong information and its nonrelevant prescriptions? The question argues an assumption: Somewhere in the Bible inextinguishable and vital truth lurks; so it pertains to the high calling of theology to fan that spark into flames of consuming interest.

III

That double-jointed assumption has a thick connection with an intuitive certainty: We cannot expect Scripture to deliver a perspicuous word until we are sure what it means to live in the modern world. For we are sure that our world differs considerably from its predecessor. Perhaps, indeed, ours is a unique historical situation; unique—let us venture to say it—in a unique way. We are in some ways new creatures, or we know how to become such, though hardly in the Pauline sense. But there's the rub—who or what are we, really? What might we make of the human stuff? Are we the creatures of sheer possibility, untutored, finally, by anything genuinely and demonstratively normative?

It is hardly surprising, given such readings of the historical situation, that so much of contemporary theology is an anthropological quest. Some theologians look to philosophy for the right method of conducting the search. Others turn to the creative arts; still others to social science. But, again, whether or not an intuitive certainty underlies this anthropological quest and determines its results, there is a great consensus in the reports from every sector: The historical situation of scientific-technological man is unique, and the full measure of his uniqueness has not yet dawned on us. And here there may be a clue for understanding the generation gap both deplored and celebrated, namely, that the adult and senior generations simply fail to perceive that the contemporary world is radically different from the world they started with and cling to so hungrily and so vainly. In that dear dead world, living now only in the unreality of nostalgia, many people, perhaps a majority, believed they lived under the canopy of Scriptural authority. The noblest and most poignant sentiments were expressed in biblical language. The national life and destiny were grasped in biblical metaphor: the Chosen People; the assured end of life "for which the first was planned" (Browning, to be sure, but often taken to be scriptural by people used to hearing their preachers quote Scripture and Browning in successive, if not the same, breaths) is an eternal happiness beyond the grave.

So—"things learned on earth we shall practice in heaven" (Browning again; practically canonical, nonetheless). But the world now around us, and within, is very very different from all of that. Most people nowadays do not and cannot believe much of the Bible, or enjoy or use it, even if they wanted to. The pious may suppose that they take their bearings from the Bible. If they really do, they are an endangered species left behind by a world lost to sight and sound.

Yet the great majority of theologians remain committed to showing that the Bible is uniquely authoritative in and for a historical situation which is itself unique. An authority dimly acknowledged and poorly served by the conventional gestures of biblicist piety, to be sure. But can the proper quality and magnitude of that authority be more easily descried on the assumption that the Bible is a massively important message coded so obscurely that only a highly trained specialist can decipher it, and only if he brings the right tools to it? How can Scripture speak authoritatively when its perspicuous and decisive word has to be filtered through grids of attitudes, logico-linguistic rules, and conceptual systems imported for this holy exercise from science and philosophy?

It may make a difference whether the key to Scripture is derived from science and/or philosophy. Let us suppose, that is, that a complex of scientific investigations, such as archaeology, linguistics, history of various sorts, is trained on the Bible. Ought we to expect from this a printout of some importance for the question of biblical authority? At first glance this is unlikely because there is no science of norms as such. Perhaps some complex of science can explain why (show how) we accept some norms and reject others. But no science and no complex (collegium) of sciences can prove that x is a real norm for y. By what *scientific* norm might we be able to show that modern science is a better way of organizing the study of nature—to say nothing of directing human affairs—than ancient astronomy or mediaeval alchemy? We have long since put our money down; now we are inclined to say that an electric can opener is proof the wager is won.

But back to the Bible. Suppose a scientific complex shows that Joshua (if he ever lived except as a character in splendid folklore narratives) was a bloodthirsty and cunning brigand better suited to a manual of guerrilla warfare than to any high and holy purpose; and that the walls of Jericho fell under the onslaught of an earthquake anyway, and not from the toot of a trumpet in the hands of a brigand. What then can properly dispose us to find something normative for us in any of his real deeds and words? Joshua 24:15 has inspired many a Christian sermon: ". . . but as for me and my house, we will serve the Lord." But the context effectively celebrates, through simple narration, the drive and dedicated rapacity of a desert brigand. In his splendid valedictory to his people Joshua says:

I gave you a land on which you had not labored, and cities which you had not built, and you dwell therein; you eat the fruit of vineyeards and oliveyards which you did not plant (24:13).

True, Joshua is not one of the loftiest saints of Israel, Old or New. But does Scripture boast human figures impenetrably divine against the artillery of scientific biblical criticism?

Perhaps authority, after all, is something faith vests in the Bible rather than something discovered there.

But we may be covering difficult territory too rapidly and too recklessly. Would it not be absurd to say that scientific explanations of how the exercise of parental authority works in a given culture, and thus of what "it really is," logically undermined that indispensable social force?

The analogy is crippled by a capital difference. Parental authority is a time-terminal phenomenon. A parent makes binding decisions for a child only so long as he is a child. In modern Western society one is not judged to be mature if one has not learned to make one's own decisions. To honor father and mother does not mean to obey them in all things forever. On the other hand, traditional Christianity has always looked to the Bible as to an authority never to be dismissed or transcended as long as time and the human world endure. If such an authority were real, it would have to be obeyed and not merely respected; whereas in intrahuman affairs it is common and proper for one to say to a parent, "I respect your wishes but I do not intend to accede to them." But we seem to have learned from some kind of science that no norms are culture-universal. We seem to have learned from some kind of philosophy that to come of age we must answer to and for ourselves alone. So even if there is God we ought to think twice before addressing him, Scripture-wise, as Father.

So whether or not theologians like it, the authority of Scripture is exposed to demands for scientific validation-invalidation. Nonetheless there are some theological questions to be asked about this situation. For example, if the authority of Scripture is exposed to this demand, what criteria are appropriate for its prosecution? It will not do to trot out specific scientific theories, whether cosmological or anthropological, that are widely accepted at the moment as true. Yet it might be legitimate to proceed in the investigation with such contingent propositions as, "If evolution is right, some parts of the Bible must be wrong; notably, the first human being was not created in a twinkling of God's eye." It is not entirely clear that there is a logical collision, head-on and catastrophic (on the religious side), between the biblical view of man's origin (if we assume that the Bible evinces any interest in that as a cosmological issue) and evolutionary theory. But we can be reasonably sure that somebody in the Christian camp feels threatened when he urges us to remember that a moment for God, a twinkling of his eye, might well embrace ten thousand millennia of creaturely time ("For a thousand years in thy sight are but as yesterday when it is past," Ps 90:4).

Of late we have not heard as much about the deadly threats to the tradition embedded in scientific biblical criticism, or about the promise of the latter for spiritual liberation, as several late theological generations had to endure. Theories about cataclysmic shifts of consciousness, at least in Western society, seem to pose a new threat to any principle of universal authority and to offer fresh promises of spiritual liberation from such ancient tyrannies. For now we hear that contemporary consciousness is radically different from consciousness in in any other era. More specifically, outlooks and value-systems of earlier stages of consciousness are now as impotent and meaningless as the pressed forget-me-not found in a book picked up at random in a secondhand shop.

A variety of observations and questions throng the mind when one attends to such theories of consciousness. For example, have they been influenced by evolutionary doctrine despite vivid disclaimers of that from their proponents? Are these theories and concepts so many Hegelian residues—chips of Hegel liberated from his rationalism? Are they simply the latest evolutionary stage of historicism?

I do not intend to press these questions here because there are some logical issues of antecedent importance, however devoid of engrossing interest they may be. I grant that posting this sort of priority involves the risk of trying to impose attitudes and methods simply out of touch with the latest stage of consciousness; and to no avail but thus to be exposed as a "backworldsman." Would that one could here successfully misappropriate Hegel and grandly say, "To be conscious of risks is in principle to avoid them"!

IV

The general view, that consciousness is a reality subject to quantum leaps, cannot be entirely reduced to that old affliction, historical relativism. There is a metaphysical sweep in the new view; it is a theory about reality and not merely about history and culture. But like some other metaphysical theories this one also contains some epistemological-logical puzzles. It may be that these puzzles are real and important only for people who do not share the view, or who have been left behind by evolving consciousness. These are risks to be embraced as cheerfully as possible.

Here, then, is one of these puzzles: How could a person caught up in a higher (or at any rate radically novel) level of consciousness know what a lower level really was? Suppose one now stands within C3 (consciousness, third level). How can that person say, meaningfully, "Ah, but I remember when I had, or was had by, C2?" The "remembering" that person now does is dictated by C3. He can (or should be able to) recall that as a C2-er he was, say, a racist, a sexist, a Fundamentalist, and a Republican. But now as a C3-er he no longer grasps *what* these things meant, he only recalls *that* he was then so constituted. He no longer aspires for those false values; known now, not then, to be false.

Thus the C3-er who has mutated from C2 (one must allow, I suppose, for the native-born C3-er) can say, as a historian, that he has designed a construct he calls C2, but the design must meet the requirements of C3. He can impute the construct to an alien people, living or dead, whom he does not, indeed he cannot, really understand. He has no way of knowing that the imputation, the projection of the construct, hits anything. Moreover his reasons for the whole business are by definition a function of C3 rather than of C2 or Cn.

So the C3-er speaks and thinks with his own stage of consciousness about the memories, records, and kindred artifacts of another and lost world. But what metaphysical presumption he exhibits when he avers that his constructs and theories are really *about* the life and world long gone, of which the evidences are cryptic and random (for all he knows) leftovers! It is one thing for the poet to declaim about Homer's Greece:

> Yet never did I breathe its pure serene
> Till I heard Chapman speak
> out loud and bold: . . .

Happily for all concerned, Keats' greatness as a poet has nothing to do with the semantic accuracy of Chapman's translation of Homer; or Homer's with the historical accuracy of his account of the Trojan War.[1] It is quite a different one for the C3-er to pretend to have given us a literally true and faithful account of any other level or kind of consciousness.

This issue can be put in abstract form. If the theory is self-referential, it admits only of intuitive certainty; it is true only for those gripped by it. If the theory is world-referential, it must be tested fairly against evidence not preselected by it. The same sort of issue haunts doctrines of election and every other systematic deterministic theory.

Some elements of this epistemological-logical puzzle harass the doctrines of historical relativism. Yet they avoided, or could have, some of the most punishing harassment by being related to a few nonrelativistic principles; for instance, that there is a logic of inquiry universally applicable though not universally applied. Which is to say that judgments of validity in principle are different from reported ascertainment of such facts that people now believe—or eat, drink, wear, or say.

But the general theory of stages of consciousness ought to give no quarter to such principles. Reason herself is a servant of a particular stage of consciousness; she wears the garb and does the chores assigned to her by the ethos. Thus one age turns Reason into an abstract mathematical genius, another into a moral genius, perhaps a casuist *Überhaupt*. Still another turns her into the fantastic wanton of the world-historical-dialectical process, leaving her bloody footprints all over the place. But whatever Reason is constrained by the spirit of the age to be, and wholly to be, she has no prospects of surviving in that role, under that guise, under the unrelenting pressure of the oncoming stage of consciousness. So where a master of the old school, such as Hegel, clearly supposed that reason is a time- and culture-embracing reality rather than a time- and culture-bound one, the heralds of evolving consciousness feel no such constraints. They may concede that Hegel was right in declaring that consciousness is self-grounded; it is not a product of anything else. But how could a hostage of rationalism have grasped the depth dimension of consciousness or understood that intellect is the great falsifier of consciousness?

Some kind of distinction between the surface and the depths of consciousness appears to be a defining characteristic of the outlook under consideration here. Here it is a child of the age, the Freudian age. Moreover the distinction has a valuational correlate: The depths are the home of the great powers of human life. The deep self is alone truly creative as well as irrepressibly vital.[2]

Here Hegel, as well as many a classical thinker, exacts a kind of revenge. For it appears that consciousness is always structured; theoreticians may disagree among themselves over the nature of the structure and its derivation, but they cannot blink away the reality of structure. Which is to say, minimally, that consciousness is not, it is never, a mere metaphysical blob. It is always, it is essentially, a structured many-in-one, a dominant one-in-many. Thus consciousness is more than the affective ambience of perceptions, conceptualities, aspirations, and anxieties. The many are ordered: Consciousness is an order of superordination and subordination. Something rules and all else is ruled. We shall hold in reserve the question whether at any given moment the monarchical principle *de facto* is the monarch *de jure*.[3]

If we say, then, that in consciousness something rules, something imposes order, are we not thereby committed to saying that in any stage of consciousness something rules absolutely, that is, that it always rules and is never itself ruled? (It is assumed throughout that consciousness is not available to babes and sucklings; they are candidates or postulants for it.) If this is the case, a radical shift of consciousness, a quantum leap, would mean that the displacement of a monarchical principle has occurred and another one has assumed authority. "The King is dead; long live the King!" But now the principle of continuity, that grand metaphysical mystery, has been itself replaced by a principle of discontinuity. The replacement is no less metaphysical. Evolving consciousness is thus heavy metaphysical global business. It is, it intends to be, far more significant than dislocations in perception and feeling caused by the appearance of great novelties on the plains of history. With its king a world dies. The new world has, must have, a new king.

Applied to what we may plausibly call the democratic consciousness, these notions reap an interesting bundle of inferences. For example, suppose that by "democratic consciousness" we mean a psychic constitution rather than a political orientation; that is, any impulse, perception, or aspiration is as good as and no better than any other. This is surely a strong contender for "Supreme Nonsense Champion." But for the moment let us blithely suppress the dictates of commonsense—a lot of philosophy and theology can be written and enjoyed without them. So we have a situation in which any inclination to suppress impulse *a* in favor of impulse *b* ought itself to be suppressed since *a*, by definition, is as good as *b*. But what psychic agent has the authority—not to be confused with the power—to order the suppression of that antidemocratic inclination? Whence that mysterious authority?

The answer to the first question is not very mysterious. In a democratic consciousness a policy is set to prevail over imperialistic impulse, that is the announced democratic policy. If this policy is properly enforced there will be no successful *coup de corps*. There may be rebellions but there will not be a revolution until the policy and the policy enforcer die and a new consciousness emerges.

It would seem, then, that the popular slogan, "Down with repression!" can hardly mean what it says. Though we have begun with the assumption that any impulse is as good as any other, any plain and honest account of human life will show that any policy whatever requires enforcement. Even if I admit that one of the most remarkable, though not one of the most uncommon, impulses of all, to jump off a cliff, is as good as any other, I have to compel it to recede for the time being; otherwise it is all over for every other impulse; and the structure of the democratic consciousness will have been destroyed. So policy cues such as "appropriateness," "reality," "fittingness" pop up all over the place. Primitively speaking I should say that impulse *a* ("Throw yourself over the cliff!") is as good but no better than impulse *b* ("No, wait a minute: yonder is an unwitting child running toward the cliff—stop her!"). But we are not in that primordial situation, and never were. Any consciousness we know and are, or have ever known and been, is structured both ontologically and valuationally. Every one of them has instated and honored some sort of distinction between ruler and ruled, between superordination and subordination.

So the slogan, "Down with repression!" is a piece of rhetorical license. It does not specify, it does not even hint of, a viable life-policy. It does express a conviction that in the dominant societal and psychical structures the wrong things are "in the driver's seat." It does not mean that the steering wheel is the perfect symbol of original evil.

What then is the mysterious source of that indispensable authority without which policy, both societal and psychical, is bootless?

Perhaps it seems most mysterious in and for the democratic consciousness; if, that is, in that context any and every impulse instinctively grasps the wisdom of the democratic principle, and is thus prepared to sacrifice the value of its own immediacy to protect the value of intrinsic goodness. We should have every right to be proud of an impulse capable of such a remarkable achievement. Heretofore, such discernment and decision have generally been ascribed to reason rather than to native impulse and untutored feeling. But that is an image of human life presumed now to be in full retreat, if not panic rout, before the irresistible forces of gut reaction, the primacy of the sensuous, and kindred allies of immediacy. Not that any of these thrives in an unstructured life. Each, in fact, is a postulant for supremacy. Each claims for itself authority *de jure*.

But elements of mystery remain. If authority is vested in the ruler—whether that be a regime in the political realm, some element in a value system, an intuition, or a faith—is it not the case that that from which authority derives and descends is itself the ultimate authority? Consider that in this nation the rulers govern in principle only by the consent of the governed. A regime accorded that consent thus rules with proper authority; but the sovereignty of the people is in no way abridged or diminished by that. To the contrary, only the people have the right of investiture. Accordingly, to act without or beyond authority is possible for all political agents—except for the people; but the people are self-committed always to act through one crew of agents or another, and by due process.

Now we seem to be threatened by a towering paradox. This absolute and empirically nonderivable right to rule must be both exhibited and validated in the forms of life over which it presides. It is not supposed to be validated by a final unilateral appeal to a presumptively absolute and universal standard whose eminence, majesty, and power defeat any creaturely challenge.

Here the voices of piety and theological tradition may be heard in chorus: "You have left out God! He truly is the ultimate sovereignty behind and beyond all rightful human exercise of authority."

The great biblical inspiration of this conviction is the teaching of St. Paul. "Let every person be subject to the governing authorities. For there is no authority except from God, and those that exist have been instituted by God" (Rom 13:1).

But suppose that we have not at all intended to leave God out of this puzzling business of authority. Suppose, indeed, we have had in mind all along that God who himself orders the faithful to test every prophet— that is, everyone who claims to speak for God—and who orders the faithful to test all forms and exercises of authority by that standard which is *Immanuel*, God-with-us.

As for the Pauline teaching, it takes a mentality already attuned to the vile hubris of autocracy to discover a rationale for it in the injunction: "Let every person be subject to the governing authorities." There is nothing in Romans that suggests that this means servile obeisance, silent or expressed acquiescence in oppression, or any sort of gesture of approval of either random or systematic cruelty. God knows, and we must not forget, that Christian people have not always lifted their voices or their hands against murderous and blasphemous despots. This illustrates a fundamental theological proposition: It is far easier to give intellectual assent and pious approbation to the doctrine of original sin than it is to discern and confess its reality in the multitudinous unoriginal sins of our very own.

Moreover, given the *God* of Christian faith, the derivation of all authority from the Almighty, All-Wise, All-Just being can never be executed in the modalities of self-righteousness, self-exculpation, and self-aggrandizement. For that being can dispose as well as invest, and there is no court of appeal from his decrees. Who knows how many despots have trembled when that has occurred to them, when it has been thundered at them by prophets of the Lord God? That is a historical-psychological question. What counts and ought to count as the evidencing of God's awful consuming wrath against the monsters of perfidy, cruelty, and egomania? That is a theological question. This essay is not devoted to answering it; such is the ascesis of methodology. Even so, one may hope to be pardoned for noting that the *God* of New Testament faith is certainly the concept of a being related, self-related, to the contingencies of history and to the relativities of all human judgments; related to these palpable actualities as a concrete absolute norm. A living norm, a standard embodied in a life, a life that is the paradigm worthy of all emulation. Such is the confession of faith.[4]

Yet there are many faiths and many lords. There are multitudes of monarchical axioms presiding in and over many forms of life. Moreover, despite the tensions and overt conflicts among contemporaneous forms of life, their respective monarchical axioms are not locked in dialectical struggles with one another. As monarchs, these principles and principalities have no "give" to them. They are incorrigible. It does not follow that any of them is infallible; an inference to that effect is a natural and self-serving error.

This is but to say again that the first principles—however constituted or derived—of a life-system are its final authority. But this does not make each such lord absolute *de jure,* even if the adherents and protagonists of a life-system do not see how a genuinely human existence would be possible on any other terms. In advanced civilizations the wise and the learned know there are other ways of putting things together; as St. Paul says, "there are many gods and lords aplenty." The really wise do not permit this piece of religious intelligence to license disdain or indifference to that being under whose tutelage the nation (or the people) has endured and hopes to prevail.

Here another piece of religious intelligence bids for attention. Lords, both visible and invisible, are served because it is profitable so to do. Monarchical axioms are embraced because the life systems they authorize are judged to be good, fair, and worthy of all acceptance. This is to say that a monarchical axiom, if it really rules, does something far more meaty and interesting than generating a set of definitions or a conceptual scheme. These lords all claim to provide vistas of the ultimate management of cosmic as well as human affairs. Thereby an indispensable opportunity for justification and correction is offered to a life-system; though this is not necessarily the intent of any of the "lords many." Think here of the ancient military-political-religious practice of taking captive the gods of the enemy: they too shall serve the *real* (winning) God. But think also of Amos's Jahweh who punishes the injustices of the *goyim* as severely as the sins of his people—and let the Syrians learn how impotent their gods are to fend off that truly divine assault! Who cares a fig for their "reality" if, like mere mortals, the heathen gods scurry for cover when the Lord thunders out of Zion? Think also of the more urbane views of such a cosmopolitan figure as Apuleius, who, in the midst of the wonderful ribaldry of *The Golden Ass*, launches a philosophic invocation of the one deity of whose splendor all the majestic members of the pantheon, all the household deities of the empire, and all the lords of alien empires are ciphers pointing to that One. To sum it up: it is a rare, indeed a bizarre, tribalism that does not know, even in its sacred bones, that Cosmos will persist, undiminished and undismayed, after the tribe and its familiar gods have vanished into the dust. The loftiest pinnacles of religious presumption are built directly over invincible intimations of mortality and corruptibility.[5]

Here one is prompted to insist that what the "lords many," and the One as well, purport to do is not good enough. There must be a way of determining whether that noble purpose—to provide a vista of the ultimate governance and its sovereignty in our lives—is really consummated. If a monarchical axiom says, "Here is the way to discern and respond to the ultimate governance of things cosmic and human," there must be a way to find out whether anything "out there" of that magnitude is perceived as it really is.

What sorts of tests are available? One possibility is to adopt an axiomatically controlled life-system. This does not mean that life-systems, whether or not they are religiously inspired and sustained, are often adopted experimentally. Indeed this possibility is so abhorrent to some theologians that they deny it categorically. In their view, commitment to a life-system is flatly irreconcilable with any hint of tentativeness about it, such as "try it, you'll like it," or "your money refunded." But what justifies this all-or-nothing view? A close and exhaustive investigation along empirical lines? Or a special *ex parte* way of shuffling the cards so that *commitment* and *tentativeness* cannot be paired? Or a conviction that God—and therefore godly people—has no patience with reservations: either you are absolutely for him (and us) or you are absolutely against him (and us).

"Experimentally" is very likely to create the impression that I am trying to smuggle scientific attitude and method into the tabernacle. That is not my intention. The proper meaning of "experimentally" is to relate a project of perception- conception-aspiration to concrete experience. So the psalmist adjures us: "O taste and see that the Lord is good!" (34:8). We ought to hope devoutly that our understanding of this does not automatically veer off toward "the proof of the pudding." But we are reminded that the goodness or soundess of a venture can be discovered only by making it; that is, by a commitment. So one may set sail upon the vasty deep. But *commitment* does not mean that I cannot change course without changing goal. Nor does it mean that I may not come to have great doubts about the soundness of my ship or about the competence of the helmsman; and yet sail on and on.

Here it must be granted that this first line of testing may yield thin results. Perhaps nothing noteworthy will transpire; life may go on pretty much the same as it did before the adoption, experimentally, of a life-system. If that happens—that is, if nothing happens—something has misfired. Perhaps the old axioms, yesterday's lords, are still working. Perhaps the convert is not working very hard or very intelligently at the new life. In other words, the tester may be fouled up; thus his reports are valuable only for clinical purposes.

Many religions, in fact, and these both sacred and secular, teach that misfiring is the fault of the practitioner, not of the truth or the community. So if one were to say, "I tasted and found that the Lord is sour and flat," the pious would surely rejoin, "Your mouth is still defiled by the dregs of your old life. So try again and again and . . . And remember that perpetual failure means that God has rejected you."

But suppose John Doe has given this axiomatically controlled life-system the best he has, again and again, and now insists that the system has failed, not he. And it has failed so thoroughly that he has no inclination to assay any other life-system that advertises axiomatic authority. So he goes off on his own. He means to find out for himself what life is all about and what the great world is up to.

What sort of venture is this? What does it involve? The venture is to find out what values there are to which to pin the varied moments and kinds of his experience. All kinds of values and of valuational procedures have been pressed upon him. Now he means to see whether this value-distributional scheme is good enough for all the traffic of his life and the world; good enough as tested by the light of some novel insights of his own or by theoretical criteria that are part of the standard equipment of criticism, such as the principle of coherence.

So John Doe's venture is to fashion a faith of his own and thereafter to test it as he had earlier tested the faith of the fathers and found it wanting. If the faith of his own stands up, we may reasonably assume that it offers him a clear and productive way of construing reality. He appears to have hit upon something that has an axiomlike power, something, that is, that generates and licenses a way of life. John Doe did not actually abandon the quest for a self-warranting and self-grounding authority. He found, by taking the turn to self—but not necessarily because self is the best thing he knows—the richest lode he has ever come upon. He may have made self the strategic center of his existence and his outreach because it is the only strategist over which he, John Doe, has direct, though hardly complete, control.

Homecoming to self, in the quest for authority, may be despair's recoil from a world in which there is an unrelenting clamor, a soul-deadening din from many gods and lords aplenty. It is quite possible that John Doe knows that he is but a "thinking reed," a terribly fragile thing. No world-ranger he, except by dire necessity. He feels in his gut that the inherited life-system is wrong. He feels its value contradictions as a particularly vivid wrongness. Being thus alienated in his spiritual homeland he sets off for a far country.

As a matter of geography he does not need to travel far. Right here at home we can offer him a social system which is a religious pluralism, one that is a smorgasbord of gods, cults, liturgies, life-styles. They do not all impose or even offer a rigorous regimen for the attainment of salvific insight or of practical wisdom. If John Doe really seeks such fruits of the Spirit, he is likely to be disappointed by many of the options in American life, or in Western civilization more generally; if, that is, he is looking for the real thing, the real substance, and is keen enough, and resolute withal, to reject plastic simulations. But if his aspirations are more modest, if he seeks a life-style largely consonant with his own fugitive but vivid intuitions, he may find a company that allows him to combine privacy of outlook and idiosyncrasy of axiom with a patterned publicity in everything else. This means—this arrival in such a company—that he is lovable as long as he embraces that common life-style. It does not mean that his axioms are vindicated.

In such a life, in such a society, who or what is the real monarch, the presiding principle of being? There is so much in our historical situation that presses the self back upon itself; but only so that it may find the reflexive spring to thrust itself into the orbit of some greater self, there to be safe, if not powerful and fertile, forever. So the self is subtly injected with an elixer of illusion: You are really *deciding* your life and destiny! —while by day and by night this same frail and faltering creature is seduced or frightened into surrendering sovereignty to the demigods of Everyday.

It is little to be wondered at that in this historical situation theologians, among many other sorts of thinkers, should have discovered alienation. John Doe is carried from faith to faith, lord to lord, by alienation. It is almost as though there were more power in the No to one or another authority than in Yes to any; as though one moves forward into something better by kicking out against something worse.

In this sort of world, who or what seems to have real authority? Apparently not the thoroughgoing systematic iconclast. We are guiltily happy when we learn that he, too, loves fame, money, pomp, sex, booze— whatever lords happen to hold the rest of us in thrall.

Could it be that the highest authority is vested in the visionary, in the one in whose imagination alienation becomes a restlessness geared to an ultimate and divine factor native to our souls? Or if not native, consenting to be tabernacled there to lure us away from idolatrous exile—Egypt, Babylon—and toward the peace and joy of the ultimate community?

This is possible. It is also discomfiting because as we habitually construe the "real" world, the visionary is an impractical alien in it. The great visionaries know about that habit; they construe it as a symptom of alienation from reality, which, of course, augments our discomfiture and induces us to find such heralds of a larger and freer life noncredible.

Yet in our better moments we are likely to acknowledge that there is something intriguing in that possibility. Surely one of the fondest dreams of humankind is of a realm in which power and authority are perfectly united. What rules there is fit to rule, and is so honored by common judgment and consent. There authority is not won or sustained by deceit or coercion. This vision has a distinguished religious history. In the Christian tradition, specifically, God is honored as king over all because in him power and authority are perfectly united. His righteousness is wholly to be trusted. His purposes are invincibly sublime—a quality not be confused with sublimely invincible.

A paradox looms in this faith. Its axioms generate an existential tension, not merely a conceptual or propositional one. For here God is represented as being absolutely inescapable; he is the affirmation of all affirmations, the negation of all negations. He is somehow present in, and not merely signified by, the comings and goings of all things. How, therefore, could we fail to acknowledge the authority of such a being? How could any denial of him be anything but a hollow verbal gesture, a tragicomic stunt as odd as that of the child who buys a round-trip ticket when he runs away from home? Nonetheless we are asked to *consent,* to extend credit, to something putatively representative of all that majesty, all that beauty, all that everlastingness.

Of course theologians insist that God does not have to solicit our consent; he orders it, or its refusal. But theologians, woefully unlike God, have to make cases for their views. They have to convince us that their claims for God's sovereignty are reasonable and true. More particularly, if they invoke the authority of Scripture, we have a right —perhaps itself divinely secured—to ask whether *that* authority does not also rest somehow upon our consent. For Scripture, too, uses over and over again such bidding terms as "come," "seek," "ask," "choose." And it seems also to acknowledge the reality of contingent promises and commitments: "If you turn again and do my will . . ." and "If you keep my commandments . . ."

Perhaps what obtrudes here is a theological version of the determinism paradox. Whatever his metaphysical colors, we suppose that the philosopher is supremely the mortal mind who believes only that for which a suitable and convincing case can be made, and believes it for that reason, whether or not he grew up in a family habituated to that outlook and attended schools where nothing else was taught and is now a member of a faculty where nothing else is deemed respectable. So we suppose that the philosophical thinker is able to stand alone, if necessary, above or away from all the theoretical options and choose the best of them. But if he is compelled, whatever be the agency therein, to accept one of those options, the image of the option-spread is false. He believes as he must, whatever linguistic spread of "freedom" he is also constrained to effect. If he speaks of freedom, it is not because he chose to do so. If he refrains from speaking of it, it is not because he deemed it wise to refrain from so doing. So the systematic determinist neither propounds nor defends his system by virtue of having appraised the option field and the cases. And, of course, in his view the libertarian is in the same boat. Yet he consents to argue with the libertarian. Each goes on looking for the best argument for his views, or at least the most stunning refutation of the other's views. But for the determinist, the debate as such signifies nothing, that is, it determines or decides nothing. The meaning of the philosophic exchange is reduced to its function as a necessitating cause.

Early and late in Christian history there have been plenty of theological determinists, though that view is no longer the dominant one in Protestant circles. It is not my purpose to argue that issue here. I want rather to observe that scriptural views of the relation of God's absolute sovereignty to human perception and decision do not fit neatly or easily into theories of absolute divine determinism. For what God demands of mankind ultimately is communion. "Demand" is surely an odd verb to associate with the supreme mode of spiritual unity. I do not say that Scripture itself makes that conjunction. The picture is rather more like this: Communion is what God purposes in his commands, it is their intention. Therefore God intends that human beings should trust him. But trust cannot be coerced. If, therefore, we are to believe that God is the cause, pure and simple, of our trust in him, shall we not also and simply believe that he attracts our trust rather than produces it? Moreover, even if God, as Holy Spirit, is believed to be the immediate and internal cause of our believing in him, we have a right to ask whether the empirical features of belief and believing are falsified by that. Piety declares: "Apart from God I can do nothing. He has done it all!" But piety has its own stake in distinguishing God's doings from our own. God

127

alone is wholly to be praised. But I ought not to blame him for my wretched hymns.

Thus the great distinguishing merit of Christian deterministic language is its promise to refine, enrich, and refocus existential rather than theoretical discernment. So if we believe properly in God, we ought to grasp divinity in the quotidian as well as in the marvelous. We ought to discern the children of God, our real brothers and sisters, behind the appalling disfigurements and disguises inflicted upon human existence in the Everyday of Western civilization. And we ought to love all whom thus we discern, without reservation dictated by pride, fear, or envy.

V

Here piety seems to have the better of us. We fall far short of such glory, we have all strayed from it. This failure is apparent in the oscillations of the spirit of the age in relation to spiritual authority. Now authority is lodged in an unreal inwardness of self. Then it flees to an equally unreal externality that stands over against the cowering ego as an alien and alienating other. To call this lunatic oscillation a dialectical movement overloads the circuit. Elijah's biting description of the irresoluteness of Israel does better: ". . . limping with two different opinions" (1 Kings 18:21).

Beneath this oscillation powerful intuitions are working. But they generate restlessness and anxiety rather than light or peace or joy. Nonetheless there may be something providential in this picture, there may be some seeds of health in those intuitions. Consider why we are restive under a regime of purely external authority once we have put away other childish things. Is it not because we know intuitively that communications from an external authority must be translated if they are to be intelligible? Not that intelligibility is a necessary condition of all kinds of obedience; but if a command is not intelligible at least its sanctions must be. It is not always necessary for us to understand the *wherefores*, but our situation is indeed forlorn if we do not grasp the *whereases*. Moreover, we have a right to ask whether translations of external commands are authorized properly. But authorized how? By whom? From this side or the other side?

There is another intuitively grounded reason for the flight from external authority. The externalistic modality reduces all encounters to surface-to-surface dealings; it precludes "deep calling unto deep." We do not naturally or normally expect all encounters to be deep rather than superficial—What I want ordinarily from the egg merchant is an honest egg, not a revelation of his soul; though a society that thinks it remarkable that he has one is in bad shape. (Being a "character" is not to be confused, though it commonly is, with having a soul.) So I show him the color of my money, or my credit card, rather than the beauty or the horrors of my soul. But when such patterns of human relationships become standardized and, much worse, normative, we rightly feel frustrated. Then the face, the talking point of the embodied self, has become a mask behind which the real person may sink into an incurable addiction: incommunicative privacy. If one is buried alive in that unmarked tomb, what can one of the most suggestive of all promises of Scripture mean? That is, that God is bringing a time when we shall all be fully known, when we shall be able to see one another in God and therefore rejoice, when we shall see God face to face. To the self sealed into privacy these are meaningless fantasies, demonically tantalizing whispers of never-never.

So there is no salvation in flying from externalistic authority to an unreal inwardness of self-existence. For then the self endows want, need, or dread with sovereignty. Whatever is thus elevated to central command will be as little disposed to proffer an intelligible rationale for its edicts as the alien Other is. This is partly because rationale is commonly taken to be an abbreviation of *rationalization*; and one of the most cherished and formidable dogmas of secularist pop theology holds that rationalization is a matter of giving bad reasons for what one wants, or is inwardly compelled, to do anyway.

VI

It is very generally supposed in modern Christian theology that *heteronomy* and *externality*, in respect to authority, are interchangeable concepts. Both, accordingly, are to be spurned for the sake of human freedom and dignity. This philosophic conjunction requires at least passing scrutiny, partly because it is not entirely clear that the territory has been definitively mapped in the great debate, Kant vs. Kierkegaard.

I take it that the proper force of heteronomy is being subject to determination and thus domination by the will of another; that will being governed, so to speak, by either secret or unintelligible motives. But does the imposition of the will or law of another being necessarily presuppose or entail externality of relationship between subject and domination? Does heteronomy necessarily entail the abdication, cheerful or truculent, of one's own will and self? Suppose that the Other is a being altogether righteous, wise, and resourceful, so that he purely wills my good as he wills differentially the good of all. The will of such a being, and the commands he issues, must appear to be heteronomous just insofar as they cannot be assimilated to or confused with my own, and insofar as I judge that I ought to obey him rather than do my own will.

This situation, so far suppositious, is not like being up against an alien power and an ineffable authority, that is, one whose intentions cannot be scanned. It is not like having to accept blindly the say-so of one who claims to know what is really and ultimately good for me when I do not recognize it as good at all, or not as good as something else. Indeed the claim of the divine good is altogether different from that. I inwardly acknowledge its goodness, the ultimacy of its goodness, and thus its full right to rule in me and over me. But my energies and appetites are already deployed along other lines. Naturally, therefore, but not rationally, I am powerfully inclined to assimilate the divine will to my extant commitments and deployments. That, in a nutshell, is the true natural history of religion.

The actual situation is more complicated even than that. My extant commitments and deployments are geared into a social world that maximizes externality while it loudly and continuously advertises its supreme devotion to individual freedom. I am supposed to choose freely a position in that world on the grand theological assumption that it is a providential orchestration of an infinite variety of private interests with competing social expectations. In fact, this is a piece of secular mystical theology. Everyday wisdom teaches us that the social world is an arena in which the big pay-off goes to aggressiveness, ruthless cunning, and mendacity. But—and here is the mysticism—if the arena is allowed to function by its natural laws, everything will work out well—for the survivors, that is. Blessed are they; they shall be called Fittest. One of the more intriguing aspects of this nation's religious history is the amalgamation of this grotesque natural theology and conventional church piety. This marriage —certainly not made in heaven—rendered plausible and precious a combination of private virtue with public corruption. He would be a hardy dogmatist who would claim that we have seen the last of this marriage and its offspring.

Thus freedom, like authority, is made to go "limping with two different opinions." It is made to hurtle from one unreal pole to its equally unreal antipodes.

I do not argue that the divine cure for this madness is a heavy charge of spiritual heteronomy. It has to be admitted that the very word conjures images of base surrender of freedom to an alien inscrutable power. But *God* in the Christian outlook does not signify an alien power. If it so appears, it is because the human citadel is now occupied by the spirit of alienation. Nor is God's design inscrutable; the demons read it and tremble (Jas 2:19). They know that the original and ultimate design is the coinherence of all life in the enjoyment of the life of God. Nothing is denied this perfection, except by demonic self-exclusion. I confess that Milton is on the track of the right questions: What life is more fit-full than that which hates its proper joy? What but the pride of an unreal self could generate such hate? (Milton is not to be blamed for "fit-full.")

VII

The problem of religious authority becomes existentially acute when religious institutions claim hegemony over the whole of life. Scripture then becomes both a symbol and an instrument of overweening and overbearing social power. I do not believe that this is an accurate and realistic description of the actual religious situation. Authority has become so acute as a religious problem because other institutions and other theologies claim hegemony over the whole of life, and largely make good on their claims. The fear of a specifically Christian heteronomy is painfully unrealistic.

The actualities can be painted in still harsher tones. Authority is being exercised largely in subliminal forms. These are overwhelmingly secular. For example, the authority figures in the marketplace are people wholly lacking pertinent, to say nothing of commanding, credentials. Movie stars urge us to buy their brand of margarine. Sports heroes promise us a variety of long-coveted satisfactions if we will use their mouthwash or deodorant. But, of course, these shills and hucksters do not *oblige* us to buy their lies. They do not try to inform conscience. They, too, are tools, weapons of an authority system designed to govern us by making a narrow and low-lying range of wants and aspirations absolute. For that purpose the system is compelled to neutralize as far as possible any interest in a rational appraisal of its solicitations and any scientific scrutiny of its products. So, in one respect at least, counterculture and the marketplace of the establishment are parts of a continuum: they are both deeply suspicious of rationality. The marketplace appeals indiscriminately to basic needs and to wants that are the inventions of the system. Counterculture makes a great thing of subrational feeling.

Is there something remotely analogous to this situation in traditional Christianity, with its vaunted distinction between truths of reason and the truths of revelation? Perhaps there (rather than, as Hegel claimed, in Judaism) is the real wellspring of heteronomy. For the truths of revelation cannot be allowed to drift in and out of human existence, coming and going on the whimsical tides of sensibility. Therefore, an authoritative church licensed to administer revelation.

In relation to that theological mentality, the instincts of biblicist Protestantism ought to be honored. What is coveted there is an authority that is both inexpugnable and assimilable to the quotidian world. The latter is as important as the former because it marks a refusal to let even God's truth rend the fabric of daily existence. Indeed no such possibility is acknowledged, even in the abstract. But in that case, what is the inexpugnable authority of the Bible? Just this: In what pertains to salvation it is not to be doubted. Moreover, what Scripture says about salvation, its conditions, and its effects (and its affects), is full of practical value for rightly ordering life in the here and now.

In this view, then, the Bible is anything but a source or instance of alienation. So understood, if Scripture is a critique of anything, it is a critique only of a sinful, disobedient, private life in a sinful social world. Once the soul is redeemed, there is a blessed assurance, a divinely absolute affirmation, of the soul called to eternal life in a world beyond the skies.

I do not intend here to rehearse the grievous shortcomings of biblicist Protestantism. They are plainly visible in the churches of that persuasion and in the larger society they helped to create and continue powerfully to affect. What ought to be noted here is that what thus emerged is much nearer the pole of autonomy than it is to heteronomy. Which is to say that the Bible has been drawn altogether into the continuum of the quotidian world; altogether, that is, as far as the Bible seems to make any real sense. Thus revelation is domesticated. Thereafter, whatever shatters, or threatens to shatter, the structures of Everyday are construed to be demonic rather than divine.

So it comes about that revelation as transcendental judgment upon this world, and Scripture as the peerless testimony to that revelation, are alike very dimly perceived by the piously committed denizens of Everyday. Piety by itself does not clarify and strengthen those perceptions. Those are tasks properly assignable to theologians. That does not mean that theologians therefore have a license to take the Bible away from piety, a license derived from systematic philosophy or produced by a flourish of hermeneutical craft.

Chapter Six

❧

REVELATION AS TRUTH AND AS COMMAND

I

In Jesus Christ, God reveals the perfect righteousness of his will rather than the fathomless reaches of his being.

This proposition functions very like an axiom in contemporary Protestant theology; perhaps as the prime axiom concerning God and his revelation. But the proposition also has a negative function: it is a theological roadblock both to metaphysical system and to mysticism.

A correlative principle shares a good bit of this axiomatic glory: The revelation in Jesus Christ of God's perfectly righteous will comes always as a command. This appears to be a direct entailment of the doctrine that God's act is his being, God is what he does. This suggests an affinity with plain philosophic sense; for to will is to order something of oneself, of another self, of an aspect of the natural world.

Accordingly, revelation is not an information communique from highest heaven. God does not act to augment man's cognitional stores. Not that he disdains making himself known to sinful creatures, but rather he imparts that practical knowledge which man cannot attain to, by, or for himself, that which contains the sure hope of salvation in the world to come and the lines of acceptable behavior in this one.

But if God communicates instructions for faithful action, for properly obedient life, why should we not call that "knowledge" in a strong rather than a derivative sense? Granted that we do not ordinarily say, for instance, that our knowledge of the world is augmented by learning how best to act and be in it. But perhaps in this scientific era we ordinarily think of knowledge as though it were the product of a fact machine rather

134

than a variety of activities yielding a variety of results. One such activity is interaction with other persons, giving-and-taking that does indeed involve discovering, by the expression of their intentions and the force of their wills, who the others are.

It is too early to say firmly whether the model of personal interactional human knowledge is appropriate, or perhaps even decisive, for the interpretation of revelation either as a general category of the religious life or in Christian thought in particular. We first have to ask what it means to say that God *reveals* his perfectly righteous will. I propose the following schematism of the possibilities.

II

(1) The persons to whom God communicates his intentions and orders now know who is to be credited with the determination of the decisive events in our lives and our world. So the Lord instructs Moses to tell the people Israel that he is the God of their fathers and will deliver them from vile bondage (Ex 3:13ff). The Lord on that occasion does not give Moses an explanation of why he permitted Israel to fall into such a wretched condition. Perhaps Moses knew better than to ask or wasn't curious about it. Subsequent theology, Jewish and Christian, has not been so circumspect; or so incurious.

In respect to the interests of Christian piety, (1) is a strong reading of revelation if one says in good faith, "God has willed it all." Such expressions may function as condensations of the Christian outlook. Not that the outlook itself is revealed, but rather, what we, as Christians, avow about God and human destiny may be credible only on the strength of revelation. If so, we need more than ever to know what sense to attach to the concept of revelation.

(2) We know what God demands of us; but we do not claim to know what sort of process "willing" designates in God. So "God reveals" means "God wants us (orders us) to do thus-and-so." The obligation to do that—whatever thus-and-so is—is divinely imposed.

This is a familiar view of revelation. It is attended by some familiar questions. A brief review of these questions may help to show what the claim involves.

(a) How do I know it is God who commands thus-and-so?

One response to this: The commandment itself, its content, is divine; that is, it opens up an ultimate good, it uncovers a primordial thrust of man's being.

There is a rather different response to (a): It is the mode of address, rather than just, or primarily, the content of the commandment, which shows it is God who speaks in it.

Now if we say that the content of the commandment testifies that it is God who so orders, we appear to have drawn either on an antecedent experience-knowledge of God or upon some independent criterion of divinity. The chief trouble with the first alternative is that it reinstates, without answering it, the antecedent question (a).[1]

But the second option seems to deify human categories. That is one of the things that revelation is supposed to interdict.

Another sort of response to the familiar question (a) is possible. God at one and the same time commands something and identifies himself as the one who commands it. This starts with the second response noted above. Let us see whether it advances beyond it significantly.

First of all it assumes that human beings have a fundamental knowledge of what it means to obey commands or follow orders, whether or not the command is given by another being or is self-imposed. It is widely felt today—and the sentiment is shared by some theologians—that this obediential capacity is an acquired characteristic, and that it ought to be radically reduced if not eliminated, at least in mature persons. Such sentiments define the band of the spectrum farthest removed from traditional Christianity, for which disobedience is the seed of man's dire wretchedness. I do not venture here to adjudicate this theological conflict, being content, or compelled, simply to note that it avails little for contestants of either persuasion to point to some all-conquering fact to decide the issue.

Along with this capacity for obeying orders and rules, whether or not it is an acquired characteristic, we know in ourselves an equally strong disposition to rank commands and obligations according to the clarity and power in which they enjoin the enhancement of human life. This does not necessarily mean that the upper reaches of this scale are, *eo ipso*, divine; though there is a venerable philosophical-theological tradition that says the upper reaches of this scale must be the platform from which our minds launch all proper conceptualizations of deity. Be that as it may, the gods which ignore or traduce that scale cannot command moral trust. We can conspire with them but we cannot commune with them.[2]

But what about the Christian insistence that God, not man, is the determiner and judge of what is really good and really evil? More specifically, what about the possibility that God has already revealed the true scale and the absolute criterion by which it is constructed? Since my purpose here is not systematically to review or propose substantive doctrines, I simply observe that such assertions (and I accept them as true) are human assertions and must be judged as to their value by reference to a scale and a criterion generally available. It is true, sublimely true, that God does not think as man thinks. The author of that (in the Old Testament; it is found in Is 55:8) is the same Christ who pressed the claims of the higher righteousness. In his representations, that righteousness soars far above the highest reaches of the natural scale. Fathers, for example, know how to give good gifts to their children (Lk 11:13); and by inference we know it is a good thing to give good things to one's children. Or again, where is the point in saying that peacemakers are (or are to be) especially favored of God unless peace is already known to be of great value? And yet again, what is so terribly wrong with legalistic nit-picking at the expense of "justice, mercy, and faith" unless the latter have a natural and commanding elevation above the low foothills of ritualistic punctilio? ("Woe to you, scribes and Pharisees, hypocrites! for you tithe mint and dill and cummin, and have neglected the weightier matters of the law, justice and mercy and faith . . ." (Mt 23:23).

The thing at stake here is not whether the higher righteousness obliterates the natural scale. The issue is whether the all-sovereign God identifies himself uniquely in his ultimate demands so that those demands reflexively, so to speak, reveal the being of the law-giver. Does this mean that since God in Christ issues the love commandment, it must be that God himself is love? There is surely an inferential route involved here. I doubt that we should call it an implication.

The inferential route may bypass the mode-content distinction imposed upon the divine command. Before we decide what gain there might be in pursuing that, we ought to have a look at *mode of address* as a theological concept.

III

If we say (2) that the real and full meaning of "God reveals himself in his righteous will" is to be discovered in the mode of address, we must be prepared to deal with several factors. The first of these is (A) the speaker.

(A) The speaker.

Contra the chorus of *The Bacchae*, let us put it down as axiomatic that the nisus of the natural scale of value is toward the overcoming of all externality in commandment in the relation of the speaker to the one addressed. In the lower and intermediate ranges, the authority of the commander looms over the command itself. Moreover, then, the being of the commander may be as mysterious as its power is great. On these levels one has a sense that the same quality and quantum of authority could be affixed to *not x* as to *x*. What one hears on these levels are such things as "Do it because it is ordered, it is simply the rule." And "You do not know what is good for you until you are told." And, "Yours not to ask/Nor reason why . . ."

It is doubtful that there is as much of this kind of measure of externality visible and potent in the Bible as we may suppose. There, intransigence ("Woe to a proud and stiff-necked generation!") is severely rebuked. But that condition is not represented as rationally or realistically grounded. When life itself is the issue of obedience, who but a self-infatuated fool would prefer to do it his way?

But whatever degree of externality is present in Mosaic revelation, later prophetic tradition in the Old Testament exhibits a powerful drive toward the interiorization of the divine command. This does not mean there is any loss of certainty that God is still the giver and enforcer of the law. So Jeremiah foretells the creation of a new relationship:

I will put my law within them, and I will write it upon their hearts . . . (31:33).

It is a serious mistake to interpret this as a great leap forward into philosophical individualism. The central concept in Jeremiah is still the People of God. That community is not a congeries of human atoms each pursuing its own well-being, each legislating for itself, and perhaps each using "God" as the name of a benign observer of the worldly scene. For the prophet God is still the giver, the keeper, and the redeemer of the Covenant. His will is sovereign, his righteousness overwhelming, his power unbrookable. God is all of this. In all he makes personal address. His law is written on the inward parts of his people. It must follow that each must make a personal response:

And no longer shall each man teach his neighbor and each his brother, saying, "Know the Lord," for they shall all know me, from the least of them to the greatest, says the Lord (31:34).

We do not need to be reminded that nowhere in the Old Testament is knowing the Lord God primarily an intellective-cognitive affair.

Eventually the nisus of the natural scale of value tracks into the autonomous moral agent who, entirely unlike Jeremiah's concept of the addressee of revelation, is a law unto himself: the purely self-warranted authority. Does that not imply that man thus becomes both (A) the Speaker and (B) the auditor of revelation?

Then what is to prevent this remarkable creature, this A-B, from acting simply and purely from his own interests? Perhaps it is a count against Providence that we do not encounter an insurmountable barrier against that. But we do have to cope with a singularly prickly fact: I cannot expect others to grant the principle of my will's autocracy unless I award them some gain from it; but then they will honor the gain rather than the principle. Furthermore, when the self begins to emerge as an autonomous moral agent, a singular conviction dawns: To live in the ethical sphere is indeed to be an agent, that is, one who acts in a representative or representational capacity. Thus the interests of agent and community tend to coalesce. To coalesce, but not therein to become indistinguishable. The relationship of moral agent to moral community is such that each is the fulfillment of the other, that neither is a mere tool or appendage of the other. In that state the Speaker (A) is the perfected community of mankind.

The idealistic strain seems to have carried the day at this point. The giver of the genuinely ethical command is the ideal self, the same being the beloved community. This being of transcendent richness and goodness looms above Everyday, the lower world in which the beloved community is neither here nor there. But in the light of the ideal, Everyday, the world "that is too much with us," is perceived itself to be an illusion, as is also the low-flying self wedded to its simulations, plausibilities, and outright counterfeits.

This is an ancient, persistent, and noble strain. Nevertheless it does not have the field to itself. There are other accounts of the process by which moral agent and moral community are to come at last to stand in mutual uncompromised and unambiguous affirmation of each other. There are other ways in which the opposed threats of purely external authority and ego-autocracy can be overcome, though not once and for all in this life. The being whose agent the nisus is, is more than human destiny calling from beyond the life-and-death of this world. That being is the I Am, from everlasting to everlasting the same, whose will is the wellspring of all goodness.

So when we name this being "God" we are not simply using a religious label for the loftiest ethical aspirations of the race. But neither are we trying to create an unbridgeable chasm between *God* and the highest ranges of the natural value scale. If, then, we say God speaks in history, we mean that he personally addresses us in all his authority. The Word is not filtered through the cosmos; neither is it mediated by an abstract universal such as Mankind.

But what then is *personal address?* It is a particular "You there!" rather than a general "To whom it may concern." It is definite: "I mean *you.*" It is concrete: "I demand this here and now."

Thus we come to (B), the one addressed in revelation.

IV

(B) The addressee.

A specific particular and concrete being is addressed in revelation. This person is to do this particular thing because God orders and ordains it. This is to be done also because the addressee, the auditor of the Word, is this particular concrete being. Thus a significant part of the divine command—part or aspect—is derived from the being-and-situation of the hearer of the address, the "object," of the Word of God.

But what part or aspect? This theological-ethical area is a veritable mine field, except that the hazards do not fall into a helpful pattern. Beneath one's feet are such threats as privatized revelation and other vagaries of subjectivism, personalistic metaphysics, and Kant's bowdlerized Christianity. But one is likely to stumble over such other horrors as a naïve appropriation of biblical talk about God-speaking, and illicit inferences from the experiences of the prophets of the Old Testament.

Would that there were a guaranteed safe route through this mine field, but there is not. We must hope for the best, and make due allowance for the worst.

What then is involved in claiming that the being-and-situation of the hearer of the Word, the addressee, is an integral component in revelation as command? Above all, an acknowledgement that the one addressed is a moral agent and that moral agents are personal beings endowed with singular powers for infusing concrete situations with novel possibilities.

It does not follow from this that God's command must always be viewed as requiring somebody, or some community, to do something in behalf of morality. When Jesus sends the "seventy" out to proclaim the kingdom of God (Lk 10:1ff), he is not ordering or authorizing them simply to fill the air with edifying moral sentiments or lofty ethical precept. In that connection, the concept of the kingdom of God has pronounced moral dimensions, of that we can have no doubt. But the authentic preaching of the kingdom of God shows forth God's absolute authority over cosmos and history exercised to bring all things to fruition in communion with him. In his own teaching, moreover, when Jesus says, "Blessed are the pure in heart for they shall see God," he surely does not mean that they shall see how purity, as one courses through this world, pays off in the next. So hold on ye pure in heart, good times are a-coming by-and-by.

We must say, also, that the divine command never falls into the subethical. Even those who say that God's command is either occasionally or essentially supraethical—and who, for these purposes, are much given to quoting, "For my ways are not your ways"—do not mean that the revealing God either commands or condones something immoral in his sight. Though what he commands may beggar merely human morality it does not exalt baseness or meanness or any of the myriad ways in which man visits inhumanity upon his fellows.

So whatever disparity between a revealed higher righteousness and human morality there may be, we must insist that the content of the divine command does not war against the personal mode of address. Moreover, the content of that command is not so general and abstract that

141

it is indistinguishable from a natural aspiration of the human spirit. Neither is it a heavenly injunction to have a proper regard for moral obligation as such, indispensable as that is for human existence *qua* human.

V

The third component of the mode of address is (C) The utterance.

What does God command? What is the revealing word in which the ultimate situation is something enjoined rather than something merely hoped for? The following distinctions are proposed with a view to casting some light on this persistent question.

(i) Protocal commands.
(ii) Strategic aims.
(iii) Tactical requirements.

(i)Protocol commands.

Obey my voice, and I will be your God, and you shall be my people; and walk in all the way that I command you, that it may be well with you (Jer 7:23).

The intention of protocol commandments is to create a situation in which unqualified respect is an unqualified obligation. Respect of this order is not contractual or otherwise conditioned by consent. There is a remote analogy to this in respect for any properly constituted authority. The respected object is given its due; it must be given its due. Though one may expect some benefit for self or society from this, that benefit is not the legitimation of that respect. Perhaps, indeed, respect as such entails a fundamental asymmetry of relationship between respected and respecter.

So God and God alone is to be obeyed absolutely. "Absolutely" means God is to obeyed more than anything or anybody else (Acts 5:29). It also means that God is to be obeyed no matter what, that obeying God admits or allows no exceptions whatever.

Thus God is to be honored as the ultimate object of loyalty. But not that this is an obligation and not a compulsion. It is a singular obligation.

Like all appeals to obligation, it has some kind of sanction behind it, a hint of an "or else . . ." In this case the sanction is a situation involving both antecedent and consequent features. "I will be your God" is the antecedent. "You shall be my people" is the consequent situation in which "it may be [will be] well with you." So, of course, there is immense benefit for Israel in giving God the respect and obedience due him. But he cannot be used as a means to an end. His majesty is too awful for that. Life with him is the end. That is purely his gift.

The protocol commandments, then, establish who is to be honored and obeyed above all and no matter what. Any alternative is unthinkable; that is, to think an alternative would be to conjure a situation utterly devoid of goodness, power, or beauty—death, exile, captivity.[3]

Accordingly, the First Commandment occupies a place by itself in the Decalogue. It is not so much a commandment among and like others. It is the one that sets the stage for the others, it is the one that creates the context of intelligibility for the others. This does not mean that the relationship of the other commandments to the first one is that of logical entailment. Not at all. The primacy of the First Commandment, the supreme protocol demand, does not by itself mean that all other duties and values are *de jure* set in motion by a uniquely religious duty and value.

(ii) Strategic aims.

"Aims" may suggest a step down from the order of commandment as an absolute imperative. "I order you to aim at x" seems to make sense only on the firing line. Otherwise, to aim is to intend or purpose something. So what sense does it make to speak of commanding an aim?

It makes a good deal of sense if the aim is already operative. Then to command an aim is to order its mode of expression or its direction, or both. Such commands do not create primary aims. The existence and the validity of such aims are assumed by such commands. Thus "Seek me and live, saith the Lord." The sense of life's value is not created by this injunction. So perhaps it is better understood as a solicitation something like:

> Ho, every one who thirsts,
> come to the waters;
> and he who has no money,

come, buy and eat!
Come, buy wine and milk
without money and without price (Is 55:1).

Granted that human beings normally want to live, sometimes even in the most adverse circumstances imaginable, the commandment specifies a strategy for fulfilling that desire.

This analysis is theologically simplistic; it may offend piety, to boot. "What? Representing God as having to resort to strategy when he is the creator and absolute Lord of all creaturely life? He has no need to acknowledge any mortal aims as already operative, as having any antecedent reality."

The import of such sentiments and convictions is that, apart from God, human beings do not know what *real* life is. God can and does command the proper aim of man because God is the giver of life itself.

Such caveats may seem to be entirely congruent with the letter and the spirit of the protocol commandment, namely to give God the glory in all things. But they suffer from two defects. One, they threaten to obliterate the *imago Dei:* man as an intending creature. Two, they may induce us to overlook the ways in which in biblical and Christian traditions God himself is represented as deliberating in his choice of instruments to effectuate his holy purposes. "Strategic aims" may be a painfully prosy way of expressing such factors. Prose is heresy, or milder disobedience, only if God has regard for nothing but poetry.

There is another way in which it makes reasonably good sense to speak of commanding an aim. It is also a way that resists being assimilated into antecedent causal explanation. An aim is commanded when there is, and there is known to be, only one strategy for fulfilling it. If there is only one way to get to x and that is through w, then anyone who wants x had better plan to accept w. One might resent this drastic restriction of means or routes to x, but resentment is not noted for any ability to open up new options. It is noted for inspiring efforts to achieve the impossible and, in consequent failure, to curse the arbitrariness of the cosmos.

Now let x equal the perfection of human life; and let w equal the demands of the kingdom of God registered here and now. Thereby an even stronger case appears for saying that God commands the aim in the second sense noted above. "There is only one way to get to x and that

144

is through w" now means: God alone sets the conditions for entrance into his kingdom, and for that participation in his life therein which is man's perfection.

Nevertheless, one can apparently reject the primordial divine intention of one's existence, and refuse the sole means of route to that end: here and now, and in all things, to obey God absolutely.

Such at least is the *prima facie* situation. Refusal to accept the ordained end or the sole route to its realization is, in fact, a commonplace of human history. Indeed "proud and stiff-necked people" have been among the makers and shakers of history. Their empirical importance is not greatly diminished by an earnest Christian expectation that such Nay-sayers to God must endure eternity in custom-fashioned torments in hell. Nor is indispensable theological light generated by the traditional axiom that God himself wills, or consents to, their intransigence and perversity. It is the cheapest sort of theater which tries to make Pharaoh a real person even though it is the Lord who "hardens his heart" each time and thus legislates the wretch's ruinous policies. It is fair to note that sometimes Pharaoh hardens his own heart. I doubt that the writers and editors of Exodus wavered between two theories of efficient causation.

Waiving here a right to register a theory of historical causation, I reiterate the proposition that divine command as strategic aim is much more of a bidding or solicitation than an order. Not that the divine bidding is like, "Please may I have your attention and thereafter your respect, allegiance, and love?" God's biddings are not ordinary importunings or petitions. "Come unto me . . . Come to the waters . . . Incline your ear, and come to me; hear, that your soul may live." (Is 55:3ff. The whole chapter is germane.)

Nonetheless, the divine invitation is not coercive, it is not inserted into the order of efficient causation, although it is absolute in the order of strategic aims. There is no life like life with God. And God rules that there is no way to x except the route he has appointed.

(iii) Tactical requirements.

These are the specifications of the way from the present situation to the perfection of life and spirit in the kingdom of God. A godly life, thus, is one that is sensitized to the day-to-day specifications of God's will. Such specifications are illustrated by the commandments which follow the first in the Decalogue. These commandments appear to lay down the fundamental moral conditions for human society—such as respect for life, family and property, and for truthful witness in juridicial proceedings—rather than unique ethical levies upon Israel, the People of God. That is, these commandments are formulated in terms so general that a very great variety of specific rules can be subsumed under them and appear to derive authority from them. "Thou shalt not kill" has sometimes been construed absolutistically. That was not so in biblical Israel, and no nation state has ever so construed it.

Consider also "Do not commit adultery." Does this proscribe sexual liaison where either party is married, or both? Be that as it may, adultery was long regarded in Christian societies as a more serious violation of a divine commandment than fornication, against which the decalogue levels no ban. And are we to suppose that Amos derives either his passion or his principle of justice, expressed in his condemnation of selling orphans into servitude, from "Thou shalt not steal"?

Familiarity with the ways in which such general rules are rendered particular in various cultures has long inspired the inference that there are no moral absolutes. The weight of this inference is augmented by formulating it thus: In order to be absolute a moral rule must be so general that the self-preservative interests of the state and the natural drives of individuals are all compatible with it. Such conditions render such rules vacuous.

But this is to move too swiftly and too lightly over demanding territory. "Thou shalt not kill" does not presuppose or entail a state of affairs in which no person ever intentionally takes the life of another. The rule, the divine commandment, establishes a basis for levying different penalties for different kinds of homicide. Thus it may be legitimate to kill enemies of the state in authorized combat. It is not right to kill prisoners of war, or one's slaves.

So also for adultery. Old Testament law is no more utopian or idealistic here than in the case of homicide. The purpose of the rule, humanly regarded, is to establish a boundary that cannot be crossed without stipulated, rather than *ad hoc,* penalty. In one sense it is correct to say that in both cases the wrongness of the act must be intuited before the levies of sanctions can make sense. It is also true that the actual levy of sanctions is an excellent way to train dim or aberrant intuitions. In any case, a rule or a law is not wrong simply because its violators do not sense the wrongness of their actions.

This is not to minimize the problem of determining concretely what kind of violation of a rule a given action may be. There are degrees (kinds) of homicide. "Thou shalt not kill" has rarely been taken to mean that any killing is as bad as any other; though death, as Agag, king of the Amalekites says, is a bitter thing in any case (1 Sam 15:32ff.).[4]

It is wrongheaded to suppose that rules are made to be broken, or at least sprung. So the prohibition of adultery was not designed to add a dash of daring to an otherwise banal affair. Nor does it make much sense to say that legislating a rule assumes the perpetuation of what the rule proscribes or regulates. The laying down of a rule does assume a general knowledge that certain things are inimical to the health and well-being of persons and to the stability of the social order. These assumptions may be counterfactual in either or both directions: that such things are deleterious may not be generally known; that the general knowledge may be wrong.

As an illustration of the density of such issues we can turn to the present scene where any sexual activity between consenting adults is held to be both morally acceptable and beyond the jurisdiction of the state—whether or not, in the latter case, it is morally acceptable. Now, are we to suppose that consenting to something automatically guarantees its moral acceptability as well as cancels the law's jurisdiction over it? Does something become good because I consent to doing it? Only if it is antecedently known to be good; or at least to be value-neutral. Murdering my neighbor does not become right or good because I consent to a plot against his life. Voluntary acceding to treason does not render it moral. I may bear false witness for a noble cause, but it is not *consent* that makes such perjury morally acceptable. So the principle of "consenting adults" hardly means more than that the parties so engaged must make their moral cases independently of the question of legality.

VI

It is high time to return to the theological claim that the Christian doctrine of God heavily capitalizes revelation as personal address. Is this capital preserved, if not enlarged, by saying that God reveals himself in the universal structure of moral experience? Have we to deal, in revelation, with a universal order of moral law fashioned for the sublime purpose of soul-making? Are we to believe that history is the divinely authorized and administered school for the moral education of mankind?

We may wonder whether the view of God as giver of universally valid law, and thereafter as the transcendent monitor of that order, is a genuinely personal view. Surely our natural inclination is to consider legal systems as being necessarily impersonal. Indeed, do they not tend to become unjust when personal factors are injected into them? Even the New Testament, for all its glorious emphasis on the tender love of God, also declares that God is the transcendent exemplification of juridical impartiality. (Rom 2:11; Acts 10:34. This principle is also clearly expressed in 2 Chronicles 19:7.)

There is another and more obvious complication, to which allusion has already been made. How can modern people have any confidence in a putatively universal structure of morality? We have been too long and too carefully nourished on the relativity of morals. And, of course, scientific philosophy has taught us, in the first place, to believe that natural law is a descriptive rather than a prescriptive concept. It is *man* who is the law-giver. We can be grateful to nature for her largely consistent behavior, though this too is something of a modern conceit. But her laws are vested in her by the scientist.

So we wonder whether a different theological option ought not to be mapped out: God reveals his righteousness (himself as righteous) in the concrete particularities of moral choices and moral judgment. In this way God reveals his transcendentally personal concern.

It seems to follow from this that the authentic Christian would not even try to guide or to understand his conduct by invoking universal, or even highly general, rules. He ought not to indulge in or cultivate the shallow perplexities of such questions as "What is wrong with adultery as such?" Now he should know that it makes no sense to think of adultery as such as a sin. It might make some sense to think of adultery as anything that compromises the personal dimension of sexual relationships; which might be anything from brutal sadism to praying aloud for the soul of one's partner smack in the middle of coitus, or whatever the sexual activity two (only?) people have consented to as mutually enriching.

In this view, the authentic Christian is uniquely free to adopt objectives, policies, and rules to fit each concrete situation in which he finds moral decision necessary. So what God commands is tactical adroitness in being loving. For the love commandment of Jesus Christ is really an announcement of an inclusive strategic goal for which support can only be solicited—it cannot be coerced. Moreover, there is nothing Turkishly despotic, there is nothing high-handed even in God's announcement of this inclusive strategic goal, because what God is after is something any properly reflective soul can grasp as supremely worthy of acknowledgement and realization.

I doubt that there is anything that more neatly illustrates theological readiness to adapt to the wisdom of the world than the development of situation ethics; as though the best of philosophic thought had completely abandoned any prospect for a universal and fertile moral principle. But I eschew further discussion of this view except to note that there are some ignoble insects in this remarkable theological nectar. One is the religious fanatic who claims total exemption from general rules because he believes God directly guides and supports him. For such a person revelation is a very special private knowledge of what he is to do in every situation. This is the occasionalism which is the corollary of ethical situationism, in the Christian context: God, too, recognizes no binding continuity between his own moments or fits of self-disclosure.

Another complication arises in a very different quarter. It is the demand to show wherein the *moral as such* is to be found in an outlook or life-style that so minimizes regard for the well-being of others. For who is the prime referent, in human range, in the claim that I am able in Christ to express my love as I want and see fit? Does my love for another obviate any necessity for rightly perceiving who he or she is and what rightly pertains to the well-being of that person? Is there something about love that sweeps away, legitimately as well as inevitably, every claim of right and every demand of duty? Suppose that out of love I visit a prisoner convicted of and incarcerated for a capital crime. Does love dictate what I ought to tell him, or what sort of public policy, in respect to crime and punishment, I ought to support? Finally, how is it that love, Christianly understood, either eliminates or illuminates every other aspect of morality?

In respect to such questions a theologian might feel inspired to declare that the revelation of God in Christ simply throws natural morality, especially any kind of rule ethic, out of gear. Does that mean that part of revelation is a divine ukase, "Let the moral *per se* cease!"? There is a more plausible explanation: that we are dealing with a theory about religion and morality that cannot be seriously or helpfully claimed to have a divine sanction. Not that the Lord of the cosmos cannot be imagined as bending low to affix his signature beneath the results of a feat of human theorizing. With God all things are possible. This is not true of theologians. A theological theory has to run as many gauntlets as any other kind, no matter how elevated its subject matter. So a theory of revelation has to take as many chances as a theory about the sexual predilections of earthworms. As many; not necessarily the same kind.

It is reasonable, then, to conclude that God's revelation of his righteous will may invalidate some element or feature of any natural understanding of the ethical. But there is no way by which "righteousness" can be divested of every connotation of "ethical." So even when, by appeal to a revelation perceptible and intelligible only to the eyes and mind of faith, natural righteousness at its best is declared to be filthy rags, it does not follow that what in natural morality is so judged to be base or vile is, by grace through faith, converted into goodness and beauty; or that what in natural morality is held to be noble and just is supernaturally converted into an obscenity. Religious people may sometimes talk that way; some of them are Christians. There are also people—so far, a small minority thank heaven—who find nothing noxious or unseemly in eating human feces. The rest of us are not likely to treat them as nutritional experts or as paradigms of healthiness.

Yet there is something properly instructive in the view that revelation establishes a significant, perhaps a decisive, discontinuity between the best of natural righteousness and the righteousness of God's kingdom. This instruction may come as a theological surprise, namely that revelation cannot be entirely subsumed under or expressed as command. There are several reasons for this. One, since the upward properly divine transformation of natural ethical standards has been achieved in and by Jesus Christ, it follows that the truth of and about Jesus Christ is not exhibited as command but as theological-ontological truth. Jesus is "the Christ, the son of the living God." Jesus Christ is thus and therefore Lord indeed. He is the one through whom and for whom all things have been created.

Secondly, this truth can be mounted as a descriptive-attributional proposition without making any appeals, covert or open, to such super-natural accessions as saving faith. One might, that is, be able to understand what sort of claim was being made in such a proposition without being able, or feeling disposed, to credit it. One may not accept as true the proposition that a man participated directly in the being of the God-head, not because he has no notion what that might be, but because he is not convinced by the evidentiary case.

But there is still more to be said on the question whether revelation is essentially command. I propose to move along into further treatment of that question by asking whether the view that revelation is essentially command does not and must not attach a rich cognitional value to obedience.

VII

Let us proceed by consulting ordinary situations in which one person commands and another person obeys, and the commandment is something to be done or not to be done. For purposes of illustration, let that go either way and let the matter be either of great importance or of little.

In these situations is one likely to learn something not otherwise available from obeying the command? Does obedience pack any cognitive weight? Well, one can learn whether the commander means business. One can learn this either from suffering the consequences of disobedience or from reaping the benefits of obedience.

Secondly, it is possible that one can learn something more than the consistency and reliability of the commander from obeying (or disobeying) his commands: the commander's wisdom, or lack of it; his kindness, or lack of it; his power, or lack of it.

But in these cases obedience is a condition of knowledge and not an instance or kind of knowledge. In ordinary cases readiness to obey is a function of knowing what is good for one, and very likely knowing also the source of bane or blessing. "Obedience is to be given to those to whom it is due" is another way of putting the same thing. So rational moral agents proceed with cognitive differentiations that are the prerequisites of obedience rather than the consequences or the content of obedience.

Suppose, however, that all analogies of ordinary experience, and all appeals to rational reflection upon it, are alike thrown down by God's direct and absolute revelation. In this he demands absolute obedience to himself alone. Does this mean that he is revealed only in his command-ment? If so, that would imply that "God" is the name of an impenetrably mysterious commander and the command is a bolt from the blue of farthest heaven. To this it is proper to object that the relationship be-tween God and commander is not analytic. So we have to ask whether the appropriate conjunction linking these concepts is itself revealed. Or is this conjunction composed of strands extracted by reflection on natural experience?

There is another sense in which we can reasonably suppose that obedi-ence is endowed with cognitive value. That is, where obedience is very like a trusting yielding to a superior power, a situation in which no absolute guarantee of trustworthiness is possible. Situations of this sort demand either a trust or a no-trust decision without petition for absolute external guarantees.

Is this something like the real situation of the authentic believer in God? How can one *know* that God is absolutely to be obeyed because he is absolutely trustworthy? The deeply poignant confession of the psalm-ist comes to mind:

> For my father and my mother have
> forsaken me,
> but the Lord will take me up (Ps 27:10).

This expresses a profound hope, it does not appear to be a simple indica-tive sentence. Perhaps it can be read as a report of experience. Life orphaned by the death or betrayal of all ordinary supports does nonethe-less go on, sometimes to wonderful attainment. Let the pious therefore say, "It is God's doing, blessed be he." Many do indeed profess that they have found God to be absolutely trustworthy once they learned to trust him altogether.

Here we may call to mind what has been called the most notorious mistranslation in all of Scripture. That is Job's avowal: "Though he slay me, yet will I trust him." We are told that Job puts a question rather than makes so wonderful a confession. The question is one of the most formi-dable of all theological questions: If he slay me, how shall I trust him?

Piety may settle for the circumstantial report: He who trusts in God does not trust in vain. But theology does business with more than experiential reports; and with more than existential anguish. "God is absolutely trustworthy" is some kind of a theological claim. But is it what it appears to be, a strong metaphysical claim, a claim about what really is the case? Or should we understand it to be a solicitation so to enter into the religious life that the benefits of its piety can be properly enjoyed?

So, viewed one way, "God is absolutely trustworthy" states something about a human attitude, namely that trust can persist beyond all normal experience and ordinary reason. So viewed, the statement "God is absolutely trustworthy" is indisputable. But so construed, it provides no instruction about the real world with which attitudes, motives, and interests must deal. It is, of course, the case that though all finite objects of trust prove unreliable, and some treacherous, one might yet say "Nonetheless I will trust God to take care of me." But this might simply mean that I feel better about the world and myself when I persist in trusting the power and intentions of the ultimate being.

There is a good deal of sound and plain wisdom in this. Being untrusting is a meaner condition than being trusting, despite the numerical strength and prominence of untrustworthy people. So even though we say sometimes of a person that he is too trusting for his own good, we do not generally mean that trust is a virtue only when practiced in calculated moderation, or that unreliability is a good thing when practiced shrewdly. Liars and frauds do sometimes have a fine time of it ("Why do the wicked flourish as the green bay tree?"), but only because they learn to blend deceit and treachery with many a fine show of honor and truthfulness.

So we are clearly on the grounds of value judgments when we say that God is absolutely trustworthy. But it is just as clear that this theological proposition is not a fact-naked value judgment. A considerable part of its intention is a conviction that trust and trustworthiness are reality concerns. They are, in fact, reality clues.

Let us, therefore, put the obvious and inescapable question: What might count as evidence or reason for not trusting God, or at any rate for not trusting him absolutely?

The second clause of this question can be discarded as nonsensical. By definition God cannot be the object of a partial or equivocal trust. This is ironclad, either as a psychological-philosophical proposition or as an ontological-theological one.

153

Thus the main and real business of the question is exposed in its first part. The answer to it is that there is no situation in which it would be either wrong or unprofitable to trust God absolutely.

This is a unique sort of claim. It is not a generalization about human attitudes, though it has no quarrel with such. It is an assertion about the total situation (the world); thus it is a framing proposition. Nothing counts against such propositions, though a great variety of other framing propositions can be arrayed over against any set of them. Thus, "There is no situation in which it would be either wrong or unprofitable to trust God" is often enough denied by "There is nothing (or nobody) in any situation worthy of being trusted absolutely." But note that this is different from a partial denial of the main theological proposition, such as, "A great many victims in Dachau found it neither possible nor profitable to trust God; or at least to say, 'I trust God.'" The major negative is also different from, "How could one trust God when all finite models of trustworthiness have collapsed?"

It is not to be disputed that a great many victims of Dachau did in fact surrender their trust in God; or so at least they confessed. But this grim fact is devoid of logical-theological thrust against the main proposition, though it can be mounted with great rhetorical force, such as: "How can you dare to say, 'I trust God' in the face of the depths of suffering created by such terrible wickedness?"

The proper theological response to this challenge is something like: The possibility and the benefit of trusting God are frequently exposed in acute vicissitude. It does not follow that these situations are divinely inspired or intended for that purpose.

The proper theological response to "How could one trust God when (if) all finite models of trustworthiness have collapsed?" is something like: It is not legitimate to conclude that unreliability or even base treachery puts trusting out of business. Perhaps in order to survive in Dachau one had to become a cunning and ruthless animal. But that is something to be held against any and all perpetrators of things like Dachau. Man's inhumanity to man can reach depths of hideous novelty. That is not a novel discovery.

The proper response to the main negative, "There is nothing or nobody in any situation worthy of being trusted absolutely," is something like: Very well; give us another frame for self-in-world and world-against-self.

There is no doubt that framing propositions have a disposition-coaching function. This is not their main function but it is part of their business. So our prime theological proposition is not a covert or tacit description of a state of mind, such as a readiness to assent or adhere to something. An illustration of the latter might be to convert "God is love" into "Let love prevail!" or "I'm for love."

Yet the main affirmative proposition has dispositional business, no doubt about that. It is something like the conversion of "God is love," because given the prime proposition one ought to be disposed to various actions and aspirations. That is what is meant by disposition coaching: the prime proposition prescribes a set for mind, heart, and energy.

But if we have here a directive for experience rather than a theologically inflated report of experience, do we have also a real assertion, that is, a truth claim? It is a truth claim of a unique order. It directs attention to a global situation and asserts that there is a way of learning what is the case about that situation. It asserts that one can learn that God is trustworthy. If one learns that, then the prime proposition is, of course, true reflexively. But the Christian believer is not supposed to settle just for that kind of truth as a precious gem for meditation. In the first article of his faith, as it is framed here, there is a prescriptive, "Keep on trusting God in every situation!"

VIII

For what is God to be trusted? What in every situation are we to look to him, and to him alone, to be and do? Ordinarily we do not trust another person simply to be trustworthy. We count on him consistently to do thus-and-so. If he does thus-and-so characteristically, we say that he is trustworthy in that respect at least. This often takes the form of discovering that a person "is as good as his word"—or not; we learn that, too, from experience.

Does this hold for the prime case, that is, for trust in God? Here we are often inclined to fall back on testimony, such as "In the day of trouble I called upon the Lord and he answered me."

But then we have to brace for the "counter-factuals." "Why do my enemies (and yours, O God!) safely jeer at me all the livelong day?" "How long, O Lord, wilt Thou abide the wicked?" In more prosaic language, how shall I say God is to be trusted for my salvation when I am undone time after time? It is no use here to say, "At the end God will surely save," because it is not what the prime proposition asserts.

The radical response to these radically afflicting doubts is something like: Absolute trust in God is the ultimate existential cognitivity. "Existential cognitivity" means knowing what bears most, and most directly, upon the self-determination of a human possibility. This is not reducible to the question "What ought I do?" because that question is properly to be subsumed by the question "What ought I to be (become)?" The latter question, the master question, cannot be answered by citing a standard imperative or by appealing to an ordinary type of moral rule, such as "You ought to be a good person." It may be that the remote goal of every moral rule and prescription is the realization of good character, the acquisition of virtue. Perhaps to admit that means to acknowledge a unique ought and rule. But I believe that the business of morals and of ethics is necessarily nearer to hand, and with matters more nearly and surely manageable. For the real force of *ought* in "You ought to be a good person" is something like: Try so to saddle the thrust of *becoming* within your being that the unforeseeable, and sometimes unbearable, contingencies of the world—what seems to be randomly directed flux—will carry you toward fulfillment rather than away from it.

So while one cannot sensibly lay upon another person such an injunction as: "Control the contingent world!" one can set for another as well as for oneself the goal: "Be prepared to be your true self in every situation." This is not the same as: "Try to be self-consistent." Self-consistency as an overriding aim and criterion rests on the unhappy assumption that one saddle is sure to fit both self-becoming and the flux of the world. Moreover the ultimate goal of self-determination is perdurable efficacy rather than sheer self-identity.

The proposition, "Be prepared to be your true self in every situation," puts very heavy demands on existential cognitivity. It requires the self's perception of its own self-becoming. It requires also a veridical perception of the flux of the world; that is, whence it arises and whither it flows. But how can such mighty imponderables be *perceived?* Guessed at, yes; we all do that from time to time. Ignored for nearer and easier gains, no doubt. Celebrated in poetic fancy, by all means. But *perceived?*

Perceived indeed, and perceived veridically though not infallibly.[5] For there is an enforceable distinction between human projects launched in the right season, that is, when the velocity and vector of eddying flux are rightly perceived, and those conceived and born in the wrong time. Luck is only a pseudoreligious name for contingency that proved more benign than human cunning, wit, or merit deserved. Moreover, it is a dubious conceit that counsels: "We know the time was ripe because the project succeeded"; or conversely: "We know the time was wrong because the project failed." Great projects do more than make a neat splash in the world's flux. They fix a meaning upon it, they modify its vector. It is not the world that rushes all unheeding by. Rather, human beings are bemused by voices of failure. They are terrified by the thunder of distant cascades. Thus they do not see how flux can be ransomed by self-becoming ordered to a determinate good.

Accordingly, it is true, but it is not the whole truth, to say: Absolute trust is the same as absolute openness to being. Openness is a predispositional factor, and trust is a disposition. Trust is a readiness, rather than a proneness, to decide to determine one's self-becoming thus-and-so rather than in some other way. Furthermore, "absolute openness" is a confused notion. What is required of self-becoming is that it should be open both to its own possibility and to its own potentialities (capabilities). The possibility of a self-becoming is not an empty space waiting to be filled, a purely indeterminate something-I-know-not-what-but-it-is-interesting (or terrifying). Possibility is a next stage, or the next after that, or after that, for the unfolding or developing of a project. So possibility is a practical inference, a concrete extrapolation, the forward throw of a purpose or aim across the contingencies of flux.

Then self-becoming is required to be open enough to being and time to incorporate whatever of the world fits the design. But self-becoming must also be open enough to perceive when and how—not if or whether —the world demands that the design be modified. Yet self-becoming must also be sufficiently closed, its apertures must be sufficiently narrow, so that the potentialities of the self are not inundated by the world, and self-existence so loses determinancy; for then the self ceases to be more than a biosocial tropism.

So the burden of existential cognitivity which our prime proposition

("There is no situation in which it would be either wrong or unprofitable to trust God absolutely") and its prescriptive inference ("Keep on trusting God in every situation!") must bear is very heavy. It is what self-becoming must know in order rightly (authentically) to relate its possibility to its potentialities in the right season of the world's flux. Which is to say that the aim is the achievement of self-efficacy.

IX

We have finally to consider another way in which command is apprehended and appropriated as divine revelation; that is, as *promise*.

Promise as the other side of commandment is not a pure monopoly of biblical religion. Wherever self-becoming is allowed or obliged to conform to a standard putatively divine, and in this to find salvation, promise is at work. Its distinctive work is to bind the phases of self-becoming into an integral agent-self, and then to link up that subject with the master pattern governing the world's flux.

Promise has an obvious and inalienable relationship to futurity. "Turn again, O Israel, and I will give you life" is the promise of the Lord. "If you obey me, you shall live; but if you heed not my word, you shall surely die" is a nice combination of promise and threat. "If I leave you I will send another in my place and he will teach you all truth" is one of the richest promises of the New Testament.

These are illustrations, chosen more or less at random, of the enormous weight attributed by biblical religion to the absolute efficacy and reliability of God's promise. That weight is so great, in fact, that it constrains us to ask whether it is possible that God will *sometime* be revealed and thus known as he is, but in the meantime, no matter how painfully or even tragically protracted the interim may be, we must, as faithful, be content with a promissory note. Perhaps Tennyson makes too much of a good thing when he says:

> Strong Son of God, immortal love,
> Whom we, that have not seen Thy face,
> By faith, and faith alone, embrace,
> Believing where we cannot prove; . . .

But perhaps poetic justice is at work here, effecting a balance with (or against) Cowper's earlier and equally famous lines:

> Blind unbelief is sure to err,
> And scan his work in vain;
> God is his own interpreter,
> And he will make it plain.

Yet the highest theological interests are not necessarily well served by the millstones of poetic justice. Why must we choose between blind belief and blind unbelief? Better yet, though, in response to Cowper's piety, we may ask how long the faithful must wait for God to make it plain, especially in a season when, to quote Wallace Stevens' "Sad Strains of a Gay Waltz,"

> The epic of disbelief
> Blares oftener and soon, will soon be constant. *

Thus the primitive question doubles back upon us and with greatly augmented energy: How is God known to be trustworthy as long as his promise has not yet been fulfilled?

The traditional Christian answer is that God's promise has been fulfilled in part. Or as some theologians have it, God's promise has been fulfilled *in principle*. I admit to some confusion on what analogy of general experience, or on what religious specialization of experience, theologians are drawing who so speak. If, for instance, I tell my banker that I consider my mortgage to have been paid in principle when in fact I have paid only a dime of interest, his outrage, replacing puzzlement very rapidly, will be as intelligible as predictable.[6]

On the other hand the testimony of piety: "We have enough but not too much/To long for more . . ." leaves a great deal to be desired.

What then shall we say? I venture this: If the primordial engagement of self-becoming with God does not take place on the level of ultimate existential cognitivity, then confidence (hope) in the future disclosure of God as promise-keeper may well collapse into a stage of self-becoming.

Both in the history of mankind and of individuals there is a stage from which the realization of high and integral efficacy seems so remote both in time and potentiality that it is indeed "A divine far-off event/Towards which all creation moves."

But once that state of self-existence has been reached, it seems to be a natural, if not inevitable, inference that at last human life has attained self-completion. That mankind has at last come of age may have been a premature announcement. But the purely human achievement of human perfection is the aspiration and aim of forms of humanism that hardly agree on anything else.

Revelation as command must then mean that, in God's giving of the command, the destiny of mankind and of concrete self-becoming is announced and pledged. So to do is God's business; it is God's absolutely.

It follows that the command itself is an instrument of a destiny divinely conceived and pledged. It follows from this that the obedience God commands is identical with: "Be prepared to be your true self in every situation." This is the existential inference of what in this treatment has been called faith's prime proposition.

We have therefore reached this conclusion: Obeying God in all things, as he commands, means looking always for that option in self-becoming which maximizes the human good as such. That option is in there somewhere. The flux of the world is divinely orchestrated to bring it out. It is up to the agent-self to perceive it and lay hold of it in good faith—though perhaps also in fear and trembling.

So God's revealing promise is a disclosure of his purpose. God also designates how his presence can be made out. That is how he is to be actually perceived rather than interpolated by us into or projected upon the flux of the world from the hungry depths of self-becoming. God in his infinite wisdom does much more than specify how self-becoming must throw itself forward toward the kingdom of God. God also declares how his presence comes to light in that world in which self-transcendence is both mandated and free; the same being the only world, the only real world, there is of divine intent.

Therefore, what we mean by God's direct revelation of his righteous will is an infinite distance away from the transmission of an inviolable moral code, and from a private-line edict for a particular person. God's command is both universal and concrete. It is universal: There is an inclusive human destiny and it must be served by all. It is concrete, individual, and individuating: Be prepared to seize that option in self-becoming which maximizes the human good as such, because somewhere in the flux of the world that option will find you out. That is God's promise. God can be perceived in its keeping. That is, God does more than eventually bring good out of evil, though that is nothing to be casually ventured either as a hope or a project. What God reveals as his present unremitting activity is the orchestration of self-becoming in all of its native tenuousness, opacity, and irresolution, with the flux of the world in all its native randomness. It is God's design, assuredly not ours or Satan's, that the absolute security of human destiny should be thrashed out at the very heart of the world's contingencies.

So destiny is grounded in the heart of man by God's act. But this destiny comes to light always as this or that option submitted to free choice and self-enactment. It is God who keeps the options open. Therefore, the essence of the divine imperative is that we shall remain open to him whose promise is the foundation of the actual world as well as the hope of glory in the "new heavens and a new earth."

Chapter Seven

HISTORICAL REALITY
AND HISTORICAL EVIDENCE

I

The attack of the Enlightenment on the historical evidentiality of the Christian faith is commonly presumed to have destroyed that particular target. Since then, Christian theologians can be roughly classified by asking how they view that feat of demolition; this exempts the few who do not believe that scriptural-traditional historical claims have been materially damaged by the Enlightenment attack or by anything since. The rest of the theological world, by far its greater part, concedes that the way history is done in the modern world, and is thought about—historiographical revolutions and secularistic philosophies of history—creates formidable problems for that pathetic creature, historical evidentiality. So there are some theologians who await its resurrection, and there are others who believe in its reincarnation in an appropriately modest form. There are still others who convert the issue into a metaphysical one, that is: What is historical reality as such?

I do not propose to distribute either a small or large array of theologians according to this crude classification. My purpose here is to look into three questions made inescapable by modern attacks on what is commonly identified as the historicity of the Christian faith. These questions are:

(1) What stake does Christian faith have in historical evidentiality? OR: Is a weak historical case better than none?

(2) Is the Christian case improved by committing it to historical relativism? OR: Is the Christian faith the most relativistic of all religious views of history?

(3) Does the Christian faith, rightly construed, contain a novel and powerful theory of historical reality?
OR: You take the evidence and we'll take the court.

II

(1) What stake does the Christian faith have in historical evidentiality?

Insofar as one is sensitive to the weight of tradition, the initial answer to this first question will be all but transparently clear: If the historical testimony about Jesus Christ is not trustworthy, then Christians do not have in faith unique access to God's righteous will; their transcendent hopes for personal and communal fulfillment are based on (and not merely expressed in) myth; and they have no existential paradigm for the life-policy of love.

Transparent truths are not always enthusiastically embraced by theologians. Since the Enlightenment, the *odium theologiae* has been more easily borne by seeming to be wrong rather than naïve; naïve particularly in respect to complexities embedded in modern concepts of historical evidentiality. The coming of age of the science of history has inflicted as much and as heavy punishment on the historical credibility of the New Testament as any other single development of modernity has done. Theologians who do not properly acknowledge this are leftovers from a long-dead intellectual world.

There is a more traditional reason for distrusting theological naïvete; that is, the apostolic injunction to which allusion has been made several times. St. Paul says, "Test everything; hold fast what is good" (1 Thess. 5:21). It is not necessary to suppose that the apostle foresaw an era in which theologians of the faith would petition a court of scientific history for a license to write drafts on historicity; and, denied that, would turn for solace to philosophical assurances that the truth of history transcends every niggling concern with factuality; and would thus confound the apostolic injunction not to invest heavily in philosophy or any other "empty deceit" (Col 2:8).

Whatever St. Paul's understanding of it may have been, there is a serious question here. To test all things by their relationships to absolute truth—which is certainly what St. Paul had in mind—is indicated when such truth is available. When truth of that magnitude has been eclipsed, something else is indicated. That something else is a variety of accommo-

dations of systematic doubt, doubt as a fundamental methodological orientation, doubt as the first lesson in mental hygiene. The great wielders
of this instrument have had various things up their sleeves, things held
to be either doubt-immune or doubt-certified, paradoxical as the latter
may seem. The practical consequences are the same. The systematic
doubters have had fall-back surrogates for absolute truth; epistemological
and metaphysical principles presumptively safe from backfire from the
siege guns of modernity.

So the apostolic injunction to test everything, only superficially similar
to the posture of modern skepticism, prompts obvious questions. Who is
responsible for all of this testing? What are the criteria? What are the
paradigms? What are its objectives? Not everybody, not just anybody, is
able to go into the universal testing business; no one works at it all the
time. What then are the proper credentials? What kind or degree of
confidence should the general public vest in the properly certified doubters and verifiers?

These questions have been with us before in this essay. Here concern
for them is confined, as far as possible, to the situation of Christian faith
held to be grounded in historical fact.

Here, then, is one of the cardinal affirmations about Jesus Christ in the
New Testament: God was in Christ reconciling the world to himself (2
Cor 5:19).

The past tense, *was*, has nothing in common with the tenses of fable
or myth; nor with deceptively tensed expressions in metaphysics, such
as: "The world *has had* no beginning in time." and "There *was* never a
time when there *was* no world." But it is as serious a mistake to impute
to this text a sophisticated, perhaps a sophistical, distinction between an
historical occurrence and a suprahistorical meaning. In this era it is easy
for theologians to slide into that sophistication. That is not necessarily
the fate lying in wait for every believer or for every theologian.

The affirmation of St. Paul, cited above, moves on the same level of
historical intentionality as the familiar creedal elements:

> Born of the Virgin Mary
> Suffered under Pontius Pilate
> Was crucified, dead and buried

Rose from the dead on the third day
Ascended into heaven.

All of these propositions, and many more like them, were accepted for many centuries as factual in the same sense as "Julius Caesar was assassinated in 44 B.C." is still accepted as factual. Since the Enlightenment, the company of theologians prepared to accept traditional historical assertions has become steadily smaller. For the larger part, such assertions are treated as symbolically valid rather than as empirically true. Yet that larger company of theologians has fought resolutely to keep some historical-factual account open for serious theological drafts.

But what magnitude of draft is likely to be ventured or accepted where secular canons of historicity reign? I propose the following sketch as a summary of the present situation.

(i)   There are good historical grounds for saying that Jesus Christ—Jesus of Nazareth, called Messiah by his followers—taught certain things about the kingdom of God. The New Testament account of those things can probably be relied on.

(ii)   There are poor historical grounds for saying that anything transnormal happened to Jesus, such as resurrection.

(iii)   There are no historical grounds for saying that Jesus was, or had, anything transnormal, despite the fact that much of that order is imputed to him in the New Testament; such as Son of God, Savior of mankind, Master of the tempest. etc.

III

(i) Jesus of Nazareth preached the kingdom of God, its ethical demands, and its imminence. As historical fact this is as well-attested as Caesar's crossing the Rubicon—a fact to which he does not allude in his own *Commentaries*— or his assassination. But what about Jesus' own relationship to that kingdom? How did he represent himself, both to himself and to others, in respect to the kingdom? Here the historical assets in the theological account seem very slender indeed. We know what the New Testament reports about such matters: a considerable variety of ascriptions and attributions. But do we know, how could we possibly *know*, what Jesus, the historical figure, actually felt and really said about them?

One can *believe*, but such beliefs sail far far from the solid shores of evidentiality.

This harsh fate, this alienation from hard historical fact, seems even more certain in the case of the grand affirmation: *Jesus is the Lord of history*. The very notion of an evidentiary case for this seems patently absurd. Ought we then to conclude that "Jesus is the Lord of history," being immune to historical verification-falsification, is a pseudoassertion? Ought we to acknowledge that this affirmation is a ringleader in a pack of affirmatory expressions dressed up as fact-assertions for the sake of emphasis?

There may be no escape from this stern verdict, but before it is returned it may be useful to inquire briefly into historical evidentiality as a criteriological concept. Specifically, what is the distinction between hard and soft historical evidence, that is, evidence adduced to support fact-claims about a past event? Hard evidence includes human records and other artifacts, and physical registrations of natural events, such as lava flow, volcanic ash, flood detritus, high-water marks. Soft evidence is comprised of opinions, attributions, ascriptions, sentiments, legends, rumors, interpretations—things for which substantiating hard evidence is lacking or is incurably equivocal. Suppose I say, "Augustus Caesar was an inveterate womanizer; he was probably also an active homosexual." In support of these pronouncements I am likely to cite the testimony of Suetonius, at least in respect to the first item. But the only thing really hard here is that no competent scholar doubts that Suetonius was the author of *The Lives of the Caesars*. Moreover, while he cites the rumors and tales of "a vicious and wanton life" invented and circulated by Augustus's enemies, early and late (sections 68–70 of his *Augustus*), he says these things are "criminous imputations or malicious slanders." But there is a question about the reliability of Suetonius as a historian. One scholar says of him: "[He] panders too much to a taste for gossip." But the same source continues: "None the less he is next to Tacitus and Dio Cassius the chief [sometimes the only] authority."[1] Another scholar, however, gives him very good marks on "his conscientious use of sources," and explains why Suetonius did not screen out "scabrous gossip."[2]

Then there is the related question of the harsh voluptuary laws Augustus laid down. What was his *real* motive for levying this famous bit of legislation? Who was the real target? Suetonius inteprets this as an expression of the repugnance a morally upright, if not puritanical, person feels when he beholds the licentious behavior of the upper classes. A novelist has hypothesized that those famous edicts sprung from Augustus's profoundly ambivalent relationship to his promiscuous daughter, Julia.[3] For all the sobriety of this novelist's imagination, he does not have to linger long over the distinction between hard and soft evidence; for his purpose he can invent both. Historians, on the other hand, may well be inclined to treat *The Acts of Augustus* as hard evidence and *The Lives of the Caesars* as soft; but surely not, one would hope, because the former is a lot of public records and the latter the work of a superior Walter Winchell. "Hard" does not mean made of stone—monuments and their magniloquent inscriptions can lie. Nor does "soft" mean such stuff as dreams are made of, though some dreams are as old as the pyramids.

Moreover, documents about whose authenticity or date there is little significant argument can be either hard or soft; both, for that matter, depending on the contested point. The Synoptic Gospels are hard evidence in support of the proposition that some people long ago and far away believed that Jesus rose from the grave; that point is not contested. Whether he *really* rose is a contested point, to say the least, early and late.

Lest we make too short work of the complexities here, we should pause to ask whether the Synoptic Gospels are soft evidence for the resurrection of Jesus simply because they report what we call a supernatural event. To this I say, perhaps a bit piously, we should hope not *simply.* The history of science in the Western world is full of a great variety of things that informed and presumably rational people refused for a long time to believe despite the elegance of the arguments and the hardness of the evidence adduced in support; refused to believe because the new things could not be squared with extant truth and reigning canons. In the case of the resurrection, however, there is no extratextual evidence that can be marshaled in support of the textual case. For example, the people who saw the empty tomb are already figures in and of the text; though "of" does not mean none of them had an extratextual existence. And as the text itself allows, the tomb might have been violated by human hands (Mt 28:63,64; 28:12,13). So also for "the five hundred brethren at one time" of St. Paul's mention (1 Cor. 15:6). Though he says, "most of them are still alive," he made none of them available for interrogation. A similar verdict must be handed down in the case of "the many proofs with which the risen Lord attested to himself" (Acts 1:3).

So far we have skirted some antecedent questions, such as: What would count as hard evidence in the case of the resurrection? And: Even if such evidence were available, could we legitimately count it again in support of such a history-summing claim as, "Jesus is the Lord of History"? I do not propose to address these questions until the issue of the distinction between hard and soft historical evidence is disposed of.

Then what is the real basis for the distinction between hard and soft evidence? It is the need to relate incorrigible belief to corrigible hypothesis. An incorrigible belief might turn out to be true. Its arrival at truth could not be accounted for simply in terms of the psychological strength of the belief; belief is perfectly capable of digging in to resist all assaults from fact-resplendent hypotheses, drawing strength to endure, if not prevail, from intuition, habit, antecedent personal commitments, or all three. But we know also that some incorrigible beliefs are fundamental expressions of self-reality, so that to correct them would be to destroy a version of that self; whereas to modify or remove a hypothesis is but to alter an account or a view of a situation in which the self appears, in one guise or other, but not so as to be constituted by that situation.[4]

On this hypothesis the real basis for the distinction between hard and soft evidence, in respect to historicity, has very little to do with the common distinction between the objective world and the subjective one. The essential difference is between kinds of human interest. There are kinds of discourse suitable for the fulfillment of those diverse interests.

Applying this hypothesis to (ii) and (iii) on pages x, xii, we obtain the following results:

(ii')   There is little or no hard evidence for saying that anything transnormal, such as resurrection, happened to Jesus.

(iii')   There is little or no hard evidence for saying that Jesus really was or had any of the transnormal things imputed to him in the New Testament, such as Son of God, Lord of history.

But is this a net gain? It would be hard so to compute it apart from a clear and cogent determination of what hard evidence would or could be in either case (ii' or iii'). Where would we look for it? How would we recognize it? Consider the resurrection. The documents (the Gospels,

1 Cor 15) clearly attest to beliefs that easily pass muster as incorrigible; 1 Corinthians 15 is a nice demonstration of belief in the resurrection digging in for the duration. But where are the conviction-free facts to substantiate that belief? That question prompts its opposite number: Where are the conviction-free facts with which to attack that belief? For that negative offensive there are hypotheses available. The disciples of Jesus—to draw on a stock item—were psychologically prepared to believe that the best (Jesus lives again!) was entailed by the worst (he suffered, died, and is buried). But there are no ranges of independent facts for the perception of which such a hypothesis can sensitize us. Factlike suppositions can be conjured for the sake of such a hypothesis; for example, suppose somebody had been there with a camera, would the risen Lord have shown up on the negative? But if he had not registered there, how could we say, "Christ is risen indeed!"?

Such fact-conjuring feats of the imagination are generally inspired by specific religious interests: Jesus was a fraud, for example; his disciples were naïve, superstitious, country bumpkins, for another. Not that suppositions of that sort, considered as propositions in the abstract, presuppose something other than a Christian religious concern. Concretely, why would one want to unseat the historicity of the resurrection unless one had an alternative to the traditional Christian outlook?

It hardly needs saying that defensive reaffirmations of a once incorrigible belief are commonly as free with supposition. One thinks here of the fail-safe interpretation of the resurrection as the *real* miracle of the rebirth of faith during the deep black night of despair.

The transformations of (ii) and (iii) into (ii') and (iii') do not mean that either the believer or nonbeliever is thus liberated from all meaningful responsibility for historical evidence. A responsibility remains not to invent evidence but to incorporate what there is of it as faithfully as possible. "Incorporation" means many things, no doubt. At one extreme it is a systematic regimentation of fact—so systematic that reality seems to be there for the sake of the system. At the opposite extreme, fact is a world that seems to impose itself wholebodied on the mind of the believer, demanding an all-or-none response. In the latter case, evidence sufficient for conviction is made available by surrender. In the former case, the route to the evidence is a dialectical one: the unfolding of the mind in and to itself.

For the larger part, we live by faith somewhere between these extremes. We sing of surrender, but we try to make a case for decision. We say the real world is what we make sense of, but we concede, with Tennyson, that

> Our little systems have their day;
> They have their day and cease to be: . . .

At our very best we intend to hold fast with the apostle:

. . . whatever is true, whatever is honorable, whatever is just, whatever is pure, whatever is lovely, whatever is gracious . . .

But we are not always or surely delivered thereby from the perplexing and perverse doubts occasioned, though not intended, by the ensuing phrases of the apostle: ". . . if there is any excellence, if there is anything worthy of praise" (Phil 4:8).

So it appears that a belief may be incorrigible but not overwhelmingly strong. It may be something to which one clings for dear life. It may be something for which one endures fire, flood, and forsakenness, but in the courage of despair rather than the courage of hope. Belief, finally, may persist, may perdure, in full recognition that the evidence for it is weak. Weak, that is, in respect to historical evidence.

What then would be a weak case for the Christian faith? Would it not be identical with a weak or reduced form of that faith? Suppose one were to say that Christianity as a faith is nothing but a belief, or a set of beliefs, about something symbolically expressed as the kingdom of God. A strong case can be made for the proposition that Jesus of Nazareth was the historical source of these beliefs. So far, to believe in him is to believe that the substance of what he said about the kingdom is true. Such a judgment, such a belief about the beliefs imputed by the New Testament to Jesus, assumes the independent validity of a truth criterion; that is, independent of the New Testament, not necessarily independent of my being or the values of the society in which perforce I live. Indeed such a truth criterion may be part of a structure of incorrigible beliefs for which I seek some sort of evidentiary corroboration; in this case from the New Testament so construed as to render it sufficiently evidentiary.

This would be an attenuated form of the Christian faith. It might be the best that a person striving for intellectual respectability could afford. In respect to history, however, it has jettisoned a major item of the Christian manifest: the conviction that Jesus Christ is the Lord of history. The vestige of lordship left to the historical Jesus is ethical superiority; superiority in precept rather more clearly than in example if one hews to the text of the New Testament Gospels. But if one's incorrigible beliefs are strongly impregnated with the democratic egalitarian ethos, the very category of lordship, any and every image of it as well, may be repugnant. In that case—hardly uncommon or atypical—the evidentiary Jesus is reduced to the teacher who rejects authoritarian social structure (Mt 20:25–27). The Christ who commanded the waves of the stormy Galilean sea and the unruly wills of Galilean fishermen recedes into the mists of arcane folklore in the one case, and into the wasteland of archaic dogma in the other.

Here we may have stumbled upon a kind of law: The more credible theological claims about Jesus become, relative to prevailing canons of historical evidentiality, the more such claims tend to become lighter and thinner as religious propositions. The more seriously one takes the canons of historical evidentiality, the less weight one is able to assign to traditional religious claims about Jesus; unless one is prepared to exempt those claims from duty in the established courts of cognitivity. If one is prepared to claim that exemption, there is no need to bother about the canons of historical evidentiality in the first place.

IV

Given this *law*, it is not surprising that theologians have turned to the consolations of historical relativism, hoping to find there the basis, perhaps even the substance, of an interpretation of the Christian faith capable of assimilating the worst possible damage from historical evidentiality. For suppose that all the achievements of a given society, including its proudest cognitional triumphs, its most brilliant raids on the realm of truth, are all historically conditioned: they all derive their meaning from coordinates (presuppositions, prepossessions, axioms) uniquely employed by that society. So even if an abstract semantic unity overarches a great variety of cultures and cultural epochs, it does not follow and it is not true that there is any persistence of a common material meaning.

Plato speaks of God. So do Billy Graham and Spinoza. These theologies have nothing in common except *theos*. More modestly expressed: In the era of Billy Graham there is no way of *knowing* what *God* meant for Plato and his audience.

How is it possible for Christian theologians to find comfort in such doctrines of history? Doctrine indeed; an incorrigible belief, it has long since transcended the provisionality of a hypothesis.

Well, consider one of the great slogans of the faith extracted from Scripture: "Jesus Christ is the same yesterday, today, and forever" (Heb 13:8). One of the inescapable facts of history is the immense variety of ways in which the same Jesus Christ lives in the minds and hearts of Christian people down the ages. The quest for the historical Jesus may be a fixation of modern theology, but even a very thin knowledge of the history of Christian art suffices to document the extraordinary variety of ways in which Christ has been represented from the earliest Christian times until now. Within the folds of piety Jesus Christ has been all things good and wonderful to all persons. In myriad guises he moves also through the world of modern unbelief.

Where, then, in this amazing welter is the *real* Jesus? The question is burdened with naïvete. It predisposes us to believe there *is* one supremely, transcendently real Jesus Christ. So challenged, some theologians, few of Protestant hue, scramble for the metaphysical uplands. Others seek to turn the historical phenomenon into theological loaves and fishes for the sustenance of the many caught in the lowlands. That phenomenon is indubitably historical—the historically real Jesus is this total, this potentially infinite representation-representability. Thus "gentle Jesus, meek and mild," is just as real as the figure of cosmic grandeur and terrible power evoked by Michelangelo.

It does not follow that arbitrariness is king and that fantasy is his consort presiding over the representation of Jesus Christ. One can, and the devout must, assay the seriousness of the religious quest in the ways in which Jesus Christ is represented. So, even if it is true that the *real* meaning of Christ is what he means to me, it is also true that my intentions are fair game for anyone who wants to ask about their seriousness, comprehensiveness, coherence, and lucidity. Every age and every believer reveals a particular degree of kind of seriousness, of passionateness, in the way in which one representation, one bodying forth, of Jesus is honored above all others.

Each successive age has done this. Every devout believer has done this. Where, then, is the critical pressure from historical relativism? It is registered most acutely in the demand that we modern people must confess that our representations of Jesus Christ cannot possibly be universally valid, though they be more precious to us than our life's blood. Indeed, insofar as Jesus Christ is absolutely real in and for us, he cannot in that form be universally valid. Not only has he other sheep we know not of (Jn 10:16), we have not the slightest idea of how he cares for them or how he represents himself to them.

The pressure of relativistic dogma does not in itself justify plunging into a solipsistic conclusion: as many Jesuses as believers—one to a customer. There are, in fact, four specifiable subjects or entities which can properly be said to be the "the real Jesus."

One: The Jesus of dominant contemporary representation. Dominant in the sense either of (a) cultural eminence; or of (b) personal (subjective) vividness.

Two: The Jesus who (which) is the sum total of all representations, past, present, and future. For phenomenological purposes, a class name.

Three: The Jesus who is the central figure in the Gospels. More accurately, the various figures in the Gospels who are called Jesus. The Jesus of John's Gospel is not identical with the Jesus of Mark's. John's Jesus is older when he dies; he has been in Jerusalem at least once before his trial and crucifixion; he claims a metaphysical unity with God the Father; his human enemies are the Jews.

Four: The Jesus who is (was) the referent of *One, Two* and *Three.* The person about whom the stories are told. The person to whom supernatural presence, properties, and power are ascribed. Commonsensically, this alone *(Four)* is the real Jesus. The others are interpretations, testimony, celebrations. Theologically, this is the Jesus of supreme perplexity. What do we really *know,* as something determined or at least certified by the canons of historical evidentiality, about that Galilean? Here a powerful temptation insinuates itself. Why not join the philosophical throngs around the epistemological wickets with a view to showing how confoundedly complex are the relationships between knowing and believing, perceiving and caring? But the sting in this seduction is the confusion of complexity as a feature of a phenomenon—such as the fall of the Roman Empire—with complexity as a feature of a conceptual-analytic and conceptual-reconstructive address to a phenomenon—such as dialectical materialism. Overwhelmed by this seduction, one grows accustomed to confusing naïvete with ignorance, or with stupidity or flat error; quite as though a naïve person were bound to be wrongheaded as well as wrong about the facts. Worse still: as though the proper cure for naïvete were a heavy charge of theory about the world perceived in hopeless innocence and expressed with artless simplicity.

The proper outcome of such lugubrious reflections is surely not to eschew any or all theological theory that inspires quarrels with religious naïvete about the real Jesus. It would be far more appropriate to ask as objectively as possible whether the real Jesus has a residual and intelligible reference to the figure who trod the dusty roads of Galilee long long ago. If one consents to putting this question, one ought to keep in mind the difference between historical investigation and reconstruction on one side and historical fiction on the other. I do not mean to suggest that the historical fictioneer can predictably be faulted for slipshod and inept research or for excessive play of the imagination; or the scientific historian for insufferable prosiness and presuppositional frigidity. Multiple representations of the great figures of history are bound to materialize from both sides of the aisle between the novelist and the historian. Thanks largely to the pressure of historical relativism, we expect the scientific historian to exhibit in his work the ethos of his cultural epoch quite as much, though not in the same ways, as the novelist does.

What then is the reality question which can properly be levied upon both sides of the aisle? To dip again into Roman history, in respect to the plurality of Julius Caesars, is it appropriate to ask whether Thornton Wilder's Caesar, or Rex Warner's, is less "real" than the figure who emerges from Caesar's *Commentaries* or from Dio Cassius? Is the Caesar of Mommsen or Buchan more real than Shakespeare's? Does the circumstantial detail of *The Gallic Wars*—cry a special boon for all the Latin students condemned to build, piece by piece, all of those bridges!—make that Julius more real than the man Shakespeare fashions with matchless strokes of poetry? Or should we become theologians again and say that the *real* Caesar is all these representations, and a numberless throng yet to appear, all held together in a transcendental unity, itself nowhere represented but everywhere intuited as an ideal? If so, Caesar sits down with Christ and the innumerable choir of persons who, save for the assurances of piety and the dicta of metaphysics, live now only in historical reconstruction and poetic evocation.

There is something missing here, or perhaps something amiss. It may be that too little has been made of the creative role of imagination in the historian's work. Surely he uses that magician's wand to render the data —both hard and soft—intelligible and coherent. The facts, the blessed facts, do not speak for themselves; they speak meaningfully when they are properly addressed. Learning that takes a lot of doing; many are called, few are chosen. So also of the artist's craft. There is nothing easy, nothing at all merely "natural"—*native*, certainly; but *natural*, certainly not—about being able to impart the sheen of verisimilitude to a fragment of a remembered world. Imagination is the fabricator of that illusion, that verisimilitude. What tempts us to suppose that the coherencies, the elegant mathematical patterns of scientific discourse, are fundamentally different from avowedly aesthetic creations and have a surer grasp of reality? What but the incorrigible belief that scientific knowledge is providentially ordained to dissolve metaphysical mysteries into material advantages for *homo sapiens;* at least for the happy few of that self-endangered species.

Here we may detect an unmistakable tincture of pathos in the contemporary pursuit of historicity. Here there is a point of convergence with the art of the historical novel. The artist may use a greater wealth of data to lend to the work of his imagination a sheen of verisimilitude. That the sheen is an illusion is beside the point. The point is to create a surface of such mirror-bright plausibility that the age in which the artist writes can read thereon the actualities of its own situation. This existentializing of the past is the fate coveted both in the historical novel and in much of contemporary theology. But the novelist does not need to worry about such things as historical relativism, whereas the theological embrace of that doctrine is a worrisome thing.

V

What is wrong with that doctrine? I detect several flaws in it. If these flaws are really there, and are as serious as I make them out to be, the doctrine is a hopelessly inadequate foundation on which to rest any of the piers of the Christian faith.

In the first place historical relativism is a theory that leads a double life: it purports to apply both to history and to historiography. It is reasonable to expect congruence between a theory of historical reality on the one hand and methodological assumptions and procedures on the other; that is, between history as lived and history as reconstructed. But congruence is one thing and identity another. In respect to history the confusion is a very heavy liability. It leads us to suppose that the instruments of inquiry endow the object of inquiry with its significance, if not with its very being. If that is the case, if it is not gratuitously suppositious, then in the interpretation of an historical event we know what we are looking *at* because we know what we are looking *for* and what we are looking *with*. Having come so far we would have very slight excuse for not going the rest of the way and saying that language is *all;* not only the dwelling-place of being, as Heidegger proclaims, but all of the inmates as well.

There are stronger forms of metaphysical idealism than this. They can be supported by stronger arguments than an appeal to the incontestable fact that everything we say is said in language.

Secondly, historical relativism is the product of a felt necessity to make a silken virtue out of a swinish fact. The fact, initially of such low repute, is the conviction that there are no value-free facts to which presupposition-free minds have access, if there were any of those—the subjunctive contrary to fact. Even if the mind were the camera eye of common sense, all of its pictures are snapped from a particular angle and at given times. It appears to follow that all of our knowledge, or surely the best of it, is thus imbued with a human richness that the very principles of modern science stripped away from *noesis.* So to the question: In respect to history is there not a gain, clear and immense, in being able—at last!—to banish the sterile inane ghost of History-As-Such, and its dismal cousin, Historical Reason, and learn to understand, thence to celebrate, the concrete particularities of this our history?

But what then are Grote's *Greece* or Mommsen's *Rome* about? Are those mighty ancient civilizations merely dry disarticulated bones challenging historians to knit them up with modern conceptual tissue and then bedeck the results with modern sentiments?

I think that the logic of historical relativism requires affirmative answers to such questions. If so, then no historical epoch other than the historian's own has an iota of recoverable integrity. Natural piety files a soft demurrer: each and every epoch once *had* its own integrity. To which tender sentiment must be added the solemn fact: in every case that has gone off on the winds of change.

So what begins with a hunger for concreteness, for the richness and density of historical life, eventuates as an absolute right of investiture. Every past but ours is what we say it is, it is our discourse about it.

Historical relativism, thus, is even more parochial than the doctrine of progress. The latter is a secularistic construal of Hebrews 11:39:

And all these, though well attested by their faith, did not receive what was promised, since God had foreseen something better for us, that apart from us they should not be made perfect.

Historical relativism goes this at least one better. Bygone ages are all suppliants at the throne of our historians.

Thirdly, there is something metaphysical-theological packed into historical relativism. It is a theory about historical reality. History as such is subject to a universal law of periodicity. There is no history of mankind as such. Rather, there is this period and that in the life of a given people. And there is the grand succession of civilizations. In this succession one can sometimes discern cultural affinities—bequests, borrowings, superimpositions. But it is arrant metaphysics, or errant theology, to impute the rise and fall of civilizations to any kind of omnibus causal agency. The logic of historical relativism rules this out. The pattern imposed upon other cultural epochs is sense-making only as far as it expresses *our* sense of life and death and our incorrigible convictions about nature, man, and God.

So the past as such does not signify. It is rendered significant in and by determinate human societies. In our culture it is supposed that there are vast cosmic ranges of space and time eternally devoid of life. But what do these suppositions signify? The shocking paradox of scientific reason, mostly. As Pascal saw, this changeling creature is trapped between the infinite and the infinitesimal. Now we should add: self-trapped. Scientific man is self-diminished and self-exalted. He is the sport of the perfectly irrational forces of nature. He is also the lord of all he surveys in the matter of cognitivity; percipience he shares with myriad forms of life, but he alone is privy to truth.

Is this some sort of poetry in wretched disguise? Hardly. If historical relativism is true, the vasty depths of space-time are features of our mythic structuring of experience. As such they are no more "real" than the cosmogonical yarns of Sumer and Chaldea. So the silent and dark universe is not the environment of our speech. It is only that odd awkwardness occurring when we do not know what to say next or when we cannot quite recall what we have just heard.

In the fourth place, much of the persuasiveness of historical relativism is derived from an historiographical postulate: The canons of signification, and therefore of significance, are necessarily determinate; they are both culture-specific and culture-categorical. From this it follows that the canons and coordinates of historical interpretation are culture-specific. They are cognitional directives only in and for a given society in one moment of its life. For that moment they are categorical (absolute).

What empirical evidence is there for this double-jointed theory? Perhaps the phenomenon of language. Do we not say, and wisely too, that *preliterate* amounts to *prehistorical?* Imaginatively, we can endow Cro-Magnon man, say, with perception of the threat of time, as well as rapacious neighbors, to the continuity of his people. In generosity of our imagination we may grant him leave to blaze trees and chip boulders to remind posterity that he passed this way in pilgrimage from silence to silence. But all that is stuff of *our* mythic life. We do not know what sense he made of things. We know only what dim dusty lines he is given in our story. Whatever he counted as heartwarming triumph, he is a piteous failure in our book. He left no word. His mind was written on the wind. Who but the Holy Spirit could decipher it?

So the past is able to signify, is empowered to become history, only by virtue of an objective—that is, object-like, thing-like—residue. If we wish we may think of these things—records, arrowheads, coins, potsherds, monuments, enciphered stone—as being the extruded skeleton of life gone in its integrity beyond recall. But not beyond reconstruction, provided that among the layers and piles of detritus there are fragments of speech.

Now we know that language is always culture-specific. Since Leibniz there has been talk of a universal language. It is not accidental that the scientific age conceives of that as mathematical, compared to which, in respect to elegance of structure, abstractional power, and consistency of rules, Esperanto is a pious joke. On the other hand universal algebra invites us to confuse genuine universality with abstract generality. So the quest for concrete universality, that modern Holy Grail, has to lurch off in other directions, and pass through such stations as the world-histori-cal-dialectical process, the pervasive and permanent neurosis, the archetypes of the collective unconscious, and the ecumenical church. These are ways in which the modern Western world searches for universality of meaning.

Surely there is something here that counts for historical relativism. Whatever the undeclared metaphysical manifest of a historian may be, he must proceed on the assumption that the thought forms constituting the structure of meaning in a cultural epoch other than his own have to be translated into the meaning-structures of his own culture. Even if there are verbal near-identities linking the two cultures, the historian dare not suppose that *cause,* for example, means now what it meant for Aristotle. For him the concept signified four different things. In our scientific age it signifies only one of those. No, *not* "one of those." The scientific use of *efficient cause* does not prescind from formal, final, and material causes; these other Aristotelian modalities of *cause* are not even formal possibilities now except in the common-sense world. So *efficient cause* has been divested of efficacy.

In the fifth place, it is far from clear that such cultural phenomena as culture-bound concepts and other elements of linguistic parochiality count for historical relativism rather than for a nonmetaphysical recognition of the finiteness and fallibility of the human mind. There are, to be sure, grave difficulties in determining when, where, and why Hellenistic interpretations of Plato, to take another example, went wide of the mark; became, that is, something that Plato did not intend. But what does "did not intend" mean? We cannot appeal to the text. Plotinus was familiar with that, it was native to his mind. Does that mean that the best we can do is to say, "As *we* read Plato's texts, Plotinus went wide of the mark here and here, and thus and so"? But what in this confession is so devastating to the cause of objective historical knowledge or so comforting to the adherents of historical relativism? Who, after all, is the "we" of that confession? Historians of philosophical ideas, each with his own history, each with his own reading of the cultural milieu; therefore, each with his own complex of biases and prejudices. But is there any evidence that a Western twentieth-century historian-philosopher is certain to produce a Plato, or a Plotinus, the likes of which have never been seen before? Is there any evidence that Aristotle had a grasp of the Platonic Ideas that A. E. Taylor or Gilbert Ryle cannot *really* understand or refute? Or that Plato's—the *real* Plato's—own understanding of the Ideas is forever irrecoverable?

The fact is that historical relativism illicitly posts an ideal object of historical investigation only to fall back in metaphysical dismay before the substitutionary character of historical cognitivity; substitutionary, not "relative."

In the sixth place, the doctrine under consideration inclines us to suppose that cross-epochal historical understanding is inherently far less plausible than either cross-cultural or intracultural understanding is. In support of this view, one might appeal to the incontrovertible fact that the doers and thinkers of other epochs cannot file demurrers against our construals of their achievements. This does not materially augment the plausibility of historical relativism. It is also the case that contemporaries speaking to each other across cultural differences do not always find it easy to make objections to interpretations either clear or convincing. We may grant that, in principle, contested interpretations are corrigible. Whether they are actually corrected depends to a large degree on the kinds of interests engaged in the hermeneutical dialogue. These interests commonly play as prominent a role as the degree of methodological sophistication and erudition prevailing on both sides.

Something of this sort is also true of contested historical interpretations within a given society. For example, is the conflict between revisionist and establishment interpretations of Abraham Lincoln any more responsive to scientific or rational adjudication because it is an intramural debate? Is it any more plausible to say that there is in principle a better chance of rational arbitrament here because the contestants share the same thought forms and are alike products of the same ethos? So far as plausibility is concerned, its currents run strongly in the other direction. When the appraisal of the ethos itself from within is the real target of historians, what great and secure triumphs of objectivity ought one realistically to expect? One party will dismiss the other for being ideologues, captives of the middle-class mentality. The other party will retort that dialectical materialism is a theological dogma, a pseudoscientific screen behind which lurks the totalitarian mentality.

Thus to a seventh observation pertaining to historical relativism. However great the chasms of doctrine separating historians from each other, they may share many important methodological principles and intentions. Mommsen and Livy, say. They may disagree over sources; perhaps over what makes a historical source really reliable. Yet both are consciously and wholeheartedly in the evidential game; neither wants to say that something happened, or that something happened for such-and-such reasons, when there is no evidence for such claims. As historians they both know they must make do with the evidence. Moreover, the story each tells is about Rome. Neither intends to incorporate myth either to aggrandize or diminish that subject beyond what the evidence allows. Each has a moral in view, to be sure, but the intent is to allow the moral, the capstone meaning, to emerge naturally and irresistibly from the story itself.

An eighth observation: There is an historiographical phenomenon for which historical relativism provides little more light than its rival theories. The phenomenon is the recurrent pattern of historical interpretation of a given event. One mentality downgrades interpretations that are too close in time to the occurrence of an event for the adequate play upon it of disinterested inquiry and dispassionate appraisal. But the primitive views may rise again after many rounds of sophistication in data-gathering and conceptualization. Of course ground-floor eye-witness testimony can be wrong. Early interpretations may not be sufficiently critical. These contingencies do not imply that reconstructive, hypothetical, and extrapolative interpretations fashioned long after the events are necessarily superior to more primitive ones. Of course, eye witnesses often disagree with one another on just what did happen. This does not mean that they are all wrong. Latter-day theoreticians may also disagree with one another. That does not mean that any of them is right.[5]

The phenomenon of recurrent rather than linearly progressive patterns of historical interpretation is sufficiently persistent to put one in mind of the policeman's slogan: "The book on an unsolved homicide case is never closed." Sophisticated generations of historians may deplore primitive methods of gathering and sifting evidence. But then what is to be said when it is made clear to the satisfaction of any reasonable person that Cock Robin was guilty after all? One can reach for that fail-safe mechanism, that well-tried-but-not-often-true ploy of asking: "But who or what is that reasonable person?" This question is easily togged out in rhetorical finery, such as, "Was Pontius Pilate reasonable? Or the jury that sentenced Socrates? Or the one that acquitted Lizzie Borden?" About all that we can do with such questions is to avoid confusing the evidentiary value of testimony with the rationality of the charge and the cogency of the case.

A ninth observation: Culture-specific canons of evidentiality, truth, and reality do not strictly entail the conclusion that knowledge is culture-specific. It is absurd to say that "The world is round," could not have been true for a people largely constrained by their cultural milieu to think it flat. Indeed some people thought it round well in advance of their culture. Does this mean that "The world is round" was not *really* true and then became true only when the encompassing thought-world caught up with the hardy voyagers who dared impossible seas?

Such commonsensical stuff may miss the drift of important subtleties. Perhaps, too, it is only when we properly consider the value realm that the cogency of historical relativism comes home; that is, the global sense of value rather than meanings of low-grade referentiality. That small handful of survivors of Magellan's incredible exploits bring back hard evidence of vast new continents surrounded by immense seas. But they are themselves the innocent unwitting presentments of a new *human* world. Its reality is not an historical deduction, so to speak, of the mediaeval world. But neither is it the premise for the deduction of our own world. How then are we able to capture the unique underivable noncontinuable world which emerged in the fifthteenth and sixteenth centuries?

For the purpose of exploring, if not resolving, such questions "historical relativism" is not the name of a well-defined philosophic-scientific school. Some plump for a unique empathetic probe that enables an historian to reach the marrow of another world. But what sort of scientific instrument is that? Is it a gift of the gods or can it be acquired by a rigorous discipline—if the genes are right? Is the historian saved by grace through faith or is he called to works-righteousness? Other historical thinkers are somewhat more consistently skeptical. They deny to the historian any magic or grace except that of being able to think the thoughts, to scan the intentions, of the doers and makers of past worlds, as far as those thoughts are recorded; as far, also, as the historian can plausibly impute to the author of such thoughts as much rationality as he discerns and exercises in himself, or—less *ad hominem* perhaps—vests in a normative paradigm of rationality.

Here the path the relativist treads is a bit slippery. He must wonder whether rationality is after all a worlds-embracing, perhaps even a worlds-generating, universal. Or is it just the most elevated, or the most heavily disguised, of self-justifying and self-referencing prejudices constituting the axiomatic matrix of modern science? (Nietzsche: presuppositions equal prejudices.)

Finally, historical relativism is a theory about historical reality, it is not just a theory about historical knowledge. We need not doubt that as a metaphysical doctrine it exhibits the pathos of the present age as surely and poignantly as the idea of progress exposed the theological nerve of the generation which produced two world wars.

If then historical relativism is a metaphysical theory, or a theory hardened into doctrine, what sort of evidence counts for it and what counts against it? Little help can be expected from the protagonists of the doctrine; being modern, they distrust overt metaphysical doctrines. This may well remind us of the equally sturdy and hardly more passionately religious conviction that Jesus Christ, as God-for-us-to-save exhausts all faithful possibilities of talk about God. God-in-himself is (damnable) metaphysics. God-for-us is our salvation from Satan's grasp; from metaphysics, too. It follows that "God, the Father of our Lord Jesus Christ" and "God, the Holy Spirit" are either pious mouthings that sinfully and futilely plunge into a realm where silence is lord, or they are odd ways of talking about *sola redemptor.*

We need not doubt that *sola redemptor,* like *sola fide,* is the best that can be done to serve some interests of Christian piety. But if those interests are allowed to become absolute, rather than preeminent, they obliterate in principle the possibility of universalizing the Christian faith.

A similar conclusion can be levied upon historical relativism. It can be universalized only by submerging its essential conviction, its primordial axiom. For on which culture is this prime proposition—"The meaning of all historical judgments is culture-dependent"—itself dependent for *its* meaning? Or, in broader terms, for what reality does does that primordial axiom hold good?

VI

The case for the Christian faith ought not to look for heavy support to a theory that is an unstable blend of inadvertent metaphysics and incorrigible beliefs relative to historiography.

What then ought we to make of a theory of history that is unambiguously metaphysical? Suppose, that is, that the New Testament Gospel is a novel way of construing historical reality. An important part of the theological task would then be to construe that view of history rather than to fit that Gospel into a metaphysical-methodological straitjacket.

Two difficulties arise forthwith. One is a philosophical resistance to any metaphysical theory of history. The second is a theological resistance to imputing any metaphysical interests to Scripture. Ontological, yes; metaphysical, *Nein!* With metaphysics comes system. Does God not despise system today as much as he loathed the abominations of Gilgal in the days of Amos (cf. 4:4)?

As for the first of these difficulties, let it be noted that indeed a considerable company of philosophers have been voting against metaphysics for quite a while, at least against metaphysics in the grand manner. In the camps of the linguistic analysts there is a general agreement not to raise metaphysical questions in the speculative mode, because in that mode such questions are an odd kind of mental pathology, or because there is only a dialectical—not a trace of an evidentiary—way of resolving them. So an analytical philosophy of history is an acceptable venture, but an inquiry into historical reality as such is not.[6] Other philosophers are willing to venture constructive suggestions about such matters as historicity, man's being as historical, the meaning of history—but not as metaphysics. That ancient and dishonorable enterprise falsely objectifies (human) being, and sins further by claiming too much for human noetic capabilities.

How then should the reality claims of Scripture be interpreted? As poetic symbols? As myth? As some sort of subrational belief? Theologians prone to trim their sails to prevailing philosophic winds have tried all of these, and then some.

But suppose the reality claims of the New Testament were to be taken at their face value, that is, as disclosures of the real and full meaning of history, of all the history there is, past, present, and future. Again, all of it, not just a cross section lifted out and elevated for God's special use, leaving its connections with the grand and wretched continuities of the rest of history wholly opaque to natural understanding; or at least to discernment, if not to comprehension.

Let us suppose such an unlikely development. What then might we realistically expect to happen? For one thing, some theologian looking hopefully toward a philosophical peer group will promptly cry, "Hegel!" and tear off a small piece of his academic robe. But do we need to be greatly frightened by such a hue and cry? What errant fancy persuades us that Hegel is the lord of all who think to see a comprehensive pattern in history which, rightly discerned and construed, allows us to say "Such and such is the import of the human story"? What, moreover, are we to think of a theological method that allows one to dispose of views by labeling them?

Furthermore, some of the arguments advanced against metaphysical theories of history are of doubtful weight. Consider, for example: Since by definition history is not yet completed (history as lived), no theory about history-as-a-whole can possibly be true. What happens tomorrow or the day after or in 2001 may give the lie to any presumptuously universal pattern which we might devise today, or to any one scheme piously accepted from our spiritual ancestors. Whence it appears that "Jesus Christ the same yesterday, today, and forever" is a slogan of pious hope. It is not a pattern able to render intelligible a world that has an open future.

This sort of critique of metaphysical theory confuses history, as humanly signifying time, with historiographical evidentiality. From the principle that evidence for the interpretation of an event ought never be viewed as complete, we are asked to conclude that there is no universal pattern in history. But surely, claims about the whole of history are really about history as such; just as theories of space and time concern space and time as such rather than abstract totalities. It is true, of course, that we do not know what tomorrow will bring. If it brings a replacement for time, we can postulate either that *our* replacements will be able to make sense of it or they won't; it matters not to us, either way. In the meantime we are under a natural and inexorable demand, as though it were a law of our being, to make sense of human actions in the ceaseless flux of time.

Nonetheless, as far as theological currents run toward biblical positivism, overtly metaphysical theories of history will have hard rowing, whether or not theologians of positivistic persuasion, in respect to Scripture, appeal to any methodological principles of positivistic philosophers. Suppose, that is, that the New Testament offers only a pictographic representation of God the Creator of all things. Suppose further that these representations are only the mythic outrigging for an exclusive existential-soteriological passion. What sort of case for a metaphysical theory of history can be made that will not seem to fly in the face of the New Testament?

Two observations may be pertinent here. One: It is worthy of note that theologians may take on board hermeneutical principles without pausing to wonder whether these are innocent of metaphysical intimations and premonitions. Two: A theologian has a right to ask what court is trying his metaphysical case. That court is surely a human one; who says it is divine has the burden of proof. Thus it is not Scripture that pronounces metaphysics religiously illegitimate. Perhaps there are philosophies that deserve to be branded "empty deceits" (Col 2:8 RSV) or "hollow and delusive speculations" (NEB). But what about the cosmic sweep of St. Paul's own views (or of the Paulinist thinker who wrote Colossians)? He says:

Through him [Christ] God chose to reconcile the whole universe to himself, making peace through the shedding of his blood upon the cross—to reconcile all things, whether on earth or in heaven, through him alone (1:20 NEB).

This is a fitting sequel to:

The whole universe has been created through him and for him (1:16 NEB).

It is true that Western theologians generally have not been very happy with this cosmological Christ. This feeling has been given a pseudorational justification in recent theological times by interpreting that Christ as a mythological figure. Behind that time- and culture-bound representation there is supposed to stand that Jesus Christ who did something historical, not cosmical; something that makes a world of difference to people immured in the Christian faith.

Appeals to the spirit of Scripture as being hostile to metaphysics are hardly more decisive than appeals to selected texts. True, John is not the same sort of thing as Aristotle's *Metaphysics.* Yet, "all things were made through him [the Word] and without him was not anything made that was made" (Jn 1:3), on its face, is as reality-inclusive as anything that Aristotle says about the Unmoved Mover, the purely actual God. John in fact claims a wider scope of divine creative agency than Aristotle allows. On the other hand Aristotle has a concern for *proving* and John is a "witness" (cf. 21:24a). But is there really a *spirit* in the New Testament that creates and protects a divine chasm between rational dialectic and veracious testimony? ". . . and we know that his testimony is true" (Jn 21:24b). There are indeed differences in the tonalities of the two kinds of discourse. The burden of proof rests squarely on those who inflate such differences into a divinely intended alienation of the two "minds" from each other, and thereafter arrogates the "mind" of John to veridical deity.

In dealing with such conflicts over the intentions of Scripture, we ought to keep in mind that it is the object of interpretation, as far as theology is concerned. It is therefore improper to invoke or subpoena Scripture itself in behalf of any theory or against any other theory. The old hymn runs: "He [God] is his own interpreter/And He will make it plain." In recent theology much has been made of the Barthian principle of revelation as self-authenticating. Both the hymnist and Barth invite us to bring incorrigible conviction to the interpretation of Scripture. For both, this conviction, if it is not God's own handiwork (election), is divinely sanctioned. Presumably, for neither Barth nor Cowper does this second (though hardly secondary) belief have as its sole object, its full and proper intentionality, the first belief. The second belief is reality-intentional: It is about God, it is not merely a psychological-cultic reinforcement for the first belief. Indeed, if a belief is really incorrigible, it does not need and cannot benefit from psychological reinforcement.

I do not conclude from this that self-authentication as a methodological principle puts a theologian who embraces it into the metaphysical game straightaway. It is a proper inference, though, that no such principle can be legitimately employed to invalidate a theological venture into the metaphysics of history.

It follows that a metaphysical theory of history may be sprung with quite as much freedom from blockage or censure from Scripture as any other type of theory enjoys. It does not follow from this that the rule in respect to Scripture is: God proposes and man disposes, blessed be the name of Hermeneutics.

VII

A metaphysical intentionality does not of itself dictate a methodological structure. There is Descartes, but there is Pascal too, Aristotle and St. John, Anselm and Barth, Whitehead and Wittgenstein.

So the Christian theologian has to make some hard choices. If he does not make the revelation of God in Jesus Christ the sum and substance of his professional endeavors, he may well find himself deducing Jesus Christ from antecedent principles. These can as easily be a set of psychosocial commitments as metaphysical axioms. In its latter days theological liberalism made a much heavier investment in the former than in the latter. The criteria and paradigms of the liberal critique of contemporary culture were very largely derived from the idealistic sentiments of an intellectualistic elite.

This is a sobering consideration. Perhaps its gravity can be balanced by the unadvertised investment of *heilsgeschichte* theology in metaphysics. There, too, one begins by declaring that Jesus Christ is the whole meaning of history. But this Lord is known only by faith. These things taken together seem to deny any intelligibility to history apart from this selectively known Jesus Christ.

Is this really the case? Is the Christian thus condemned to being a know-nothing about the history of his nation, or about the history of Israel? Surely it is one thing to believe there is a scheme of salvation in which one's life and destiny are rendered profoundly and productively meaningful rather than merely endurable. Just as surely, it is quite a different thing to suppose that the entire cosmos and the whole of mankind, past, present, and to come, must pay tribute to that pattern or be cast into the outer darkness—of our ignorance and contempt. "Jesus is all the world to me" is a tender sentiment of piety. It is a terribly incomplete one if it encourages the Christian to look away from the Christ of John who says:

I have come down from heaven, not to do my own will, but the will of him who sent me (6:38).

And also:

I do nothing on my own authority but speak thus as as the Father taught me (8:28).

I do not intend here to quarrel with the incorrigible conviction that salvation history means more than any other kind. The quarrel is with the all-too-human propensity to posit zero-meaning as the disjunctive twin of most-meaningful.

Finally, the strongest possible claims for the centrality and uniqueness of salvation history are so many advertisements of competence in identifying what *real* history comprises; that is, what it means to have a history, what it means to be an historical agent, and what it means to say that history has an end, and that end is thus-and-so. This is a very remarkable range of truth opened to faith. No wonder Calvin called faith a superior kind of knowledge. No wonder Barth will not settle for a fideistic principle.

There is a softer version of the claims of salvation history. For the true believer, Jesus Christ is the be-all and end-all of history. This is more a matter of what the heart of faith acknowledges as its food and drink in a dry and thirsty land than of the eyes of faith beholding celestial splendors imperceptible to purblind whorish reason.

Why should one quarrel with so circumspect a confession? Theological troubles set in when confessionalism is absolutized, and reaches out for support to historical relativism. A relativistic theory of history cannot consistently be arrested short of metaphysical generality except by turning the science of history into biography and autobiography.

VIII

The principal components of a general theory of history must now be sketched. I do not claim that this pattern is contained in Scripture. It remains to be seen whether it distorts or violates whatever is there by way of clues for the interpretation of history.

(1) *Historical subjecthood:* What it means to have a history.

(2) *Historical agency:* What it means to be a maker and doer of history.

(3)   *Laws of history:* Transition to questions of evidentiality.
(4)   *Importance:* The transcendental criterion of historicality.

(1) *Historical subjecthood.* What does it mean to have a history? What does it mean to be an historical being? Here as well as elsewhere "subject" is used in various ways. One of these is visible in the common-sense view that history happens to certain people as something imposed upon them; they are subjected to it.

This view stands in the minds of many people as an incorrigible conviction. Some of them combine it with considerable philosophical sophistication, much erudition, and profound passion. Indeed who is not from time to time inclined to think of the great bulk of the world's peoples, past and present, as but fodder for the guns of history, as a great mass of raw material out of which a genuinely historical being might be fashioned?

Thus, to have a history means to be caught up in events over which one has no control, as though history were executed over us and upon us.

Having a history also means more than this. To have a history is to have the import of certain events imputed to oneself irrespective of one's own intentions and efforts. To have a history is to participate in events in which one was not and could not have been an agent, an actor, or a doer.

I do not suppose that to say such things is to propound indecipherable mysteries. Historians have long used "event" as a time-binder rather than as a time-isolater. Sometimes the unitary character of event is construed as a causal continuum: the fathers have eaten grapes and the children's teeth are edgy. It makes as much sense—actually a different kind of sense —to think of event as a fabric of meaning overarching a quotidian world: an intentionality unifying multitudinous intendings.

So to have a history is to participate in lives and events that have chosen "me"; I have not chosen them. They intend me antecedently to my consciously relating to them. I can, of course, choose whom in this history I shall deem to have been the saints and whom the mischief-makers. But there are limits to the exercise of arbitrariness in such choices. I can ransack historical remainders to confirm my predilections. Perhaps Burr was a more honorable man than Hamilton or Jefferson—isn't it too bad that so much of history is either written by or in behalf of the winners? Perhaps Judas Iscariot was the real hero and Jesus Christ the real scapegrace. Perhaps the humanly great future lay with the *Baalim* whose priests Elijah, that ferocious barbarian, slew on Mt. Carmel. And then people believe that God has picked the winners!

The revaluation of historical events and figures is a common phenomenon. It is part of what being-in-history means. But it is important to discern whether or when a move to revaluate history is a detail, a tactical component, of a massive "transvaluation of all values." That move calls for a show of the ethical cards—the metaphysical ones, too.

The meaning of one's own history can never be told simply as autobiography. One's personal history has importance for others only if it illuminates the life of the community which embraces both the writer and his readers. It is not enough that the autobiographical self and his audience partake of generic humanity, are representatives of the human condition. The autobiographical, self-reflective ego comes to life only in a specific community of values. Apart from such an organic network, the autobiographical self is a specimen of *homo loquens* enshrined in amber of its own secretion.

So far, then, to have a history is to be empowered to share a value-charged time that incorporates the life of the self. In relation to that history a perspicuous self readily confesses, "Another has made us and not we ourselves" *(The Book of Common Prayer)*.

One of the most intriguing aspects of contemporary culture makes it difficult for us to grasp this properly. That is the unconsciously rigged hostility between the creative self and the acculturated (conditioned) self: Sartre (of *L'Être et Néant*) vs. Skinner. Mounted as metaphysical propositions these incorrigible convictions cannot both be right. But to make that judgment important, as well as logically neat, one must first endow the principle of excluded middle with metaphysical validity. Which is to say: Is it irrational to think that Sartre and Skinner are both wrong?

That question does not need to be answered assertorially in this context. We may observe, though, that the Sartrian self must acknowledge a determinate, though not a determining, situation; and the Skinnerian self thinks the present world can be improved upon. Thoreau might wonder whether either freedom or dignity can march to the drums of *Walden II*. And Kant might wonder whether the self-creative self brings enough firmness of structure to bear upon the givens of the situation; enough, that is, to make an intelligible and discernible difference.

191

These are wonderments, not arguments. Under their cover, I return to noting how easily we are led to construe the first category of historical reality in terms of the self submerged in, carried hither and thither by, all-encompassing, all-determining social (metaphysical) forces. We are led thither as often and as powerfully by vividly rendered images as by doctrines evangelically proclaimed or by cases brilliantly argued. We are haunted by images of vast inert human masses divested of any power of self-determination: an interminable sea of faceless anonymous humanity.

Such images are only superficially similar to the New Testament image of "a great multitude which no man could number, from every nation, from all tribes and peoples and tongues . . ." (Rev 7:9). This is a human mass far far greater than "a hundred and forty-four thousand sealed, out of every tribe of the sons of Israel" (7:4). Far greater, and here unnamed; but not for that or any other reason diminished in dignity and glory (7:10–17).

This contrast may well remind us of another paradox. That is, the liberal confidence in which we reserve the individual, as an unrivaled ethical achievement, to modern Western and Christian culture; and blandly surrender the rest of history to various combinations of mass-man and heroes. Yet all the while we feel inordinate pressures to represent the generality of our own kind as "ordinary" or "average" people, powerless either to change themselves or to change the course of history.

There is little to be gained by minimizing the objective correlates of such images. Corporate life in our society has very heavily capitalized the acquisition of power. It has as ruthlessly and systematically diminished the value of genuine individuality. So it has come to pass that uncritical assent to the dogmas of individualism is a formidable obstacle to the attainment of individuality. Thus, the affluent can afford a range of self-indulgence not open to average and subaverage income; so long as that self-indulgence does not exhibit the wrong outlook or suggest any erosion of commitment to the "American Way." This means that rebels are driven to adopt life-styles that flaunt rejection of that primal faith; thus often confusing individuality with external eccentricities.

Both components of this awkward and sterile dialectical minuet are prone to forget that they often embrace a common anthropological doctrine: Generic humanity is divided into two camps, the small company of the masters and the vast hordes of slaves; the overlords and the underlings. Thereby historical subjecthood is rendered inauthentic at both poles of a false dialectic. Not that the categories of lord and slave have ever stood empty for long. The point is they should not be absolutized in order to swing man, the historical subject, everlastingly between them.

Let us put this first thesis at last in positive terms. To have a history means to live in and through a concrete dialectical process for which neither a determinate self nor an antecedent community is the magnet to which the other is irresistibly attracted. The self is not a conditioned reflex of society. Society is not a shadow thrown by great personages. So the history of the community is not externally imposed upon the self. Indeed if I am to become an authentic subject of that history, I must embrace it, I must set myself to live it out. If I do not do that, I fail to emerge as a subject of history from the realm of humanity-as-possibility. Failing to do that I dream life away immersed in the gossamer stuff of possibility.

The everyday world does not place such failure under public obloquy, nor does it heartily encourage its victims to waste away in private remorse. Yet its greatest—not its most lucrative—honors are reserved for those of all degrees and conditions who "keep the faith" at whatever cost to themselves. It is as though the essential meaning of our history could be grasped and expressed only in their self-sacrifice.

That "as though" is not a pure subjunctive-contrary-to-fact. It may overstress the martial virtues. It may also remind us that the forward throw of a life in the face of the cruelest hardship, and of death itself, may have far more of freedom and dignity than any niggling anatomy of motives can possibly account for, and which no hedonistically oriented human engineering can conceivably generate.

What then does it mean to say that historical subjecthood emerges only when persons are able to participate vicariously in the storied past of their community? What is the connection of this feat of imagination with being disposed to enact the essential meaning of that common life in ways appropriate to the present situation and within one's powers?

The proper answers to such questions lie in the notion of *participation*. Participation in the storied past of the community means that one learns how to hear the story of the community. This sort of listening calls for more than disciplined passivity. When Moses cries, "Hear, O Israel!" he intends to rivet attention. But he cannot do that by himself. Israel must

give attention. Israel must *devote* attention because through Moses the
Lord is delineating the absolute conditions of her life and destiny:

Hear, O Israel, the statutes and the ordinances which I speak in your hearing this
day, and you shall learn them and be careful to do them (Deut 5:1).

Then the prophet proceeds to cite the historical foundation of the
Lord's absolute demands:

The Lord our God made a covenant with us in Horeb. Not with our fathers did
the Lord make this covenant, but with us, who are all of us alive this day (5:2,3).

Moses does not assign overwhelming significance to the ear-witness
testimony of "all Israel" gathered in front of him that day. They know
from memory what God ordained. But it does not follow that the Israel
of posterity will have to rely primarily on the transmitted memories of
the founding fathers, so to speak. The Israel of posterity will live in and
through the patterns of obediential activity the first generation created
as the objective faith-keeping of the Covenant.

Thus, authentic participation in the covenanted community involves
discernment of the actual situation and dedication to its well-being.
These are as much involved as stated celebrations of its divine institution
and glorious messianic future. These are all elements of living out the
history of the community, "all Israel." The community is called to perform these things; not an elite, not a peerless paradigm, but all Israel.

We ought to be careful about giving such features of Israel's history an
unnatural tilt toward religious democracy as we conceive it and purport
to practice it. On the other hand, it is only just to note the dynamical
features of "hearing" in the faith of Israel. The Hegelian canards about
that faith as the absolute triumph of externalistic transcendence still have
residual life. Animadversions about the Religion of the Law for being
static or sterile live on in mainstream Protestantism.

The Old Testament history of Israel is altogether convincing testimony that "all Israel" did not consistently remember and obey. There
she is one with the rest of religious mankind. But what other religion has
left us such a ferociously candid portrait of its own faithlessness? Who
of the rest have given such skimpy support for the Great Man theory of

history? Perhaps it does make a difference whether a religious community sets out to glorify God rather than man or nature—or history.

Israel aside, we know from our own experience that at any given moment there are human beings whose emergence into historical subjecthood has not yet occurred, and there are others from whom it has been interdicted. There are those who hear and do not understand. Others hear and understand only in part because a full range of participation is denied them. How long shall we persist in believing that anybody fully hears, fully understands, fully lives out our history, as long as any of our people have far less to look forward to than the "resident alien" in ancient Israel?

Another cautionary note is in order. We ought not lightly to suppose that anyone wears constantly the toga of historical subjecthood. Even of the Lord Jesus Christ, Christians believe that he sometimes found that robe unbearable. Perhaps there were moments when he yearned to swap it for the breechclout of an unhistorical Galilean fisherman.

To be a historical subject, to have a history, means to participate personally in the storied past of one's people. But that is also to live out the destiny pushed ahead by the achievements and hopes of that community.

IX

(2) *Historical agent.* We generally begin thinking of a historical agent as one of the real makers and doers of history. Such people make things happen. The world is their oyster; they know how to crack it and season it. They experience themselves in the world and career through it in the active voice, not in the passive one. Thus the first and most persistent claimants for the rank of historical agent are the great men and women, the heroes and heroines, the demigods who stand boldly out of the masses; just as the event in history stands out from the mere passage of time. Taking the two together we say at the outset that the real historical agent is the bold, all-wagering creative genius who creates an event out of a moment or any other arbitrary measure of time.

This way of understanding historical agency has had to cope with very heavy seas in recent times; so heavy, in fact, it is a wonder that there is anything left of it. It has been battered by convictions that the great person is only a symptom, a node, of omnipotent social forces. This is a fearsome descent from dignity and importance. In the Old Testament,

Cyrus of Persia is not diminished as a historical agent simply because God chooses him to be an instrument of his holy purpose (Isaiah 45:1–6). Societal omnipotence is a very different matter.

Add to this battering wave popularized Freudianism—which makes a hero of Freud—and we have to improve upon the eighteenth-century cynical insight, "No man is a hero to his valet," with "No man is a hero to his own varlet," that is, his id. Here the full incorporation of the self into generic humanity entails an irrecoverable diminution of individuality, of self-causality and intentionality. Some brave souls who accept this outlook spell it *humanism.* That is clear triumph of piety over reality.

Yet the Great Man doctrine lives on whether or not we deem it a gibbering anachronism. It lives on in strange places: in Marxist Russia, where incorrigible philosophic belief holds that consciousness is always a product of social forces and the first person singular is "a grammatical fiction." And it lives on in Maoist China. But also in social policy drawn from rigidly behavioristic physico-psychology. There the conditioners will be the lords of all they survey. We begin by telling them to give us what we want. But they are the ones who know what we want, so they can turn us on and turn us off. Armed with that power, they must see intransigence—the ghost of individuality—as a mechanically resolvable kink in the flow of neural energy.

Perhaps there is a point, then, in trying to see whether there is a kernel of truth in the chaffering of philosophic dogmas, a kernel such as this: The great person is more than a symptom and less than a demigod. In himself he is not a symbol. But his actions acquire a symbolic magnitude of significance by a certain reflexivity of history. But not just his actions; his character as well. Thus Abraham Lincoln has become a symbol of the tragic travail of the Civil War, but not simply because he was overtaken by martyrdom. The heroic figure in the Lincoln Memorial is a powerful representation of the man who bore the nation across the awful blood-red river of internecine strife. That he did not live to weave the peace of his immortal envisagement is a vital part of this nation's experience of tragedy.

We come now to ask what are the principal elements of historical agency?

(i) *X* is an agent if he was measurably and personally responsible for an event in which the community discerns, sooner or later, the meaning of its existence. This certainly does not mean that X did it all. It does mean that without X that event would not have transpired. There may have been a run of occurrences, surely *something* would have been happening. But these occurrences would not have been gathered up as that event for which X was responsible. But note: (a) "X carried the day" does not entail (b), "There would have been no day if there had been no X." (b) is a speculative proposition. It may be true, it may be false; we have no way of knowing which. A readiness to believe it testifies to the place X holds in our esteem. It does not throw much light on history. Nevertheless it is true to say that if there is a historical event of which X is the prime agent, it may fairly be called an X event. Some of his critics called the Civil War Mr. Lincoln's war. They were wiser than they knew, more truthful than they intended.[7]

(ii) A historical agent is a person whose difference-making action was intentional. But what does it mean to say that X intended e, and intended it efficaciously? The following factors seems to be involved:

(a) It does not mean that X intended everything that happened at or during e. Nevertheless e bears the stamp of X's intentions. So it is absurd to say that Lincoln intended the disaster of the Crater in front of Petersburg on July 30, 1864. Yet he approved of Grant's strategy for crushing the Confederacy; just as Grant approved Burnside's (reluctant) consent to the mining of the Confederate fortifications.

(b) X pursued what he had envisaged. He took the proper steps to make the envisaged e event occur.

(c) X must have found it necessary for the sake of e to correlate his resources with those of other agents. Human agents are all finite. All are fallible. These incorrigible beliefs are unassailably true. So in the Gospels Jesus has to incorporate others into his kingdom mission even though his power and authority are vastly greater than his disciples'. And even without imputed prescience he must have known someone would let him down. Endowed with that supernatural power, why did he not separate Judas Iscariot before he could work his mischief—why did he not pass Judas by in the draft? The New Testament sketches answers to such questions. That indicates, I suppose, how promptly in Christian history the pressure of a unique formation of the problem of evil is felt.

(d) X must have found it necessary to entrust his project to unforseeable contingencies. This is so obviously true as a historical generalization that we may, again, cash it in as a metaphysical principle. Sooner or later necessity will drive hard upon it. Contingency may be crushed down into illusion. One of the most sobering facts in the history of metaphysics is the readiness of philosophers to let the plainest generalities of experience go down the drain on the grounds that such stuff is honeycombed with inconsistencies and obscurities.

Taking (c) and (d) together we acquire (e): X's intention is thrown around forces he cannot identify in advance, and he will not be able to control them perfectly once they take shape.

(f) Nevertheless X intends that these forces shall coalesce in the form of e. This is a project, not just a hope or a wish. Ordinarily we think of this as foreseeing difficulties and being prepared to counter them, if not to overcome them. Thus X's intention is realized when the difficulties, the counterthrusts of circumstance, are themselves countered.

Part of the natural metaphysics of the general mind crops out here. We are predisposed to say of X when he succeeds against a veritable sea of adversities, "He was lucky. How could he possibly have known that the fog would lift?"

What shall we say to this? X didn't *know* the fog would lift. If he was really sagacious, his plans included sketches of the worst possible conditions, even though his plans weren't based on the worst case. Only one *worst possible* is omitted in that prevision: his own failure of nerve, his own loss of faith in the project. If he is really sagacious, really faithful, he will anticipate his own failure of strength, his own death. Even in dying he intends to fling forward the grand intention. Where it lands on ahead is God's business.

A proper emphasis on agency, on history in the active voice, should not blind us to the realities of quasi-agency and pseudo-agency. Parts of the e event, in other words, may have been accomplished by people who just happened to be caught up in the action through no intention of their own. Some of these dragged-along participants may have supposed, or even hoped, that the project was something other than what eventuated. Others may have cast themselves as innocent bystanders, uncommitted observers, only to find the net of a compelling intentionality settling around their shoulders. This is a familiar device in fiction; here art imitates history.[8] So people who have not been intending e are caught up in it, not as dumbly acquiescent puppets but as actors. Even a walk-on character deserves a place on the playbill.

Two potent intellectual forces unite to forge an incorrigible belief that all individually intentional agency in history is an illusion. One of these is the Augustinian Christian denial of affirmative agency to humankind. In this view the only thing Adam does on his own is to commit the first history-determinative event, the fall. The other monolithic theological enemy of personal agency is classical Marxism, here a doctrine extracted from Hegel. Who can read *Reason in History* without being deeply impressed by its homiletical power? Whether exalted or depressed is another question. But Hegel *redivivus* appears in other ways and places, too. We have had a glimpse of him in the current doctrine of consciousness as a global reality in which personhood, concrete individuality, is an incident, a symptom. It must be a heady experience to feel that as a writer delineating a stage of global consciousness, or as a thinker uncovering the tracks of reason in history, one is a point—why not, come to think of it, *the* point—at which the whole thing becomes transparent to itself. Just imagine: the whole cosmic process, every moment and detail of human history, straining forward to this *kairos* of fulfillment: a Book-of-the-Month Club winner.

A final cautionary note. The Great Man view of history is much too easily convertible into its dialectical twin for it to be more than a thinly plausible candidate for historical agent. It is not necessary, and it would be unseemly, to deny that there have been great persons who have left time-resistant marks on the body of mankind. But the Great Man doctrine of history makes far too little of the factor of the consent of multitudes of unremembered participants in historic events. Not the "lumpen" masses alternately pummeled and hoodwinked into compliance with a Führer or with a ruler elite; but free people who agreed to throw in their lot with great ventures, win, lose, or draw. So Shakespeare's Henry on the eve of Agincourt:

> God's peace! I would not lose so great an honor
> As one man more, methinks, would
> share from me

For the best hope I have. O do not
  wish one more!
Rather proclaim, Westmoreland,
  through my host
That he which hath no
  stomach to this fight,
Let him depart. His passport
  shall be made
And crowns for convoy put
  into his purse.
We would not die in that
  man's company
That fears his fellowship
  to die with us (*Henry the Fifth*, IV, 3;31–38).

Of course kingly Henry is the hero of the tale. That he could not have been without the sturdy yeoman who elected to stay; and thus

. . . shall be remembered—
We few, we happy few, we band of
  brothers.
For he today that sheds his blood with me
Shall be my brother (59–63).

If then we are still disposed to employ Hegelian rhetoric purged of Hegelian metaphysics, we may speak of the "cunning of historical reason"; now to suggest the ways by which individual historical agents have succeeded in throwing the net of personal intentionality around massive social forces and the brutal play of chance. Success in these ventures has not always appeared in the lifetimes of the prime movers and designers. Perhaps not often, in fact. This gives historians something to do, something other than hieratic scanning of some past world in order to discern the fate of this present one.

We may not have sufficiently noted that a considerable part of the appeal of the idea of progress was the incorrigible conviction that human life emerges into history from its biosocial matrix only when destiny is positively correlated with general enlightenment and universal freedom. It is not the case that this humanistic dogma was driven aground and broken up by the tidal waves of two world wars. Its most formidable enemy, indeed its executioner, was the totalitarian society. In that abomination of desolation, systematic brainwashing is substituted for general enlightenment, and the freedom of the state to control its citizens is substituted for personal self-determination.

X

(3) *The Laws of History*. Is history a nomothetic affair? Where the study of history is regarded as a science, history must be treated as law-observant. Otherwise the science of history would be merely a logically organized guess about the past.

Serious as the issue of the scientific status of history may be (though its gravity seems to register more heavily in the philosophy department than in the history wing) we shall consider first the attribution of a nomothetic structure to historical reality.[9] What then is implied by this imputation?

(i) Historical reality must have an internal nomistic structure. Otherwise the past, or, more generally, human experience as temporal, would be all randomness; it would be just "one damned thing after another," or it would be a random assemblage of contemporary forces adventitiously producing significant results. Now whatever one's metaphysical prepossessions, no one of any intelligence thinks practically of his experience, or of the past as such, in these terms. If B follows A, it is either because of A *per se*, or because there is a pattern in things obliging B to follow A.

But what sort of pattern? There's the rub. Consider how the prophet Amos proceeds from one kind of pattern, largely commonsensical, to another kind, largely historical-theological.

> Do two walk together,
>> unless they have made an
>>> appointment?
> Does a lion roar in the forest,
>> when he has no prey?
> Does a young lion cry out from his
>> den,
>>> if he has taken nothing?
> Does a bird fall in a snare on the earth,
>> when there is no trap for it?

> Does a snare spring up from the
> ground,
> when it has taken nothing?
> Is a trumpet blown in a city,
> and the people are not afraid?
> Does evil befall a city,
> unless the Lord has done it?
> Surely the Lord does nothing,
> without revealing his secret
> to his servants the prophets.
> The lion has roared;
> who will not fear?
> The Lord has spoken;
> who can but prophesy? (3:3–8).

So two men walk together because they have planned to. Animal cries signify. People understand alarm signals and react accordingly. None of this is transcendently rational but it is all lawlike. *A fortiori* then: "Does evil befall a city, unless the Lord has done it?" But what sort of a law is this? The sequel is even more mysterious: Surely the Lord does nothing, without revealing his secret to his servants the prophets.

Adverting to the first verses of this chapter of Amos we may find something of an answer:

Hear this word that the Lord has spoken against you, O people of Israel, against the whole family which I brought up out of the land of Egypt:
> You only have I known
> of all the families of the earth;
> therefore I will punish you
> for all your iniquities (3:1,2).

In the light of this we might say "lawlike" at best, because the analogy of an autonomous nomothetic structure is very remote. Amos is talking first of all about the Covenant grounded in God's pure electing grace. The reverse side of that gratuity is the certainty of punishment for faithlessness. And along with that certainty, but not as a logical entailment, comes another: "The Lord has spoken; who can but prophesy?" Surely the prophet knows that ever so many people will be able to decline that hazardous and thinly rewarding honor. Ever so many more will howl with one voice against the rank presumption of him who claims to speak for the Lord—especially when he says that the long-awaited, desperately yearned-for Day of the Lord will be darkness rather than light.

In the Old Testament prophetic interpretation of history, then, the historical "law" is God's ordinance for the people of the Covenant. Beyond that "law" is God's relentless insistence on the absoluteness of the covenant relationship. The prophets do not say that the moral structure of reality eventually exacts requital for moral evil; it is the jealously righteous God who does that. But he also accepts a contrite heart and fruits worthy of repentance in place of legally exact punishment.

(ii) This sojourn in the realm of Old Testament prophecy is intended to suggest a contrast between biblical representations of the laws of history and modern beliefs about such laws. Science has been the great teacher of law in our world; science, not the prophet of the Lord. From science we have learned to think of nature and man as law-observant in every detail of being. Granted that molecular detail eludes observational determinateness. All such, nonetheless, sing a song of the most exquisite mathematical perfection.

There is a conspicuous fly in this wonderful ointment. It is a sort of two-headed monster; or one whose eyes rotate without relation to each other and thus report worlds wildly disparate. On one side is a causality principle stripped of real agency, demoted to perceptual regularities of sequence. (Hume: a mental habit; a purely psychological datum.) The other side is a global determinism. So in one eye of this strange creature nothing whatever in nature happens *because* of law. You might as well say, on this side, that I vote Democratic because 57 percent of this county votes Democratic as to say that a stone falls to earth at a certain rate of acceleration because Galileo said it must. But in the other eye of this awkward monster every event is a *real* (not an academic) deduction from the immediately antecedent state of the entire universe.

Now if one is infatuated with this second eye—or is, in one's own view, but a speck in it—the historicality of a human event is not at all unique compared to a nonhuman event, observed or not, anywhere in the cosmos. Thus a ray of light from Betelgeuse, 270 light years away, is the cause of our perceptions of that red supergiant; just as truly, and in the same sense of truth, the pious Christian says his behavior is caused by the light streaming from the cross of Christ. No, come to think of it: the argument favors Betelgeuse. We can, and some say we must, draw on Freudian dogma to explain the odd behavior and attitudes of the pious Christian.

It appears, then, that modern conceptions of causality deny any uniqueness whatever to historicality. But the appearance is slightly deceptive. If *cause* simply and purely denotes a mental habit rather than a cosmical one, then a genetic account, that is, a historical one, becomes exceedingly important. So the evolution of Betelgeuse does not stand on the same footing, or mayhap even share the same world, with the development of a mind. Moreover, if Hume is right, we cannot sensibly say that the mind is *made* to conform either to biological demands or to sociopsychological forces. We could deny that minds exist; a proposition that would not have Hume's unequivocal blessing. But then we would have to scurry mindlessly around looking for real, not linguistic, equivalents for such cognitional oddities as denying, affirming, arguing. Some profess to have found such benison in biocybernetic models of the brain. They are welcome to the job of correlating those models with intelligence making sense of the practical world.

Apart from such extraordinary efforts in behalf of such extraordinary causes there is another sense of *law* that moral experiences may induce us to impute to historical reality. That is the law that renders intelligible the experience of moral agents. The moral law commands but does not coerce. On the strength of such a law we cannot predict what we shall do. We learn from it only what we ought to do. It instructs and monitors intention; it does not bind it into an efficient-causal nexus.

(iii) Why should we not think of the laws of history as something like the moral law? Rather than saying we know (conjecture) what Caesar *had* to do, as though he were the product of necessitating forces—his ambition, forces he had already set in motion—why not say there was a rational constraint emanating from his intention; something, that is, he had to do if that intention were to be actualized. True, that intention, that internal law of his being, may not have been sufficiently moral. It may have been as ruthlessly self-aggrandizing as his enemies charged. But even if this question is moot, the locus and function of such a law are clear enough. The "law in the members" (Rom 7:22,23) is not a mechanically coercive power, however potent it may be in the realm of the dispositions.

This is very far from what the Laws of History theologians, Christian and other, want. They contend that things happen because of the laws of history. Thus Toynbee's law of challenge and response, Marxian laws governing the evolution of capitalism and the rise of the proletariat, Spengler's laws of organic maturation and decay, and Buckle's laws governing the rise and fall of civilizations. A recent writer says of Buckle:

The moral drawn is that the ineluctable laws of historical development should be permitted to take their course freely and without impediment.[10]

If the laws of history are indeed ineluctable, what cogency can devolve upon an *obligation* to let them operate "freely and without impediment"?

I hope that question is neither captious nor perverse. It seems only fair to ask a Law of History thinker whether he supposes that these laws make things happen, or on the contrary, whether everything that happens exemplifies them—happens to exemplify them, we might add. The latter option claims, at most, that historical events are rendered intelligible by laws borrowed or devised by historians.

(iv) If the laws of history are stripped of specious causal efficacy and left with some measure of interpretational validity (or perhaps only with velleity) what would be the fate of an event that did not "obey" (exemplify) a law of history?[11] Would such an event have to be recast to fit the laws? Or should the laws be reformulated?

The latter is patently the course of wisdom. There is, however, a serious question whether mundane wisdom can scale the heights to legislate changes in laws of history that are actually metaphysical principles. Such laws are so many ways of imposing order upon the hurly-burly of history. Historical reality represented as following that libretto is a triumph of faith. Its faith-full character is not diminished by the display of immense historical learning.

(v) There is a way by which the Law of History concept can be largely relieved of its fideistic-metaphysical character. That is to see it as analogous to the law of moral agency. There *law* stands for a structure of obligation that imparts intelligibility to intentionality. On this basis the Lisbon earthquake of 1755—that terrible catastrophe that sent so many shock waves through Christian theodicies—is deficiently *historical* until we know what steps were taken to alleviate the suffering of the survivors, bury the dead, and discover why some areas of the city were more easily destroyed than other parts. This is to say that the human response to horrific natural occurrences is the decisive clue to their historicality. "Human response" is to be distinguished from the tidal waves of either spontaneous or manipulated reactions to stupendous occurrences. Thus "human response" implies intentional projects to restore a humane order.

Much in this view runs afoul of prevailing conceptions of history and historicality. Massive academic traditions predispose us to call historical any age or element of the past that investigative entrepreneurship can recover and reconstruct. What was life like in the twenty-fifth dynasty? What caused the abandonment of the ancient Mayan cities in Yucatan? Why were the splendors of Copán, Quirigua, and Piedras Negras left to the mercies of the jungle and pilferers centuries before Christian white folk arrived on the scene to lay waste in the name of Christ and the Spanish crown?

I do not believe that the damage done to a general theory of history by empirical historical investigations is very great or particularly perplexing. The historian, ancient or modern, is not only trying to make sense of his evidence. He is also working from the grand axiom that the people whose world he is trying to reconstruct tried quite as strenuously to make sense of their existence. Which is to say that *homo sapiens* never becomes historical by letting nature take her course. A team of anthropologists reports that "whatever its specific meaning and symbolic function, Barrôles's sculpture associates symbols of rank and warlike attributes with maize agriculture."[12]

So the absence from the record of the names of the mighty kings, counselors, and shamans who commanded and directed such activities in no way diminishes the historicity of the Mayan people thus engaged. Moreover, whatever they reckoned as the complicity of the gods in their endeavors again in no way diminishes the purposefulness or intelligence of their behavior.

What then are we to say about those grand confessions of faith in which the entire *raison d'etre* of history is the drama of divine salvation? In this view the absolute nomothetic structure is God's eternal decree, the heavenly uncreated scenario which dictates the lines man speaks, except, in the Augustinian version, that awful word with which Adam, generic man, elects his own good rather than God's manifest will.

What are we to say to this if not that it arrogates all genuine historical agency to God who by definition lives beyond history? That the Augustinian theologians are content with this is strongly suggested by the zeal and consistency with which they have always fought off the attribution of any real causal efficacy to secondary agents, such as human beings. But at least this affirmative thing is to be said about theistic absolutism: it maximizes the intentional model of causal efficacy since all things manifest God's righteous creative purpose. So while man's intentional efficacy is a very remote analogy of the divine, human causality is not an illusion perpetrated by the Absolute upon itself, an Absolute that rejects all personalistic attributions. The Augustinian God adjures his image, man, to take his creaturely responsibilities with the utmost care. But does this mean that human beings are the real makers and doers of history? Yes; in respect to other creatures. No; in respect to Almighty God to whom belongs the entire drama of salvation, the beginning and the end of history.

XI

(4) *Importance.* Subjecthood and agency are indispensable components of a Christian theology of history, of any genuinely intelligible general theory of history, for that matter. Less ought not to be said of *importance* as a category of historical explanation. How so?

We have already seen that historical experience means more than having a past. Historicality is the past, or a segment of it, weighted with importance. Personal memory may be directly involved in the determination of importance, but this is not a metaphysical necessity. Memories may supply many of the data-strands to be woven into importance. We can imagine, for instance, that interviews with Wovoka[13] might have revealed many fascinating things about his intentions. (They were pacifistic as well as apocalyptic.) But the importance of his messianic revivalism was threshed out on the terrible winnowing floor of Wounded Knee on December 29, 1890. Not even the painfully vivid memoirs of Black Elk[14] suffice to fix the importance of that massacre. Its importance is the place it occupies in the story of the nation; in this instance a chapter of mindless cruelty and unshriven sin; of total disregard of treaty commitments for the sake of defrauding the Indian of whatever noble Paleface coveted.

And all under the obscene theological banner of Paleface Providence.

Memory is part of the raw material of historical importance. It would be of hardly more than passing interest if there were no intersubjective and transsubjective structure of meaning to clarify and amplify it. Sometimes we profess to find a well-written autobiography or autobiographical novel interesting or gripping. But unless it can be placed in a larger frame, unless the subject was an actor on a stage where the interests of a community were clearly at stake, we do well to refrain from saying of that autobiographical piece: "It is important." Importance denotes a transsubjective structure of meaning. Much of the psyche's affairs can be placed somewhere on a scale of interesting-uninteresting. Thus Hell for the alienated psyche is tedium. The affairs of history must be placed on the scale of important-unimportant. So the personal immoralities of Talleyrand are interesting or not, depending on whether one believes that history is the stuff of boudoir comings and goings. But Talleyrand's achievements at the Congress of Vienna are of monumental importance for the subsequent history of Europe.

There are degrees of importance. Not all historic events belong to the watershed or "axial" class.[15] Too, some events achieve a rich symbolic rank greater than their linear consequences alone would argue. Gettysburg has a far richer symbolic importance than Vicksburg in the popular view of the Civil War, though many historians claim that Vicksburg sealed the fate of the Confederacy, as Gettysburg did not.[16] Or take Lee's decision in the summer of 1864 to send General Early on a wild dash up the Shenandoah Valley and across the Potomac to "threaten" Washington. He hoped this would relieve the Petersburg-Richmond defense of some of Grant's pressure, and exacerbate the hunger for peace in the North. The capture of Washington would have been a symbolic victory at best. Even that was denied Early. In fact, an aggressive counterattack would have destroyed the Confederate forces committed to that symbolic gesture.

Perhaps the foregoing observations are a sufficient reminder that importance has several kinds of lives in and for history.[17] The important events in the history of a people may constitute a causal chain; for example, the events beginning with Caesar's crossing the Rubicon.[18] But events oftimes gain multidimensionality of importance from being infused with heavy symbolic meaning by the prophets and poets of the community. Consider in this connection two events, Pentecost and the Exodus. Traditionally, Pentecost is regarded by Christians as the founding moment of the church. In Judaism the Exodus has a similar weight. There is little reason to doubt that the people Israel was created in the Exodus experience. So also of Pentecost: here, as far as empirical rather than transcendental history is concerned, the Christian church begins. But this distinction between empirical (real) and transcendental (mythological) history is a modern confection. Wrongly applied, it becomes an enemy of genuine historical understanding. It may induce us to misconstrue the fabulously rich prehistory the writers of the Old Testament ascribe to the pre-Exodus life in Palestine—the age of the patriarchs. So we scurry for help to the students of literary genre, under the conviction that such wonderful stuff cannot be *real* history. So father Abraham is transmuted into an avatar of Judaic and Kierkegaardian piety, or perhaps into a totem figure of the tribe. And Joseph's reality is preempted and restructured by Thomas Mann's incandescent weave of historical fiction and metaphysical lucubrations on time.

Pentecost does not fare much better. The incorrigible convictions of modern historiography and of contemporary theories of historical reality cannot credit any authentically divine institution of the church at Pentecost. Indeed it seems to be a fair question why historical methodology and philosophic outlook should be adjusted to assimilate such stuff. The modern disposition is to believe that even the most scientifically rigorous methods can only expose the historian's mind to himself. So the only way the dry bones and stones of antiquity might live again would be to have them bedecked with our humanity, tattered and befouled as that is.

Actually the story is not quite so desperately parochial. A discerning eye can see how ancient historical narrative is part of the remarkable mechanism by which importance accrues to the past of a community. This accrual cannot be reduced to a fictive inflation of tradition in the interests of glorifying the present or trying to make it endurable. Neither the Old Testament nor the New evinces the slightest interest in deriving their several histories from the "giants" that were in the earth in the old days. In fact the *nephilim* of Genesis fame (6:4) are anything but heroes of God's election, though their children were "mighty men that were of old, the men of renown." Later on, the faithful in Israel have to persevere in the face of monstrous creatures, "men of great stature" so formidable that "we seemed to ourselves like grasshoppers, and so we seemed to them" (Num 13:32,33). This report, of course, turns the courage of the people to water, and they yearn for the hard life and predictable death in Egyptian bondage. Not so Joshua and Caleb; they also had seen the frightful giants. But with the eyes of faith they had also seen ahead of them the land of God's intent for his people (Num 14:8,9). So whatever the flat historical reality the *nephilim* may have had in their own right, in Israel's story they are only tests of courage and faithfulness:

. . . do not fear the people of the land, for they are bread for us; their protection is removed from them, and the Lord is with us; do not fear them (14:9).

This hardy counsel is not quite what the people, struggling now against their ordained historicality, want to hear:

But all the congregation said to stone them with stones (14:10).

So also in Pentecost. The disciples are not transformed into god-men. Rather, they are endowed with the powers which are to define the church's mission in the world. These powers are from God, to be sure. But their *historical* importance is that they define a new community in which faith, hope, and love are given supernatural potency until the kingdoms of this world have become the kingdom of Jesus Christ, the Lord of history.

Importance, then, presupposes a community. Something or somebody in that community epitomizes its true nature and its high destiny. For these purposes it does not matter whether that primal event or that larger-than-life hero is the cause of the existence of that historical community. Cause, as we now understand it, is too weak a concept for such purposes. It would be accurate to say that certain persons and certain events are the concrete presuppositions for the persistence of the community through harsh vicissitudes and alluring temptations. Elijah the Tishbite saw the terrible dangers to Israel's unity and faithfulness in the Canaanitish fertility cults Jezebel, with Ahab's compliance, sanctioned. The story of his attack on those "modern" religious innovations is one of the great narratives, sacred or profane. Its historical importance, however, outstrips its world-literary rank. Through it Elijah becomes an epitome of faithful Israel. He alone of the prophets is assimilated to the messianic order of importance.[19]

So far I have been arguing that importance is a transsubjective category of historicality. The intent in this is not to minimize or ignore the obvious fact that people often disagree vehemently over importance, both among themselves and with assessments of importance filed by earlier generations. But what are they arguing about? What would avail to adjudicate such arguments? Surely the fundamental issue is not interestingness. The crux of the matter is the objective magnitude of an event, together with the role of intentional agency in bringing it to pass. For example, in English history the murder of the nephews of Richard III was a very important event. Shakespeare's consummate villain says: "Shall I be plain? I wish the bastards dead. And I would have it suddenly perform'd" (IV,2:18,19). Here the dramatist sides with the house of Lancaster against the last of Yorkist kings. His dramaturgical interests are better served thereby than history is, if by "history" we mean "what really happened"; that is, what convergence of factuality with importance has the strongest evidentiary support. The question of importance as a category of historicality, in other words, reaches far beyond such questions as: Was it important to Richard to maintain an iron grip upon the throne? It was obviously so, for him. His failure in the end—whether or not it was presaged in horrific dreams, as Shakespeare has it—brings peace to an "England [that] hath long been mad, and scarr'd herself."

But now "civil wounds are stopp'd, peace lives again . . ." (V,iv). Which is to say that the health of the body politic—surely a major passion of the master dramatist—has an importance vastly greater than the self-serving ambitions and cunning intentions of mortal errant kings.[20]

This is not just a matter of estimating the linear consequences of particularly momentous decisions. Above all it is a question of the clarity and power in which the soul of a people is exemplified in certain events, and the shape of its destiny. Nations are not undone by a wicked monarch. The outcome rests on the ability of the people to grasp the import of his villainy for their common life.

So importance, a paramount criterion of historicality, is a value-laden and value-essential concept. It is not a substitute for factuality. It is, rather, that pattern of meaning which makes the ascertainment of factuality a significant endeavor.

This emphasis placed upon importance is not intended to minimize the role of individual personal efforts to transmute a series of psychic occurrences ("experiences") and natural events into historicality. Think, for instance, of the transmutation of mortal terror in Crane's *The Red Badge of Courage* into an almost equally mindless martial valor; and without any sense, in the participants, of the historical magnitude of the battle. Tolstoi's account of Borodino is a much more weighty philosophical treatment of a comparable theme. The hapless hero-infatuated wanderings of Stendhal's Julien Sorel at Waterloo is in much the same vein (vanity). But the novelist, whatever his philosophic agenda, can hardly deny, or seriously question, that history was made at Borodino and at Waterloo; or at Chancellorsville, the putative scene of Crane's story. We may agree or not with Tolstoi that Napoleon himself was a pawn in the hands of a mysterious providence, or of chance. That is a theological question. Historical reality is the infinite variety of ways in which personal experiences and sundry features of the natural environment are transmuted into a historic event.

Such transmutations put the alchemists' dreams to shame. These historical transformations work with a fantastic collection of base metals: despair and confusion so profound they seem irredeemable, ego ecstasies and ambitions so anarchic as to defy incorporation into a public order, closed-circuit alternations of tedium and terror so heavily insulated as to render even putatively divine interference ineffective. Yet the job gets done. If it is not done, the community at that point dematerializes; it may leave behind it a hope for its reincarnation.

Thus a vast stock of psychic occurrences is transmuted into public events. Some of these events acquire such magnitude of importance that private sorrows, guilts, and joys are given no choice but to link up with that historic event or go down the drain as infinitely precious but dumb and inert reminiscence.

Walt Whitman's "When Lilacs Last in the Dooryard Bloom'd" allows us to see this process of transmutation at work, this miracle by which private grief is lifted into a public historic reality. The second stanza concludes:

> O helpless soul of me!
> O harsh surrounding cloud that will not free my soul.

But then his attention is caught by the lilacs in the dooryard—"with every leaf a miracle"—and his heart and mind are carried to the ulti-encompassing mysteries of life and death. So now he sings of that encom-passing death.

> (Nor for you, for one alone,
> Blossoms and branches green to coffins all I bring,
> For fresh as the morning, thus would I chant a song for you
> O sane and sacred death.
>
> All over bouquets of roses,
> O death, I cover you over with roses and early lilies,
> But mostly and now the lilac that blooms the first,
> Copious I break, I break the sprigs from the bushes,
> With loaded arms I come, pouring for you,
> For you and the coffins all of you O death.)

And at last:

> Comrades mine and I in the midst, and their memory ever to
>   keep, for the dead I loved so well,
> For the sweetest, wisest soul of all my days and lands—and this
>   for his dear sake,
> Lilac and star and bird twined with the chant of my soul,
> There in the fragrant pines and the cedars dusk and dim.

In one of the middle passages (stanza VI), he sings the funeral cortege across the land in a threnody from which the last remnant of self-referencing grief has been ablated in the suffering nation.

Let us now apply some of these things to the overtly religious life. The essential life of the community is exhibited in liturgical events able to transmute subjective states and occurrences into objective public struc-tures of meaning. So, in the liturgies of mourning for a fallen leader, we are not licensed to weep for ourselves as private egos. We weep as and for the entire community. It is permissible for a child to ask, "Why are you crying for President Kennedy—you never knew him?" But discern-ing children knew that personal acquaintance was not relevant to the occasion.

So the rounds of liturgical events, both in church and state, are celebrations of the essential life of the community running downward into the depths of time, and straining upward and forward into the vast future of which only God, no creature whatever, is master. And so again comes to mind the liturgy marking the passing of a monarch: "The king is dead!" The factuality of this announcement is the indisputable base line of meaning. But an immense superstructure looms above that base line; the ordered life of the people does not end with the passing of the monarch. Hence the next phase of the liturgical canon is as ordained as the rhythms of the galaxies: "Long live the king!" But here the modality of the base line is not harsh factuality. It is a prayer for the preservation of the state, not only from the depradations of usurpers but also from unforseeable natural calamities. So at the end of *King Lear* Albany says,

> Friends of my soul, you twain
> Rule in this realm, and the gor'd
>   state sustain.

And at the end of *Richard III,* Richmond, in a proper benediction declares:

> And then, as we have ta'en the
>   sacrament,
> We will unite the white rose
>   and the red:
> Smile, heaven, upon this fair
>   conjunction,
> That long have frowned
>   upon their enmity! . . .
>
> Now civil wounds are stopp'd,
>   peace lives again:
> That she may long live
>   here, God say *Amen!* (V,iv) [21]

XII

It is a commonplace that Christianity is a historical religion, as are Islam and Judaism. The three are one in claiming that God has spoken in history. They are also one in believing that history as a whole is under the canopy of divine providence. Thus each exhibits an incorrigible belief that the images and categories appropriate for the interpretation of history are irreducibly religious. And where, in each instance, this primal belief has been amended by more rational and/or scientific elements, each of these historical religions has lost its organic, its religiously coherent, character.

The primal belief of Christianity is that God came into history as Lord Incarnate and he remains in history as its sustaining spirit until his primordial convenantal purpose is consummated.

The evidentiary drafts on history are therefore extremely complex for the modern theologian. It is one thing for piety to sing, "God is His own interpreter/ He will make it plain." An earlier stanza of Cowper's oft-quoted poem is even larger with promise:

> Judge not the Lord with feeble sense.
> But trust him for his grace;
> Behind a frowning providence,
> He hides a smiling face.

A rather different sentiment of the same poet is not so widely employed in services of worship:

> But fixed unalterable care
>   Foregoes not what she feels within,
> Shows the same sadness everywhere,
>   And slights the seasons and the scene. [22]

I do not mean to make light of a sweet soul tortured throughout his life by emotional disabilities. Nonetheless it is legitimate to say that Cowper's "fixed unalterable care" is rather more like a "haunt" for the modern theologian-historian: What historical evidence counts for the Incarnation?

It is surely clear that this question is not on the same footing with such a question as: Did Julius Caesar really intend to establish himself as an absolute rather than a provisional dictator? What would count as historical evidence of the Incarnation is already under the control of an incorrigible belief; that is, that the testimony of the New Testament is the Lord's own doing, he himself is its self-determined historical subject. If we attempt to put that up as evidence in the same court in which the case of Julius Caesar is heard, we shall be obliged to confess that the New Testament witnesses to what the first Christians *believed* happened and to whom they identified as the supreme historical subject-agent. There is no reason to doubt that they believed what they had reported as real events and that God himself had done these things. But the more strenuously one argues that the disciples were divinely inspired to see and speak those inestimable truths, the less available for purposes of historical evidentiality, as these are now conceived, the whole business becomes.

Nor will it do much for the traditional Christian case to say that, after all, the admissible evidence in the case of Julius Caesar suffers from ambiguity, incompleteness, and partisanship. The charge is true enough. But such judgments about the historical evidence are not dictated, in the case of Caesar, by people who claim to have privileged, if not sole, access to the absolutely decisive evidence. Nor can we permit theologians to try to settle the Christian case by imposing on the court a novel theory concerning the nature of evidence and evidentiality. Of course Cowper is religiously right in warning, "Judge not the Lord with feeble sense." This hardly means that the historical senses of theologians are endowed with an acuity and perspicuity denied earthbound journeymen historians.

I do not mean to suggest that there is something logically odd or pernicious in the proposal: "Just look seriously at the New Testament. There's all the evidence one needs or has a religious right to ask for." Yet we must ask what this proposal means. On its surface it is something like this: Do you want to know what happens when people *see* Jesus Christ as God Incarnate? That is, *see* him as such and not just believe that he is that. Then you must take the testimony of the New Testament at its face value.

In this sort of claim the New Testament is not employed as though it were a unique cache of historical evidence the weight of which, the truth of which, could be assayed only by people under direct divine inspiration. Indeed here the stakes are quite different from those generally put down on theological concepts and religious celebrations of inspiration. Here the preeminent question is: Is it really possible to see—that is, to construe —the whole world and one's whole being as the dwelling-place of God Most High and as the objects of his ultimate solicitude?

If one says Yes to that question, what artillery of historical evidentiality need one dread and flee? One may be depressed by the scorners and cynics who say all the day long, "Where now is your God?" The pious, in the misery of persecution or persiflage, may wish that God would have struck down Sinclair Lewis on that famous Sunday when he stood in a Methodist pulpit and dared God to do his worst. But why should God have been seriously tempted to match worsts with such a mountebank?

Yet Christians do claim that a certain order of evidentiality is opened in the New Testament. It contains clues on how to go about seeing God in Christ. None of these clues comes easily under the heading "Wishing will make it so." Moreover, some guidance is called for in order to interpret the clues correctly. This is something for theologians to do. It is not theirs alone to do. One's sainted mother may be as divinely inspired for such purposes as the author of *The Summa Theologica* or of *The Institutes of the Christian Religion.* If, that is, the main business is learning to see all things in, of, and through God.

XIII

We have come at last to what may seem a distressingly negative conclusion: The historicality of the Gospel of Jesus Christ is bound into the witness of faith about him. Historicity of this sort does not share footings with modern questions about historical evidentiality. Therefore, how much religious value is there in the latest word from technical New Testament scholarship about Jesus of Nazareth? How much faster is the pulse of faith supposed to race when one hears from that quarter that there really was a Jesus of Nazareth and he probably did preach the righteousness of God's kingdom pretty much as the Synoptic Gospels report; and for this, probably, was liquidated?

Such historical probabilities are light years away from the historicality absolutely central to the New Testament and to authentic Christian faith ever since. What is paramount there is that Jesus Christ preached the kingdom of God with an authority and presence the realities of which are not entrusted to the portfolio of historical research.

So if one is moved to say of Jesus Christ, "Verily, he was not the Son of God and just as certainly did not rise from the dead," one should not suppose for a moment that, in so testifying, one is reporting a verdict rendered by minds occupying a uniquely commanding spot in the world historical-dialectical process, a spot from which the evidence can finally be weighed as it ought to be and dismissed as it deserves. In biblical terms, such a one speaks as those who have eyes and see not, ears and hear not. Or in more mundane terms, it is possible to be so caught up in another story that the New Testament story cannot have the ring and resonance of history.

It is possible. Many voices in many quarters testify that it is highly probable.

Chapter Eight

❧

STORY AS THE ART
OF HISTORICAL TRUTH

I

This is Livy's version of the legendary founding of Rome, "the mightiest empire the world has known—next to God's":

The Vestal Virgin was raped and gave birth to twin boys. Mars, she declared, was their father—perhaps she believed it, perhaps she was merely hoping by the pretense to palliate her guilt. Whatever the truth of the matter, neither gods nor men could save her or her babes from the savage hands of the king. The mother was bound and flung into prison; the boys, by the king's order, were condemned to be drowned in the river. Destiny, however, intervened; the Tiber had overflowed its banks; because of the flooded ground it was impossible to get to the actual river, and the men entrusted to do the deed thought that the flood-water, sluggish though it was, would serve their purpose. Accordingly they made shift to carry out the king's orders by leaving the infants on the edge of the first flood-water they came to, at the spot where now stands the Ruminal fig-tree—said to have once been known as the fig-tree of Romulus . . . and the story goes that when the basket in which the infants had been exposed was left high and dry by the receding water, a she-wolf, coming down from the neighboring hills to quench her thirst, heard the children crying and made her way to where they were. She offered them her teats to suck and treated them with such gentleness that Faustulus, the king's herdsman, found her licking them with her tongue. Faustulus took them to his hut and gave them to his wife Larentia to nurse. Some think that the origin of this fable was the fact that Larentia was a common whore and was called Wolf by the shepherds.[1]

It would be natural for us to feel that Livy here demonstrated the right sort of critical historical judgment, at least minimally. He allows that the Vestal Virgin had reasons for declaring that the father of her twins was a god, but he puts no money down on her claim. He cites the wondrous tale of the providential she-wolf and adds that the surrogate wet-nurse may have been a "common whore" instead.

Virgil, Rome's mighty epic singer, takes the ancient legend more seriously. But after all he was a poet and was therefore free to use any tradition and any rhetorical device that suited his grand overarching purpose, namely to celebrate the greatness of Rome. But in respect to that aim Livy gives away no weight to the poet.

Events before Rome was born or thought of have come to us in old tales with more of the charm of poetry than of a sound historical record, and such traditions I propose neither to affirm nor refute. There is no reason, I feel, to object when antiquity draws no hard line between the human and the supernatural: it adds dignity to the past, and, if any nation deserves the privilege of claiming a divine ancestry, that nation is our own; and so great is the glory won by the Roman people in their wars that when they declare that Mars himself was their first parent and father of the man who founded their city, all the nations of the world might well allow the claim as readily as they accept Rome's imperial dominion.

But to this the historian immediately adds:

These, however, are comparatively trivial matters and I set little store by them.[2]

Livy is one of the progenitors of historians who want to "tell it just as it was." We may in fact be disposed to say that he regarded his prime responsibility to be ascertainable factual truth. No less patriotic than Virgil, he had an allegiance to historicity, to historical truth, different from that of the poet. Virgil works with a poet's license. As a historian Livy ought to be bound by the facts.

Distinctions of this sort have long dominated the modern historical consciousness. It is hardly too much to say that they largely define that mentality. Surely the rise and meteoric career of science in the modern world has had a great deal to do with this. Science has demonstrated what dedication to the pursuit of factual knowledge can accomplish, provided that sufficient attention is paid to refining technical instruments for ascertaining the facts and conceptual schemes for rendering them intelligible. For the facts which matter most in the paradigmatic sciences are not ascertainable by gross perceptions and are not rendered intelligible by concepts refined out of common sense.

Now the long hegemony of physical science over the whole realm of truth is being challenged with fresh vigor in many quarters. This is certainly true in the discipline of history. In that quarter we now hear such questions as: Is history best understood as the quest for general laws from which particular events or series of events can be deduced? Are the laws of history more than fairly loose empirical generalizations that pertain only to particular historical situations that have some features in common? If the laws of history are richer than such things as "Tyranny tends to run to excesses," by how much do they miss being incorrigible convictions about human reality as such; that is, being metaphysical? It hardly matters that many who believe that there are historical laws that can be exactly formulated are avowedly anti-metaphysical. As Peirce long ago suggested, the soaring ambitions of speculative thinkers do not give metaphysics a worse name than those who do metaphysics unconsciously.

Questions such as those cited above express a marked reluctance to accept scientific models of explanation as normative for the interpretation of concrete human activity in the round. Behind this reluctance there is an incorrigible conviction that to make fullest sense of human activity, and thus of history, one must allow the shape of interpretation, thus of sense-making, to emerge from an interplay of creative imagination with historical factualities, an interplay at the antipodes from the realization of mathematical form. Science cannot do this. It cannot allow that interweave of imaginative structure with gross factuality. The putatively objective interpretations of science consist of the reduction of phenomena to causal laws expressed mathematically, the same being the shape farthest removed from any order of gross fact; unless one has in mind counting on one's fingers.

One may well wonder where the revolt against the hegemony of rigidly mathematized science over the realm of truth is likely to go. Should we so capitalize creative imagination in the service of existential needs that the distinction between fact and legend is threatened with a loss of meaning or power? Should we try once again to devise, or profess to discern, a hierarchy of spirit in which some truths are higher and richer

221

than others? Should we profess that truth is many kingdoms rather than one, and that over each province its own fit monarch rules?

In respect to the last question one may well wonder whether the poet's famous credo, "Truth is great, and shall prevail," says rather more, confesses rather more, about the unity of the human spirit than it does about a realm of truth.[3] Spirit, that is, as a unitary reality in all and withal its multitudinous interests. Given systematic conceptual articulation, this is idealistic metaphysics. But it is also a fundamental intuition of human historicality. Its metaphysical inflation ought not to obscure that fact.

II

Every religion, though not every metaphysics, has one kind of stake or other in historicality. This is true even of those faiths which inspired Whitehead's famous dictum: Buddhism is a metaphysics in search of a religion; Christianity is a religion in search of a metaphysics.[4] Happily we need not tarry here to ponder the plausibility of that aphorism.

We have seen that Christianity has an exceptionally heavy and unique investment in historicality; in historicality rather than in mere historicity. Everything from galaxies to gonads can lay some claim to being historical. To say that is hardly more than to say that time infects all things. How rich is the poet's dream:

> Where beauty has no ebb, decay no
> flood,
> But joy is wisdom, time an endless
> song.

Little wonder that the child who voices these sentiments is forthwith told:

> Awake out of that trance—and
> Cover up your eyes and ears.[5]

For in the real world time is that "ever-rolling stream that bears all her sons away."

In Christianity the essential claims concern the actual historical occurrence of those things in which Christians believe God's real being and true purpose have been revealed. Thus *revelation* is a historical category. It is in many ways the primal category for the Christian interpretation of history. Statements such as: And he dwelt among us, full of grace and truth (Jn 1:14) and: God was in Christ reconciling the world to himself (2 Cor 5:19) have traditionally been understood to be fundamental acknowledgements of historicality. Historical statements, yes; that might simply mean that once upon a time there were people who said and purportedly believed such things. The claim for historicality is the claim that in such astounding events the inner core of God's dealings with man is exposed; with man, that supremely temporalistic creature. It is almost as though the metaphysical-ethical weight of those events created a new criterion of historicity, or perhaps even a new definition of it.

Moreover, Christians have believed that New Testament stories about the wonders worked by Jesus are true as such and attest to his divine power and authority. Finally, traditional Christianity has put an immense weight on the historical factuality of the resurrection of Jesus Christ. Here St. Paul says it all: "If for this life only we have hoped in Christ, we are of all men most to be pitied" (1 Cor 1:19). The conversion of this primitive affirmation of absolute historicality into a timeless symbolic truth is not much more remarkable than the triumphant appropriation of Easter by couturiers and florists.

Thus *revelation* traditionally bespoke a range of divinely determined historical events rather than a human elevation of quintessential wisdom to the order of eternal truths.

III

We have seen that Protestant liberalism is a protracted retreat from unqualified historicality to a position felt to be essentially consistent with the presumptively rational criteria and methods of modern historiography; as though the fundamental issue were how to do history rather than what to believe about its reality. So there seemed to be some digestible and nutritious marrow in the bones picked clean by critical historiography: perhaps some truths about history that do not depend upon particular historical facts.

It does in fact seem that the worldviewing perspective of any given historian, the spirit which informs his performance, is a case in point. Spengler does not learn his pessimism from particular tragic episodes in history. Bury does not acquire optimism from basking in the bright sunlight of some happy moment in the eighteenth century or since. Indeed, why should we not say that history offers a moral, an overarching and pervasive meaning, only to those who have imparted to history an intelligible structure, a pattern of meaning? Nor need we worry unduly about that fine old-fashioned word "moral." Historians aspiring to admission to the mystic order of science flinch at the word. But to the extent that they presume to have told the real story—for instance, about the financial burdens inflicted upon the peasants by the building of the cathedral of Chartres—they have in effect said: "See, this is what Chartres *really* means; very likely, too, what the ecclesiastically ordered society of medieval Europe meant, as well."

"Intelligible structure," admittedly, may not run quite as far as a developed worldview. It may stop with the delineation, or at least with the positing, of methodological principles. Whether any of these is unique to historiography is a nice philosophical question around which, happily, we can detour at least for the time being. The point here is simply that the interpretation of history, whether or not it is a sky-challenging philosophy of history or an earth-crawling theory of historical explanation, brings various pieces of intellectual equipment to bear on historical events and subjects in order to tame and instruct them. It was R. G. Collingwood who claimed that the historian lends authority to his data.[6] Did he mean that the past speaks only the lines the present assigns to it? I doubt that he meant that; I doubt that it is true. It is true that every historian must excogitate or borrow a sense-making conceptual structure. That fact does not lend more credibility to any one theory of historical reality than it does to any other.

But are there structures of meaning and methodological principles built into any respectable study of the past? Or are all such structures heuristic devices calculated to interpret historical events rather than to explain them?

Such questions lead us to wonder whether there is any sort of helpful analogy linking historical investigation to the natural sciences. Perhaps, for instance, there is something of an analogy in the relation of the physical sciences to the grand principle of the uniformity of nature. This principle necessarily holds for the entire domain of natural science. But there is no particular positive science qualified to establish the validity of the principle. Philosophers of science may worry about the logical-epistemological foundations of the principle, but scientists tarry not for their decisions, demurrers, or caveats. Nor do the rest of us going about our affairs in the everyday world. We know intuitively that our confidence in the daily rising of the sun and the setting of the same does not rest on the principle of the uniformity of nature. Indeed it was neither science nor philosophy which put Phoebus out of business. That was an accomplishment of a generalized *religious* desacralization of the cosmos: the sun is no god, it is God's luminous creature. As such it has no more divinity than the uncertain glow of a candle in the wind. People may continue thereafter to worship the sun in diverse ways, some of which invite cancer. But some people also continue to use bear grease to treat pneumonia. Religious habits atrophy and perish more slowly than almost any other kind of habit, not because the facts eventually gang up to quash them but because sundry human interests and anxieties have not yet discovered a productive alternative mode of expression.

So it is the case that no particular science of history, no particular scientific investigation of any historical period or of any range of historical data, can establish the validity of any methodological axiom. The validity of a methodological axiom consists entirely of its ability either to produce or to justify certain results. That these results have ever been or shall ever be universally and unambiguously gratifying is at best a hope, a very generous hope.

Let us be more particular. Every historian assumes that the subjects and agents of the period or the culture he studies are axiomatically historical. That is, they were human beings. They conceived themselves to be doing some things on purpose; they assumed that some value was thus served, however slender, ephemeral, and non-nutritious when they complained that they were caught in "the fell clutch of circumstance." So they were not merely *homo faber, homo sexualis, homo ludens,* though they were all of these. Preeminently, they were *homo historicus.* They knew themselves to be creatures of time; knew it infallibly. But they also believed incorrigibly that in some strong and important sense they were also masters of time, time-binders. For as *homo historicus* they had a story to tell and to hear. The proper hearing and telling was a celebration. It was a celebration thrown forward. The epic sings the mighty deeds of the heroes from whose mind and heart and loins the people have descended.

225

But the thrust of the epic is a time vector oriented toward the future. Mayhap we are lesser creatures than the ancient heroes, but we are pledged to live and to die for the community of their creation.

Thus mere history is taken up into historicality. In every epic, history may be partly fictionalized, consciously or otherwise. In the true epic the intention of such invention, of such poetic license, is to render the historicality of the community more luminous. The aim is to display the transcendent importance of that historicality.

So there is surely much that is sound in the Protestant liberal interpretation of history. Why should we not cheerfully and in good faith agree that narrow factual questions about the resurrection cannot possibly be decisive; such questions as what really happened at the tomb or on the dusty road to Emmaus? What matters ultimately is what the stories say about the human situation as such; that is, how the threat and reality of death are properly appropriated by authentic faith.

Thus the logic of history which Protestant liberalism exploited, though did not invent, called for the translation of every fundamentally important fact-claim of Christian history into an intentionality-claim: a claim about the structure of consciousness (spirit) in relation to its world. Or at least such fact-claims must be seen as the outer garments of intentionality-claims.

So, to ask whether the resurrection really occurred is to ask, essentially, how the members of the Christian cult in the first century construed the thrust of life against all-consuming death. This question cannot be answered by detailing their beliefs because we know, as they did not, how important the unconscious depths of spirit are in shaping perceptions, attitudes, and commitments. But as far as our concerns are theological rather than simply historical a further step is ordered for the Christian today. He must suppose that those New Testament intentionalities were essentially true despite their bizarre habiliments. Those intentionalities were and are existentially valid.

IV

A fair-minded account of the revolt against the despotic reign of natural science in the realm of truth must take into account another factor. That is, the philosophical discovery of the distinction between truth-about and truth-of descriptions. I propose to cast this distinction as the difference between *verisimilitude* and *fact-confirmation*. Faulkner's *Absalom, Absalom!* drives for verisimilitude. Gibbon's *Decline and Fall of the Roman Empire* drives for fact-confirmation.

Faulkner's epic has as its immediate subject the rise and fall of the Sutpen family. There is a larger subject behind that: Jefferson, county seat of the mythical Yoknapatawpha. There is a still larger subject behind that: the rise and fall of the fortunes of the South. But isn't the really real, the ultimately real, subject the human condition as such? Or at least the genius of American history?

I am reminded here of one of Mr. Lionel Trilling's remarks to the effect that the real subject of the novel as a modern art form is the human community. Translated into philosophical jargon, the conclusion emerges: The real intentionality of the novel is a historically given structure of consciousness in a historically particular world.

We seem by this to be instructed to say that the truth of Faulkner's story is its truthfulness, its verisimilitude. Since Faulkner's Jefferson, Mississippi, does not exist in the "real" world, however much it may resemble Oxford and a host of other southern towns, how does the commonsensical question come up—who *really* are the Sutpens? And the Compsons, the Snopeses, the De Spains? Surely the proper answer to that question is that the characters of Faulkner's great stories haven't the slightest obligation to be "real" personages artfully concealed in or by laminations of poetic fancy—though people will go on believing that is the case, with various satisfactions. No, the really sober question to put to the story is whether the Thomas Sutpens of the world really behave and think as Faulkner's character does. Note that we must say *behave* rather than *behaved;* what is at stake is historicality. Given the character Sutpen brings to a specific historical context, part of which is his creation, are not his motives and behavior clearly recognizable?

Perhaps we should go a bit further and ask whether it is not legitimate, or perhaps necessary, to apply something remotely like the principle of the uniformity of nature and thus see whether Thomas Sutpen obeys— or at least illustrates—universal psychological laws. If he fails this test, this sort of "reality principle," Faulkner may be accused of having produced a mere stock character, a type, not a person, not an agent capable of carrying the history of the community. We might well draw back from proposing that the actions of a Sutpen must be predictable, except in retrospect, the safest of all predictions. But we should also want to say that they are intelligible. So that in the end we are not found saying, "If there were any Sutpens, this is the way they would act." Rather we are prompted to say, "This is the way the Sutpens of the world are likely to act. Whatever they do these are the motives and these are the results." Thus, whoever makes all things and all persons "adjunctive to the main design," as Sutpen confesses he has, is sowing the whirlwind, though each such sinner faces a unique reaping. Not all, God knows, are cut down by a scythe in the hands of an outraged servant.

But why do we say that Faulkner's story has the ring and aura of truth? Why do we award it the accolade of verisimilitude? Why should we not be content with saying simply that it is very meaningful and full of insight?

There is a history behind such questions. It is a history surrounding a lately incorrigible belief: that *truth* should be reserved exclusively for inquiry rightly ordered to get at the "real facts." True, this conviction is often a curious mixture of garden-variety skepticism—"seeing is believing"—and a reverential respect for the wonders of scientific fact-determinations where what is seen is at best a crude sensory signal requiring the most ingenious mathematical-logical deciphering.

But now let us turn an eye toward Gibbon's *Decline and Fall of the Roman Empire*. Gibbon also tells a story. He is a narrative historian, not a mole grubbing in the subsoil of economic indices. And what a story he tells, and with what artistry he tells it! With what sophisticated and carefully polished artistry, at that.[7] But since he is a historian we expect him to ride with the facts, as far as he has access to them, and not spin a fanciful tale in the once-upon-a-time vein. His is the fate of the mightiest, most durable, and most humane imperial system man has created: an engrossing plot. No novelist or epic singer has come as close as Gibbon the historian to doing it justice.

What then is the chief difference between Faulkner's verisimilitude and Gibbon's responsibility for the facts? It is certainly not that Gibbon has to mine his facts while Faulkner simply draws upon his creative imagination. The facts for Gibbon are necessarily archeological: monuments, records, inscriptions, coins, antecedent historical studies. And of course it is true that Faulkner does draw upon his creative imagination. But notice how he constructs young Compson's performance as a historian, that is as one who grapples with the reality of the past. He too has data: an old watch, time-withered family letters, oral traditions.

But not all of Gibbon's facts were archeological. Before him there were many generations of historians whose subject was Rome, some of whom, like Polybius, "spared no efforts in his research for detail, accuracy, and unbiased truth."[8] So Gibbon had a considerable store of second-order facts to consider as carefully as he scrutinized the archeological data. The second-order facts were the great range of interpretations of the so-called prime data. This does not mean that what earlier historians had said was as important for him as the primary data. But he was functioning as a member of a community of scholarship that incorporated both the quick and the dead. Its principles and paradigms were not lightly to be regarded. To reject them was as unthinkable as to ignore or deface archeological data. Moreover, that community of kindred minds largely shared a worldview as well as principles and paradigms normative for the interpretation of history.[9]

Faulkner as a novelist did not have to answer to the same kind of community. Nevertheless there was, and is, a community whose traditions and expectations figured for Faulkner as an order of secondary fact: the community whose story was his own. This story also demanded to be told in the appropriate language. But unlike the historian, the novelist must meld the story and the language into an organic unity, as though there were but one way of telling it that made real sense. On the other hand, whatever we may think of Gibbon's style, it would be absurd to say that there was no other language in which to tell that story.[10]

It is apparent, then, that historian and novelist are committed to making sense, each in his own way, of some range of the human story. Each must immerse himself in tradition and in whatever else passes muster as primary data. But each must also immerse himself in historicality. For each, the real and inescapable subject is a particular adventure of the human spirit in the dense thicket of the world.

The historian *per se*, of course, has unique obligations. He must gain control of first-order facts as far as these are available. He must also be familiar with the second-order facts—he must know the interpretations already in the field. If these facts are defective—wrong, obscure, incomplete, or prejudiced—he must be able to show that this is the case. He must draw on his imagination to give proper shape to the facts. He must carefully consider the prevailing criteria governing sense-making in the peer community of scholarship. I propose now briefly to consider these obligations.

(1) Control of the facts may well involve complex discriminatory judgments. Sometimes the historian must ask, "Is it likely that there is anything to this story?" But what does *likely* mean? Surely not a mathematically precise calculus of probability. Here the historian is applying canons of credibility that seem to be profoundly influenced by a worldview. "Seem to be" is dictated by such observations as the following.

Of Mommsen's work, "an unmatched re-creation of Roman society and culture," it is said:

His liberal politics prejudiced his view of ancient history; his German contemporaries are clearly visible on his Roman scene. Although a great admirer of Caesar, he vigorously denounced Caesarism.[11]

Of Dio Cassius's histories of Rome it is said:

They are a reputable source of the period of the later republic and the first two centuries A.D. Dio Cassius tried earnestly to study all available sources in the light of a moderate scepticism.[12]

In our time the "moderate scepticism" of a historian is very likely to be a bequest of natural science; it may be as incorrigible a belief as Dio's convictions about the monarchy. Thus today the man of science will protest that there are things he simply couldn't believe even if he wanted to. To believe them would threaten the worldview he accepts as normative and thus precipitate a major crisis of faith as well as a crippling loss of prestige in the scientific community. As clear and terrifying a risk of double jeopardy as one could imagine.

So the historian's control of the facts demonstrates his ability to screen out trivial and dubious data, using as a filter a "moderate scepticism" dictated by the scientific spirit of the age.

(2) The shape a historian gives to the adjusted net budget of facts is a product of creative imagination whether this structure is a conceptual system or a regal image or some combination of the two.

So far then there is some warrant for saying that *story*, quite as much as conceptual schematism, may be signified by "shape." At the outset this hardly means more than that historians write narratives. Narratives, though, are more than sequential accounts of events—B following A, C following B. History as narrative has a story line. The story line may not be so lean and controlled, or so ambitious, as that announced by Thucydides:

> . . . it may well be that my history will seem less easy to read because of the absence in it of a romantic element. It will be enough for me, however, if these words of mine are judged useful by those who want to understand clearly the events which happened in the past and which (human nature being what it is) will, at some time or other and in much the same ways, be repeated in the future. My work is not a piece of writing designed to meet the taste of an immediate public, but was done to last forever.[13]

But the narrative structure is there: who did what to whom and for what reasons and to what effects.

The *who* component calls for the identification of the historical subject-agent, as we have seen. This identification involves a sustained effort to flesh out the character of either an individual person or a group of persons. So the historical work of subject-agent identification runs far beyond specifying the name of the person or the group primarily responsible for the event. We have a right to know what sort of person he was, what he thought, what his motives were, how he perceived things, what his beliefs were, how he rationalized his beliefs, how he habitually acted and how he justified his actions. So far this is only a crude impressionistic review of what it means to identify a historical subject-agent.

There is no person in history about whom even the first range of impressionistic questions can be answered without drawing upon both creative imagination and discriminatory judgment. Nor does it matter whether there is a great mass of putative facts from and about a given person. What were Julius Caesar's real motives in establishing the dictatorship which contributed to the destruction of the Republic? Did he have an unmanageable lust for power, an urge to be godlike—odd in a man who did not take religious *auspicii* seriously? Or did he earnestly and correctly see that he alone could restore order and power to a state horribly torn by civil war? The debate goes on and on.

And what did Jesus really intend to accomplish by driving the huck sters out of the Temple? And who really gave the order to murder the little princes in the Tower of London? And did Lincoln really intend to destroy slavery with the Emancipation Proclamation?

The point in this random selection of moot historical questions is to ask what is the force of "really" in such questions put to the "facts." Here are some of the obvious candidates:

(i) Which of the stories should be credited above all others? Many of his contemporaries believed Julius Caesar was cunning, depraved, ambitious, able, and wholly unscrupulous. Can a modern historian test adequately these appraisals? We know that Cicero had his reasons for giving wide currency to stories about Caesar's gross lubricity and homosexuality. Dubious motives for repeating slander do not necessarily invalidate its truth. But if a man's character is known to be sleazy, what should the jury make of his testimony? Or should one say that such appraisals are necessarily retrodictive, and may thus be taken to be so many guesses ventured to make the actual events intelligible? But they might also be so many attempts to vindicate a policy for or against Caesar's usurpation of power.

(ii) What will render the behavior of the historical subject-agent intelligible? This question has both a general and a particular application.

The general application assumes that there are universally valid criteria for determining when a person is acting rationally and when explanations of his actions are themselves rational. For example, the Synoptic Gospels tell the story of Jesus going out into the wilderness to be tempted by Satan. There is nothing unusual about a man seeking solitude as he confronts a critical decision. So rational-irrational may apply here, but not very helpfully. Being tempted by Satan is a very different matter. A modern historian will be predisposed to say that anybody who believes that his life and decisions are being complicated by Satan is irrational, because there is a very wide consensus on the religious-metaphysical proposition that Satan does not exist. In more abstract terms, "There is no X such that he (it) is Satan." This consensus, moreover, must seem wholly rational to modern minds. After all, it was not the historians who put Satan out of commission. It was theologians discharging a philosophical obligation to get at the essential Gospel by stripping away the supernatural husks. This means that the question, "Is there a Satan?" is not a question the historian *per se* has any business flirting with. He can only report that modern historians prescind from the supernatural on methodological grounds. This does not speak to the metaphysical question.

On the other hand it would be a reasonably responsible judgment if an historian were to say that the Jesus of the Synoptic Gospels did not habitually behave like an obsessive personality. His followers believed that he exorcised demons. There is little evidence that he was possessed by them. How could he be if demons do not exist?

There is another vexatious part to this particular story. The Holy Spirit led Jesus out into the wilderness. This is vexatious first because all kinds of historians, not just Luke, are forever imputing necessitating causes of one sort or another to their subjects. But this "cause" is filtered out by our prevailing canons of rationality. Not that Jesus and his disciples could not have believed it; likely they did. But it cannot be true; that is, it cannot be verified or falsified by appeal to fact or theory naturalistically generated. *That* is certainly true. But what has happened to the criterion of universal rationality that was presumed to be the bedrock of our scientific historiography? Is it ever rational to decide that some metaphysical beliefs, such as that God exists and guides some people one way and some another, are false or "meaningless" simply because regnant philosophical presuppositions are hostile to them?

There is an obvious though oblique rejoinder to this. Why not say that it was by the Holy Spirit that George Washington was led to make his famous crossing of the Delaware on December 25, 1776, and bag the Hessians at Trenton?

In the abstract there is nothing grossly wrong in such an interpretation of Washington's actions on that occasion, though there is no evidence that Washington subscribed to it, and it is hard to suppose that the Hessians did. In the concrete, however, the Holy Spirit is a character, so to speak, in the story of Jesus Christ. *God the Spirit* is a conceptuality that can be theologically extrapolated to cover every detail and the whole run of human history. Freud's oedipal complex is another conceptuality that can be inflated and extrapolated to cover the whole run of human history —except for poor old Oedipus himself, whose relationship to his wife-mother can hardly be called a complex.

Let us pause here to observe that it is quite unreasonable to expect historians to pitch their professional tents on territory from which they have personally cleared all philosophical underbrush and defused all logical land mines. It is not unreasonable, on the other hand, to note that a public larger than the professional peer group of historians has a stake in appraising their work if historians want their work to matter to a larger world. In that case it is not enough for them to say of their methodological commitments that, after all, this is the way their professional work is done. Plumbers also have ways of working that do not uniformly convince the public that they are well and justly served thereby. The most obvious difference is that historians seem to be claiming that the reality with which they deal cannot be rendered intelligible any other way, whereas a householder can stop a leak in a pipe with a wad of bubblegum. Not permanently of course, but perhaps for about as long as historians are sometimes able to nail things down.

There is an obvious form of the issue of intelligibility that must surely commend itself to us as essentially reasonable. That is a historian's testing for consistency in the behavior of his subject. If, for example, Lincoln generally acted one way and on occasion acted in a strikingly different way, what ought we to conclude?

(a) He was an unstable person.

(b) That means that at least some of the time his behavior was irrational. But at what times? When he fired McClellan? McClellan thought so. Historians tend not to agree with McClellan.

(c) Perhaps the reasons Lincoln announced for some of his actions were inconsistent with the actions themselves. He wanted to spare as many lives as possible but he supported Grant's strategy in 1864 for crushing the army of Northern Virginia. The grisly harvest of death which ensued appalls us even today, after two world wars. And what are we to make, come to think of it, of the Stimson-Truman rationale for using the atomic bomb?

(d) If Lincoln ascribed a supernatural cause of or warrant for his actions, we would have him. He did not oblige.

(e) If we say that Lincoln's behavior was sometimes unintelligible, we might mean that his general line of preachment and his general line of conduct cannot easily be reconciled with each other. Here we would have to assume that he generally meant what he said and that he was usually in control of his behavior. If there are facts that disqualify either of these assumptions, the intelligibility appraisal itself is in serious trouble.

There is another possibility. (f) One might say "Lincoln is unintelligible" when there is no clear or fair basis for judging what evidence there is that is both fair and definitive, as well as admissible. But then "unintelligible" is a judgment that would, consistently, have to be rendered about a great variety of circumstantial cases. In such a situation a historian might feel constrained to draw upon his powers of invention to put the evidence together in a pattern more to be commended for its coherence than for its fact-determination. Thus an historian might give a new shape to the facts in the fond hope that at least his story made sense even though the fundamental factuality questions were as recalcitrant as ever.[14]

V

(3) Now we may be tempted to say that what makes sense is very little dependent upon the facts and very largely dependent upon the criteria accepted as normative by the community of historical scholars. The facts have to be there. The criteria of sense-making are just as much there, just as given, as the facts, though, one might suppose, not given in the same way.

A painful bind develops here. Something bids us believe that science has thrown a novel and perhaps definitive light on what is really rational, not so much by defining it as by being it. What modern historian does not believe that his methods of fact-ascertainment are incomparably superior to those of the Venerable Bede, Malory, Luke, Thucydides and even of that towering historical-literary genius, Gibbon? But something else bids us believe that what we call really rational is a gratuitous compliment paid by modernity to itself. Is our way of doing history really more rational than Livy's or Luke's? Within the parameters of their perceptions and incorrigible beliefs, were they any less rational than Mommsen or Rostovtzeff, Acton or Gay? Archeology is of course immensely more sophisticated and far-ranging than earlier ages had any reason to dream it could be. But how much more about historicality are uranium 238 and carbon 14/6 supposed to tell us?[15] In fact the suspicion grows that the power and the glory of history as an art have suffered immeasurably from its physical science techniques for fact-determination. Here I find Buckle's observation remarkably prescient:

The most effective way of turning huge masses of observations to account would be to give more scope to the imagination and incorporate the spirit of poetry with the spirit of science. [16]

There is a thoroughly modern poignancy in this bind. Do we not believe that the sentiment of rationality is a very thin and fragile epidermis covering drives that are intrinsically and incorrigibly subrational? To be modern is also to believe, perhaps incorrigibly, that psychological science has at last thrown precise light on those anarchic depths—though "light" is an odd metaphor here. So we expect biographers, psychohistorians, to plumb the depths of the unconscious of their subjects, using tools that are not quite so precise as carbon 14, of course.

Here the methodological-philosophical bind becomes acutely painful. For who remains really rational, now or ever? Logically, we cannot tolerate the psychologist's self-exemption from the degradation of reason. Nor can we afford to be more charitable with persistent and systematic confusions of *explanation* with *justification*. We may decide that Caesar's justification for defying the Senate and crossing the Rubicon won't stand up. But won't stand up to what? Some theory of unconscious motivation? Then how will a historian fare who refuses to accept Caesar's "reasons"? What moves in the anarchic depths of the historian's psyche to compel him to reject Caesar's "reasons"?

VI

For various reasons the conviction grows apace that doing history must be much more like doing a story than pursuing a science, save insofar as some of the material for a history may have to be dug out by archeological techniques.[17] So now we must ask what it is that bestows verisimilitude upon a story. What do we mean when we say that a story is *likely?* Is it when a story reveals the way things really are? Very well; what things? Surely we do not mean that a story must replicate actual situations and the actual subject-agents in them if we are to say that it grasps reality and renders it intelligible. But on the other hand we are not likely to bestow the accolade "reality" upon poetic fancy that soars high and free above actuality in search of some general truth; a truth that may very well turn out to be an old saw.

So we say provisionally that the reality-power of a story is closely related to the authenticity with which it represents human life. But "authenticity" is a big word. The volume of traffic directed over it must be monitored.

Let us say next, then, that we do not ordinarily mean that a full complement of details of speech, costume, and manners necessarily adds up to an authentic representation of human existence in a particular setting. A masterly command of the externals of human society and behavior is not a viable substitute for deep and discerning perceptions of the tangled knots in human relationships and the fearful involutions of the soul. Being able to place the characters in a story in the right time and place without anachronism or anomaly is a fine accomplishment. It is not a viable substitute for the delineation of multidimensional characters who speak their own minds rather than prate the doctrines of their creator.

Hence what a good story enables us to identify is real characters interacting with other real characters in situations recognizably mundane no matter how heavily charged with importance they may be. To identify with such a character in such a situation does not mean that we empathize with him or otherwise put ourselves in that situation; though we may come to do both. What is first of all at stake in identification is recognition of real individuality whether or not it is admirable. Thereafter may come acknowledgment of the actual powers which move those individuals. "Well," we may say then, "ambition does things like that." Or, "True, love like that is uncommon but it would probably make an uncommon difference, too."

The next thing we should want to say is that the shape of the story matters greatly to its intelligibility if by "shape" we mean the devices which draw individuality up out of a dense background and the progression of events in which characters express themselves, whether or not they control those events or are borne away by them.

So a story may be truthful, that is authentic, whether or not it is factually accurate. Which is to say it may square with our perceptions and value structures even though it may be faulted by our memories or by some public instrument for ascertaining the facts. This does not mean that we ought to be patient with careless transpositions of events or with dogmatic denials of fact. But the story is out to shape and vivify our perceptions rather than to prove that the barn we remembered as red was really yellow.[18]

VII

What is now leading us to believe that the proper theological interest in truth is best served by story rather than by fact-oriented history—to say nothing of metaphysics?

One reason for this is the discovery that a naturalistic and positivistic historical methodology does not allow for any interaction of human agents with supernatural powers. This discovery was made a long time ago. Decisions against the supernatural were often announced by historians such as Gibbon, but the case was settled by metaphysicians, some of whom were disguised as scientists. We must of course grant that the antisupernaturalists among the historians had a real point: what *empirical* gain could be registered by saying that the stars in their courses fought against Napoleon? But the supernatural as a vision of reality ought not to be confused with the supernatural as the x-mysterious cause of the disappearance of the hosts of the Syrians.[19] It is possible, of course, that the whole army came down with a case of hallucinations. It is also possible that the hosts of the Syrians were dissolved by rampageous dysentery. The modern historian can legitimately stop with the trots, whether or not his religious sensibilities are offended by God's use of such low methods.

On the other hand a story can sketch interactions with supernatural powers, and represent them as decisive, without engaging the gears of a metaphysical system. Metaphysical convictions, to be sure, but not a metaphysical system. For example, the miracle stories about Jesus do not imply that nature is the veil of flesh which Spirit can render diaphanous at will. But the naturalistic historian believes incorrigibly that miracles cannot occur and, therefore, that they have never occurred. Thus ensnared in a metaphysics he does not feel obliged in any way to defend, he has then only to explain why people ever *supposed* miracles occurred. So whatever is noncongruent with his incorrigible metaphysical beliefs must be treated as though it were purely a psychological problem. As one philosopher used to put it, since we know God does not exist, we have to explain why some people, insufficiently or crookedly philosophical, persist in believing that God does exist.

A second factor in the theological turn to story is almost as imposing as the first one. This is the realization that the representations of reality indispensable for the Christian faith are far more comprehensive than the most ambitious latitudinal panorama a naturalistic historian can legitimately project. The big picture drawn in the New Testament is certainly cosmic rather than provincial or anthropocentric. But are these stories, this mighty drama of salvation, *really* about man? On the strength alone of the texts involved, one might quite as plausibly ask whether the Big Bang theory of cosmic origins isn't *really* about man.

One of the persistent elements in the big picture of the New Testament is the mortal combat between good and evil. Human history is but one theater of this action. Beyond us the powers and principalities of darkness scour the cosmos looking for victims; perhaps they have been spoiled by the ridiculous ease with which they have engulfed man. To believe this one must first believe that the differences between good and evil are very real and ultimately important. In itself this belief does not entail a cosmical inclusiveness of the conflict. That entailment rides in on the conviction that the good-evil distinction is, above all, God's business, and Satan's ultimately insoluble problem.

This very factor seduces many theologians into supposing that the big pictures of the New Testament are myths; or, at any rate, that their intentionality is mythological. Much of the damage thus inflicted upon the historicality of the New Testament is supposed to be mitigated by the theological application of literary-philosophical theories about myth. The line runs that myth, or some myth, is a conveyor of existential passions, but not of truth. Myths are not reality-apprehending; they are passion-expressing. So their importance is anthropological, they are not the stuff of real history. This is a fairly crude question-begging distinction.

Now it is clear that the metaphysical incorrigibilities of many modern historians and theologians compel them to ignore or to distort some simple facts involving central features of the New Testament. For example, the Synoptic Gospels go about their business in a very prosy way. Even the miracle stories are straightforwardly reported rather than expatiated upon. The age, to be sure, was saturated with wonder workers of every degree. In the New Testament such stories are clearly intended to tell the reader something about God's intentions for mankind rather than to illustrate eternal truths or apotheosize a religious hero. And since these stories are patently about God's presence, power, and intentions, they cannot possibly be classified with flights of poetic fancy calculated to distract one from a grubby world; or with metaphysical dramas devised to illuminate the human condition rather than to exhibit God's intentions for it.[20]

In this connection it is important to note that the Gospels do not discourse at length about the human condition. It is assumed that the human condition is sufficiently well-known and understood not to need special illumination as the basis for other doctrines or as their "real meaning." One might speculate a bit about this to the effect that the first Christians were all Jews and therefore had a common stock—a historical, anthropological, apperceptive mass—of convictions about the human condition. But some of the Gospels were aimed at Gentile ears. Why then did their writers not stop at the appropriate places to say, "Now by *sin* we mean . . ."? Or, "By *salvation* we mean . . ."? Or, even stranger, why did they not pause to say, "Now by *God* we mean . . ."?

Perhaps it is sufficient for the moment to respond to such factitious queries in this wise: Mature human life everywhere operates with a small stock of primordial intuitions about the human condition. No item of this metaphysical stock is extirpatable except by implantation of an incorrigible belief. That stock includes such things as: life is short; the world is hazardous; we are all driven by conflicting interests. The wrong resolution of these conflicts produces the "first death," variously identified as tedium, stagnation, sterility.

But now along comes a theologian—Barth—who says that man does not know what sin is apart from Jesus Christ, the God-man who saves us from it. This is rather like saying that people don't really know what suffering and death are apart from textbooks in pathology and rites for the dead; unless Barth intends only to say that we faithful Christians *really* know how to use the word "sin." I do not suppose that Barth meant to deny that other people know anything about moral conflict, guilt, the fatal loss of self-respect, and kindred phenomena. Even so, I believe extraordinary measures ought to be taken by religious people, and by their theological advocates, to avoid the pride and presumption impacted in saying anything like, "Now there's a person who doesn't *really* know what suffering *really* means because he hasn't read Job, Sophocles, Wiesel, Rubenstein, Luke.

It is also to be noted that New Testament faith is built on the assumption that certain propositions about God are so true that no case has to be made for them. We can say that the sense of these truths is conveyed by the story. We must also say **that** the story is the fundamental clue to learning how to construe life and the world in the light of such beliefs and with the images in which they are set forth.

The reality of this situation is seriously misperceived by reducing it to: "Well after all the first Christians were religious Jews." That they were, but what does that explain? It does not explain why they believed that the God of Abraham, Isaac, and Moses is now in Christ Jesus, present in power, later to come in glory.

The first Christians did indeed believe that human and cosmic history is fully under God's direction and not merely subject to his influence. Through the proclamation of the Gospel they now see what that direction is and how God effects it.

Such claims—and claims they are, not just just confessions—are metaphysical through and through. They are intended to grasp solidly, not in abstract theory or speculation, the reality in which human life is grounded in all its wretchedness of spoiled splendor, and through which the entire cosmic spread will in God's time be completely reconstituted.

So the Gospel stories are representations of Jesus Christ as the fully human, fully divine embodiment of that reality. As human he is as historical as Pontius Pilate and Joe Namath. He not only occupies a volume of space and a temporal sequence but his actions are as fully palpable as theirs. He does not float above the world nor dream through it. As God, Jesus Christ's actions adumbrate in absolute faithfulness the shape of things to come. This adumbration of the kingdom is altogether different from prophesying when and how the kingdom will come in glory and who among those now living will witness that wonderful and awful end. Concentration, both pious and scholarly, on Jesus the apocalyptic prophet has often produced monumental confusions about the New Testament witness to the presence of the kingdom in Jesus Christ. Thus historian-theologians feel constrained to say, "See, he was wrong! The old world crucified him and buried him. So it goes, on and on." But the Gospel *story* never asserts that God's promise is faithfully represented only in apocalyptic visions. Quite to the contrary there are flat warnings against *any* human calculus of probabilities about the coming in glory of the kingdom of God.[21]

I do not intend here to dogmatize on the issue of authentic vs. apocalyptic eschatology; it is an ancient quarrel. I think it is noteworthy that in the supremely apocalyptic New Testament book, *Revelation*, there is a striking, really wonderful, distinction between the visions in which the eternal beauty of God's kingdom is represented and the melodramatic visions of cosmic and historical disasters announcing the end. And I suppose that the greatest single problem an apocalypticist has, apart from the empirical falsifaction of his predictions, is his persistent inability to take historicality seriously. He imagines a connection between cosmic events and historicality. But he has never been able either to conceptualize that connection or show it forth in images faithful to the New Testament story.

VIII

The Gospel story is full of metaphysical resonances. It is also true that New Testament writers do not reach for conceptual structures with which to validate metaphysical claims. The reason for this is neither mysterious nor uniquely biblical. A reality-intending story works by employing a metaphysical vision, that is, a reading of the human situation in the world. But the story as such does not argue the case. Modern historians have spent an immense amount of energy in presenting the results of incorporating a naturalistic metaphysics. It is unreasonable to ask them as historians to make the metaphysical case as metaphysics. What they have done is to so construe their subject and the evidence involved as to confirm an incorrigible belief that the laws of history are readouts of general experience and therefore admit of no exceptions. That is an important *therefore*. That these readouts are rendered intelligible only by employing paradigms lifted from science is equally important.

Reality-intending stories work by employing metaphysical visions. "Visions" is as important as "metaphysical" in this proposition. The storyteller ought not to be saddled with the responsibility of presenting a logically articulated conceptual system. In *War and Peace* Tolstoi stops the action from time to time to present his philosophy uncut, so to speak; often in order to pay his respects to the philosophical lightweights buzzing around him, but also to formulate the true doctrine about history. (Perhaps this is why some of us prefer *Anna Karenina* to *War and Peace*.) Even so, *War and Peace* is not a metaphysical system set to music. It is one of the world's great stories.

It is unreasonable to ask the novelist to fly his theological colors on his mast. It is not unreasonable to probe the reality-intending story for its metaphysical beliefs, its theology. For the game is bigger than still-life portraiture. The aim is an authentic disclosure of the real forces which move human beings to act as they do in the real world; which, of course, is what Tolstoi was after, too.

Here we must distinguish between what the characters in a story take the real world to be and what their author knows it is. For example, Thomas Sutpen in *Absalom, Absalom!* is instinctively certain that the real world is governed by the rule of dog eat dog. So the thing to do is to grab what you want, person or thing, and fight to keep it. Much too late in the day to make reparations, he puzzles over what went wrong. Could it have been that the design, to which he had tried so persistently and ferociously to make the world adjunctive as far as possible, was faulty? It does not occur to him that the basic policy itself was radically wrong. The world itself will not allow itself to be rendered adjunctive. It submits here and now, in this person and that. But then the retaliatory muscles of the world begin to flex, and the dreadful harvest begins.

So if Sutpen supposes that his fortunes and family are ruined by mere luck, by fortuitously destructive events, he is pitifully naïve. In Faulkner's view the mysterious governance of the world is moral in its own way and time. It beggars all our conventional schematisms of right and wrong. It destroys all the proud towers of human ambition.

The point here is not to ask whether we agree with Faulkner's theology. The point is that his characters are shaped, made, and unmade by powers of the world they misperceive.

Another illustration of this is provided by the relationship of Joanna Burden and Joe Christmas in Faulkner's *Light in August*. We may feel strongly disposed to call this a sick relationship. Faulkner himself describes it as abysmally corrupt and in the grisly end absolutely corrupting.[22] But what is this sickness? Does Joanna Burden become so demonic an engine of destruction because at last the powers of the id explode under the rigidly Puritan superego (burden) and hurl lethal fragments of her ego in all directions? Or has she been as ruthlessly exploitive in her way as Thomas Sutpen was in his? And as much an outrageous child of outraged pride?

It is not necessary to suppose that we have stumbled here upon a historical dialectic. But putting the questions thus disjunctively may help to settle an issue that can be raised as yet another question: Why should we think that the first possibility is scientific rather than theological-metaphysical? Suppose, that is, we do believe, perhaps incorrigibly, that the burdens of the world are first of all victims of a terrible conflict between id and superego, between the residual puissant nonhistorical animal and the historical forces of civilization; so that thereafter they victimize others as they lunge in uncontrollable passion against a world they feel has grossly cheated them of love.

This view is pervasive enough whether or not we believe Faulkner espoused it. But note that it is a mundane expression of what many contemporary theologians take to be cosmological myth. The struggle between good and evil has now been driven indoors. That does not make it less theological-metaphysical. It is metaphysical not only or primarily because it imputes to the id a power as impersonal and universal as electromagnetism, and thus in principle responsive to and describable only in universally valid mechanical laws. It is metaphysical also because something is identified as the bedrock nonhuman reality above and upon which self and society construct the fragile doomed human world.

I think there are decisive reasons for saying that this is not Faulkner's theology. As he sees human life it is, of course, exposed to incursions of cosmic powers, but these are more than the forces and laws of nature. Human beings are interlocked with one another and with cosmic powers brooding over the human scene. The interlocks which matter ultimately are those derived from human choices. These choices are deeply flawed by pride, guilt, outrage, fear, and hatred, but they are not always or necessarily blind choices. As Faulkner sees the human scene, no person is simply self-created. But no one is simply a pawn of morally blank biophysical forces or of his social environment.

There is a more accurate way of putting this. Faulkner's world is drenched in historicality. This does not mean that everything believed—and hated-cherished—to have happened actually happened. Indeed we learn over and over again from him how memory and story have warped the facts. But the corrections which matter most, in respect to history, are not corrections in fact-determinations. Leave those to the mole historians. In respect to historicality the decisive corrections are all personal, perceptual, dispositional. Can one come to accept the story? Can one come to see that it is one's own story, that one's own reality is contained in it? Can one come to see that one's reality is not a *product*, a mechanical toss-off, of the past? Can one come to see that one is an actor in the story? For rightly to tell it is to reenact it passionally.

With what superb sagacity and perspicuity Faulkner thus closes out *Absalom, Absalom!*

"Now I want you to tell me just one thing more. [This is Quentin Compson's Harvard college roommate speaking.] Why do you hate the South?"
"I don't hate it," Quentin said, quickly, at once, immediately; "I don't hate it," he said. *I don't hate it* he thought, panting in the cold air, the iron New England dark; *I dont. I dont! I dont hate it! I dont hate it!*[23]

The issue here is larger and more demanding than the right interpretation of Faulkner's stories. The crucial question is whether reality-intending stories can work without foundational metaphysical beliefs. I think they do not and cannot. But I do not intend to argue that case here because there are related issues that have priority in relation to this one.

One of these concerns the metaphysical substructure of history. Another is a question about the conscious, if not reflective, expression of that substructure. Finally there is the question of the rationalization of these metaphysical beliefs.

IX

Like the novelist, the historian's subject is man. The historian wants to illuminate some part of the human story.[24] We may suppose that beyond this point the ways of the novelist and the historian divide as the historian seeks to provide a causal explanation of human behavior and the novelist does what he can to represent faithfully some of the realities of the human community.

This supposition is incorrect and misleading. The novelist is no less interested in accounting for the actions of his subjects. That his characters may not have been drawn from life is beside the point. If they fail to behave naturally, he has so far failed to pass the test of verisimilitude.

The historian, for his part, tells his story as artfully as he can. Some historians have been woefully short-suited as stylists; the fact is as irrelevant as it is notorious. It is also the case that some historians have used their rhetorical gifts for homiletical and cosmetic purposes. That does not count for much in this connection. What counts far more than these facts about historians is a rather different sort of fact: If a historian really believes that truth is really in those tax records, church subscription lists, conciliar documents, or what not, he has to mine that truth. Then he has to give it intelligible structure. He has to tell us what it all means as a cross-section of the human world. He has to tell us how his miniscule picture fits into the giant jigsaw puzzle of human historicality. Modesty or deficiency of interest may disincline him to respond affirmatively to such demands. But let him not suggest seriously that he knows nothing about historicality. No matter how minute his field of investigation, or how inert his data, his real subject is *homo historicus*.

This is not at all to say that the historian and the novelist alike are captives of an ideology the merits of which they sing willy-nilly. There are ideological novelists and historians. But metaphysical beliefs are not lightly or dogmatically to be identified as ideology if by that we mean doctrines accepted or rejected simply because of their sociocultural connections. Here we ought to pause briefly to applaud the young man Marx for insisting that there was one set of metaphysical beliefs which could not be tarred with the ideological brush; though he could not have been happy about hearing that set of principles called "metaphysical beliefs." Marx was supremely confident that he had in his hands the factors which altogether determine the course of human history. Perhaps he thought that these had been delivered by a superior kind of science. Whatever he thought about that, the principles themselves are as triumphantly theological as Augustine's *De Trinitate*. It does not greatly matter that Marx spent seventeen years in the British Museum mining the facts to fit the doctrines.

Lesser minds are likely to accept their metaphysical beliefs as ukases emitted by intellectual overlords. So there is nothing that prevents a

Marxian from becoming as much of an ideologue as the president of the Chamber of Commerce. They entertain different dogmas but neither will yield to the other in displaying proper reverence for what each accepts as ultimate truth.

Are we to say, then, that both the historian and the novelist are as much interested in purveying a worldview as they are in making sense of the world or a segment of it, as though both were preachers hewing to their respective texts? This does not follow, and there are many novelists and historians for whom it does not hold. Nevertheless, both the historian and the novelist build their structures of sense-making upon a substructure of metaphysical beliefs. Under critical fire each may acknowledge that the hermeneutical key to his work is a metaphysical vision, a worldview, not just an angle of vision but a perceptual-appraisive filter. Justification for this may begin as a defense of a method of fact-ascertainment. But if the critical pressure is maintained, the line of justification is very likely to become a claim that one structure of interpretation alone exhibits the importance to be attached to that story, whether it is a story or straight history.

Now suppose the next critical question is: How do you justify that perceptual-appraisive filter? This is to ask for the case for so viewing the real determiners of human destiny in the real world.

Such questions are not intended to require either the historian or the novelist to put on the philosopher's hat. There is considerable uncertainty today about what sort of head that hat is supposed to cover.[25] Happily it is not the theologian's responsibility to clear up that matter.

What, then, do we have a right to expect from the novelist and the historian in the line of philosophic reflection, broadly understood? It is reasonable to ask for a fair measure of self-awareness, and an acknowledgement that a particular perceptual-appraisive filter is really fundamental in the work of both the historian and the novelist. Furthermore, we have the right to ask for candor when either of them, or both, has depended on some other mind to make the case for his metaphysical beliefs. There is nothing dishonorable about saying, "Well, I believe X has made the best case for my beliefs." This is an autobiographical-confessional expression. As such it adds nothing to the cogency of the beliefs or to the weight of the case. I think this is worth mentioning because there is an odd notion prevalent that confessions of one's real faith ought to be viewed as being more magisterial than the confession that one prefers chocolate to vanilla or Pushkin to Pynchon. But surely the gravity of mien in which a confession is made is a very dubious clue to the passional depth or the conceptual clarity or the illuminating power of one's metaphysical beliefs.

But now if one's *real* faith consists of incorrigible beliefs, what can case-making possibly mean? Not that you must respect such beliefs of mine as you must respect my right to life and justice. But, if I insist that not only do I in fact hold such beliefs but that they are true, you do have a right to be shown what sense they make of the human situation in the world.

Finally we have a right to ask whether the way the story is told begs the critical questions about the human situation. Is the reality toward which the characters, real or fictitious, aspire, or beneath which they sink, itself the metaphysical vision of the historian or the artist? Are the characters allowed to struggle for their own self-awareness, or are they just so many stations of the cross borne by the author? Has the author, artist or historian, evoked the world in which we all do and must live, or has he projected upon that world either a private vision or a doctrinaire theology?

X

There are historical events that overturn all extant persuasive schemes of interpretation. Such events mark the beginning of a new era if not a new world. How have people on the scene during such "shaking of the foundations" gone about the deeply perplexing business of making sense of such events? Of making sense, which is more, much more, than registering the terror inspired by the crumbling of the old world.

Augustine in *City of God* provides one sort of answer to that question. It is a theological analysis of the forces which have brought the proudest of earthly empires to its knees on the edge of its grave. But, above all, Augustine seeks to show how Almighty God has controlled and directed those forces for his own sublime unalterable purpose.

But does this mean that Augustine's main line of response to the end-of-the-world events is a barrage of theological-metaphysical doctrine? It does not. The doctrines are there, to be sure. But in *City of God* Augustine, by intent, is supremely a *biblical* thinker. And the biblical account of historicality, from beginning to end, is set forth in images, in metaphors, in figural representations. So over the whole complex history-making enterprise of *City of God* itself a monarchical metaphor reigns: kingdom.[26]

I suggest, then, that a historical generalization is an order concerning responses to radical threats to the continuity, coherence, and fertility of organized human existence—to devastations visited upon the city of man. At such time there is an all but instinctive resort to imagination for devices with which to grasp the import of events that seem to signify the end of a world. For things that defy understanding may have nonetheless to be practically apprehended. The powers of life have to be regrouped in response to presentiments too massive and too opaque to be adequately comprehended; there are only moldy crusts and dry bones for the reflective understanding. The pious sing, "Sometime we'll understand why"; but in the horrific meantime some kind of sense must be made of life in a world gone mad.

For these purposes, events that augur the end of a human world must be represented as efficaciously as possible. "This is the way the world ends . . ." But no imaginative or figural representation of the world's end is a net thrown to catch it that it might be mounted on the walls of the mind. Images of the ultimate event are cues for human action; as though it still mattered, or perhaps even mattered infinitely, how, at the end, human beings comported themselves.

This is surely one of the most poignant aspects of historicality, this effort to sum in a final gesture all one has been and all one's beloved community has been. Some Christian martyrs sang hymns as they went out to their deaths in the arena. Some victims of the Nazi gas chambers went into those technological triumphs repeating the ancient assurances of Old Testament faith. But is any of this *rational* behavior? Do we not feel that Dylan Thomas must somehow, somewhere, be nearer the truth with "Rage, rage against the dying of the light"?

But what sort of rationality are we appealing to here? What sort can possibly matter here except a sense of what fits, of what brings it all together, brings it all together as circumstance seems to be taking it all apart? The rationality coveted here is much more than being willing to die for what one really believes. Hitler may have done that, for all we know. Rather, the essence of the matter is dying, or hoping and trying to die, as one has tried to live: that is, in a sense-making pattern.[27]

Images are the ordained instruments for organizing the elements and energies of the self in the face of incomprehensible events, the better to preserve, or attain, that unity without which the world itself is a "sound and fury signifying nothing."

Granted that the representation of world-consuming events is figural rather than conceptual, does it follow that the nexus of such images is or must be story? It seems not to be so. One thinks of apocalyptic literature, ancient, mediaeval, and modern, in which the decisive images are set forth in homiletical modalities: exegesis of ancient prophecies; exhortations to patience, courage, and faithfulness; condemnations of giddy life and careless thought in the face of the end.

But even if the homiletical modalities appear to be the last chapter, the chapter the last person of the dying world can write—what we were doing at the end was (will be?) praying, beseeching, cursing, remembering. Even so the exordium makes sense, will make sense, only in the light of a remembered story. Apocalypticism makes sense only as the summation of a history. Indeed the apocalypticist uses the most formidable of all events to illuminate not only the whole course of history but the true and ultimate meaning of the cosmos as well.

If this is the case, then the history of which the most formidable events frame the conclusion, and perhaps the beginnings of a "new heaven and a new earth," is grounded in those principles we have been calling theological. For the criterion to which sense-making itself is accountable is a set of intuitions about the world and the place of human beings in it. These intuitions are richly meaningful, they have an efficacious life, only when they are articulated as a linear story rather than as a miscellany of insights or a body of dogmas. The Wisdom Literature of the Old Testament presupposes a historicality that is not established by wisdom but by faith, hope, and love synthesized by memory.

XI

Science and scientific philosophy are the major springs feeding the acute eschatological anxieties of the contemporary world. No matter what the apologists of science say, it is certainly science that has inspired our pervasive doomsday mentality. "Pervasive" is a giveaway. As a people we stagger out of one crisis into another. So part of the time we are profoundly cynical about the latest announcements of world-ending emergencies; and then we take to reading the sports section first. But then fresh winds of disaster start up, and again we want to know how to make do between now and the end, on the assumption that *this* time doom will fall. But right through this alternating circuit of hope-despair courses a dire certainty: we know that the civilized world and much of the face of the earth can be destroyed by our weapons.

But if these acute apocalyptic terrors are clearly built upon scientific realities, the storyteller has as clearly emerged as the prophet self-charged with the responsibility for mapping the dimensions of the eschaton. This is not because the artist as such has unique and transcendent gifts for delineating the pathologies of the human spirit. It is because the power of plumbing the future, be it bane or blessing, is very largely vested in the creative imagination. Science can map the possibilities but only as far as the possibilities are abstract hypotheticals. Thus: (1) If the population of the world continues to grow at x rate; and (2) if the production of food expands at only y rate, then (3) by the year 2000 . . . Every now and then a morally impassioned scientist proclaims that (1) and (2) are not hypotheticals, so (3) is our just and certain fate. But every such scientific prophet is criticized by other scientists for not having his facts straight, for overlooking some facts, or for drawing illicit inferences from the facts.

The range of facts for which the storyteller is responsible is not defined, or at any rate not bounded, by things like (1) and (2). The storyteller seeks to delineate the condition of the human spirit. Not that (1) and (2) are unimportant for that purpose. But if people now are powerfully threatened by meaninglessness, if they feel themselves drifting haphazardly on boundless waters 50,000 fathoms deep and no familiar shore in sight, the plight of tomorrow's children is not likely to command full or devoted attention.

So even if the scientific prophets were right, if the sequence (1)–(3) were factually and logically unimpeachable, we should still need to know why so many of us do not absorb the prospects of an Armageddon of cosmic magnitude. But what sort of answer do we want most? A social-scientific theory? Or something that reveals how in our world the heart cools at a rate and to a consequence that together reduce the scientific law of entropy to a true but existentially trivial theory.

It would be perverse even to suggest that the storyteller's imaginative penetration of the future runs inevitably to the death and final damnation of historical humanity. Representation of the future as an ultimate fulfilment of humanity is just as familiar an achievement of story even if, at the moment, it is less persuasive or is too frequently and egregiously laced with escapist inauthenticity.

In respect to an affirmative view of the future, the storyteller's sovereignty is not uncontested. Science has its utopians: those who dream of human life rendered immortal scientifically; and those who dream of a race purged of genetic flaws by sound breeding. Philosophy has her utopians, too: those who posit an end-state in which the true brotherhood of man will last forever as a classless society, as a genuine community from which the last trace of alienation has been dialectically expunged.

But how do such theories and visions become potent in the general consciousness? They do so only if they are woven into the fabric of the common life by the creative artist; only if they can thus be seen to be a fitting culmination and climax of the human story.

This has not yet happened to any of the utopian visions of science and philosophy. I do not believe that the principal reason for this remarkable failure is a vestigial claim of religious traditions upon the general consciousness. The principal reason is that modern scientific eschatologies depict an end-state in which creative imagination has been completely volatized because human conflict has been totally resolved. The scientific affirmative visions of the future depict human life governed throughout by a banality very thinly disguised as invincible social equilibrium achieved by the satiation of every ego-need the state accepts as licit.

Popular religious eschatologies boast similar features, to be sure. But the art of the story has long since left those traditional eschatologies behind. Perhaps it is odd that one of the most remarkable storytellers of our times, Flannery O'Connor, gives at least one very powerful account of lives in which the negative visions of Christian eschatology dominate everything else. Yet even there the negative visions are supposed to reinforce "the terrible speed of mercy." So the burning zeal of the true prophet drives him to bizarre and terrible extremes in order that a sinful world might repent and live again in Godly ways; or if not the sinful world, then the children of God in it.[28]

252

XII

Unless the heart be strangely and powerfully warmed again, a new Ice Age ensues. That is something like the song today's storytellers are singing. Scientists are welcome to study—at public expense—the loss of affectivity in the urban world, that interior desert out of which spring the burgeoning symptoms of insensitivity to suffering and desperate need. But we have to see in the round—not just in theory and on graphs—what this says about the future. We have to see what it *proclaims*— bodies forth, adumbrates, figurates—not what it hypothesizes, not what it permits us to infer. For the proclamation assumes a time in which to repent.

But it is not up to the storyteller as such to tell us what we ought to do once we believe that the story is true. As a moralist, an artist may think he knows that, too. But his policy recommendations do not have a natural advantage over those of politicians, scientists, or ordinary preachers. We have a right to ask the prophetic artist, "Watchman, Watchman,/What of the night?" But he does not have to answer when we press on: "How shall we gird for the dawn?/How shall we pray if night never ends?"

XIII

The true masters of the sense of time, the arch specialists of historicality, are the tellers of tales. Theirs is the art that weaves past, present, and future into the habiliments of verisimilitude. Of that truth, alone among the truths our minds reach unaided, it is both sensible and inevitable that we should ask ourselves: Do you hate it or love it?

We may feel that young Compson's response to that question, at the end of *Absalom, Absalom,* betrays a deep, perhaps incurable, ambivalence toward his history. Yet in his passionate protestations we may catch the authentic pulse of our own true and irresolvable ambivalence about the human story. We all have histories. We are creatures defined by historicality, not merely imbued with it. To embrace it, to consent to it altogether, thing of beauty and thing of horror that it is, is a work of grace. I agree with Mauriac that it is beyond the novelist's power to represent authentically the supernaturally engraced life. But it may be that God has scattered the seeds of grace across the earth and the heavens too. A theological consideration.[29]

XIV

Some theologians feel that "the Christian thing" is either a story or it is nothing that can speak to contemporary sensibility. This is a counsel of despair. The New Testament faith is not just a story. It is also a strenuous effort to show how the import of the story must be made out: not only understood but, above all, appropriated. That requires theological work. Moreover, both as story and as theology, the Christian faith has now, and has always had, to compete with other stories and other theologies. So I think it is a fundamental and far-reaching mistake to suppose that telling the story is the whole thing. What one makes of the world and of one's own existence on the strength of the story: that is the pay-off. That is what real and decisive case-making is.

NOTES

INTRODUCTION

1. Unless otherwise indicated, all biblical quotations are from the Revised Standard Version (RSV).

2. A prosy but hardly less effective account of the failure of once dominant faiths (he calls them ideologies) can be found in Alasdair MacIntyre's *Against the Self-Images of the Age* (New York: Schocken, 1971).

3. There are two noteworthy attempts to escape from the subjectivizing of revelation. One is to the speak of a Divine human confrontation. (Cf. E. Brunner, *The Divine Human Encounter* (Philadelphia, 1943.) This is identified—to be consistent one could hardly say described—as an event utterly decisive for the human party to it. It is also an event that utterly eludes the subject-object distinction. The other theological escape hatch is to speak of revelation in terms of commanding images in a social memory; and thereafter of a "social existentialism." (Cf. H. R. Niebuhr, *Christ and Culture* (New York: Harper, 1951) and *The Meaning of Revelation* (New York: Macmillan, 1941). I do not intend to discuss these theological moves here. They are cited as illustrations of ways in which contemporary theologians continue to struggle to make hitherto key theological concepts clear and viable.

4. A Marine Corps chaplain once related a story of a very pious Christian soldier in his outfit who had been preserved (as he believed) from all injury in the jungle-fighting in southeast Asia in World War II by a voice instructing him in exact detail what to do in combat situations. Of course this innocent lad was the butt of much humor, little of it kind, much of it unwittingly theological. Then one day this lad asked to be excused from patrol duty because he had a hunch the voice would not guide him that day. That was the day a sniper got him through the head. . . . The chaplain said this incident provoked a great deal of discussion as well as many guilt feelings. Not even the conventionally religious believed that the *real* God would (or could?) provide such particularistic revelations. But of course the skeptics (and there are atheists as well as skeptics in foxholes) were prompt then to ask: So what else is your God good for?

5. Here it little matters that the later Sartre turns to Marxism, that is, to his version of that theology, for his soteriological doctrines.

CHAPTER ONE

1. All around are the hospitalized and the walking wounded, of every chronological age, who have never forgiven Daddy's ultimate departure. These trauma are excruciatingly paradoxical: Since Daddy is really gone there is little use in blaming *him*. So *reality* has to be blamed and punished—one's own reality, very likely; but equally likely, too, only as an access to a hateful world.

2. I have arbitrarily ignored for present purposes that the psalm is part of a traditional liturgical structure.

3. It is surely one of the narrowest and thinnest of Christian conceits that only in Christianity are believers enjoined to pray for their enemies. Or should we indulge this presumption in this context on the grounds that in the Bible the men Job is ordered to pray for—as pray he does, and efficaciously, too—are called his "friends"?

4. This is his "ontological" argument, as it was much later to be called. Rare now is the theologian who would take it to be an answer to prayer, at least not to any of his. But it has kept a lot of philosophers busy for a long time; they are still at it. God does indeed move in mysterious ways.

CHAPTER TWO

1. Yet Herbert's God expresses a striking reservation:

> "For if I should," said he,
> "Bestow this jewel also on my creature,
> He would adore my gifts instead of me,
> And rest in Nature, not the God of Nature:
> So both should losers be."

From "The Pulley," *The New Oxford Book of English Verse* (1972), p. 258.

2. I am not speaking to the question whether one ought to display a reliable knowledge and decent respect for the achievements of the giants in one's realm. Nor do I mean thus to speak to the question whether any philosopher or theologian has ever driven any particular bit of nonsense from the field once and for all.

3. The poet sings:

> God is his own interpreter,
> And He will make it plain.

But there is no doubt but that Cowper is talking of something God, Christianly conceived, does.

4. See Austin Farrar's *The Glass of Vision* (London, 1948) and his *Rebirth of Images* (London: Peter Smith, 1949) for striking expressions of such views.

5. One of the intriguing questions about Jungian theories of the archetypal images is whether as creations of the collective unconscious they are not as fully transhuman in origin, and as transcendentally important, as the figural revelations St. John of the Apocalypse received from on high. A preference for images of depth rather than for images of height may tell us more about psychocultural predilections than about anything else.

6. "Bar of reason" is something of a rhetorical flourish. It is much more likely that proponents of a particular philosophical method of analysis will put theological-metaphysical propositions on trial and pronounce them either meaningless or false; a bit like being given one's choice of execution by hanging or gas. What is the justification, extradepartmental shall we say, for this drumhead process? Something like this: "This is the way we do philosophy here." A great variety of things conspire to inhibit speaking for reason as such. But shall we then have to learn to speak with less hesitancy about science as such? Or about philosophy as such? Or about religion as such?

7. The reference is to the story in Luke 10:38–42. On the strength of this text preachers almost always treat Martha roughly; sermonically, that is. Often enough the sermon in which Mary's superior spiritual wisdom is celebrated is followed by a plea to the congregation to underwrite in full the projected church budget.

8. The influence of Plotinus on formulations of Christian doctrines of God is great. But he concedes—insists, rather—that the rational-mystical discipline, his version of the dialectic, cannot guarantee the mystic vision and mystic union. This does not mean that he regards those ineffable perfections as pure divine gratuities. But if God (the One) is not coy or capricious—unthinkable thoughts for Plotinus—in granting the greatest of all boons, must it not follow that there is a built-in defect in the dialectic? Or shall we permit him to say, too, that the spirit is willing but the flesh is both weak and capricious?

8a. In *An Essay on Metaphysics*, Oxford, 1940.

9. Strictly speaking we cannot say that we now see what those absolute presuppositions *are;* we can only sense what they were, that is, what their power was. But even this is an inference from the kind of social order which rested upon them. . . . We must also allow for those periods when darkness covers the face of the whole earth; that is, for the times when nothing seems surely grounded and all things are in flux. Should we then ask the skeptic what his absolute presuppositions are, and hope to get such an answer as Augustine or Descartes says the consistent skeptic must give if he is rational? Or should we simply ask: what makes it worthwhile to "suspend all judgment" and steer by guesswork?

10. It will be said that theologians, in the great epochs of *God's will,* turned to

Scripture for elucidation of that supreme Light-giver. That is a mistake. From Scripture they learned how to use that language, how to foster that belief: the language of, the belief in, that God who dwells in light unapproachable (cf. 1 Tim. 6:16).

11. I do not mean such a time as when a particular philosophic devastation of Christian theodicy is widely accepted in academic circles as the torpedo that finally sank *God's will.* Perhaps Voltaire—whose following was hardly limited to academic circles—believed that he had destroyed, with that wonderful torpedo *Candide,* the Leibnizian "best of all possible worlds." I doubt that Voltaire was that kind of fool.

12. We might have considered, for example, the absolutizing of an attitude toward inquiry into experience and the world: openness, readiness to abandon any theory, principle, paradigm, or dogma in the face of empirical contraindications or promising conceptual revolutions. But this attitude, often recommended as normative, or at least as worthy of all acceptance, is very much like being open to conviction. But to what conviction, kind of conviction, range of conviction? No material conviction and no decision rationally derive from such an attitude; nor, indeed, from any *attitude* as such.

13. Here we are not to suppose, apparently, that there is anything in the least measure provincial or non-rational in seeking to formulate the laws of history. It seems—its rationality, that is—to depend on who discovers and formulates them: Marx rather than Hegel, Hempel rather than Toynbee.

CHAPTER THREE

1. Such as R. E. Palmer's *Hermeneutics* (Evanston, Ill.: Northwestern University Press, 1969).

2. I do not want here to press the difference between "bearing on" and "exhibiting." Viewed one way, Tillich has taken the hermeneutical route: he is out to construe tradition and religious experience in the way which makes most sense to what and who we are at this historical moment.

3. Not that the Lord's self-naming as I-am-that-which-I-am hasn't kept exegetes and theologians busy enough as it is.

4. I do not intend this way of putting it to pass as an underhanded way of answering the question whether faith itself is purely and absolutely God's gift.

5. In Matthew 25:14–30 (esp. v. 25) the lord of the establishment does not deny the charge. He turns it around on the unworthy steward thus: Since you knew I was a severe master why didn't you act more prudently, that is, do exactly as you were bidden?

6. Hegel was the first philosopher to propose and execute this categorical shift. But subsequent theological appropriations of this ought not to be debited entirely to his account.

7. Such conclusions pertain so far only to the representation of the Gospel as

a report of facts, that is, of events in which the purpose and power of God are registrations of God's presence. This is not to throw the game over to theologians who say that such events have the *value* of God's presence; that is, they are ways in which Christian people interpret reports whose factual basis or elements are forever past reliable ascertainment. These issues are addressed more directly in Chapter Eight.

CHAPTER FOUR

1. Little is now being written under the heading of theology of hope. There was a flurry of discussion of Moltmann's essay, *The Theology of Hope* (London: SCM, 1967); but since then attention has moved on to other things, such as political theology, a novelty in western culture, at least as old as Plato's *Laws*. But it is worthy of passing note that part of the explanation of the recrudescence of hope as a systematic theological concern was the tilt given to Marxian eschatology by the philosopher Ernst Bloch, and by other thinkers who wanted to show that true Marxism was a true humanism, in distinction from the brutalities of Stalinist totalitarianism.

2. Here "lords" refers to social forces, not to specific persons.

3. This may be as good a place as any to take note of the standard distinction between wish and hope—standard rather than systematic. It is not always important to honor the distinction. When we do, the results are something like this:

(i) To wish for something is to shift into the subjunctive—"I wish I would/ I wish I might." "Would that it were so."

(ii) To hope for something is still to move in the indicative. One's hopes may be unrealistic, but we do not ordinarily write drafts on the fantastic in our hopes. In respect to what we hope for the actual world may be counterindicative; but the hoped-for does not float free and clear in never-never.

(iii) But there is nothing at all odd in: "O I wish I had never written that letter!" Imagine substituting *hope* for *wish* in that sentence. True, we can imagine or remember: "O I hope I only *dreamed* writing that letter!" There is nothing fantastic about that, since one is counting on a future development to ease or erase a present distress. In the meantime one can only wait.

4. Marxian orthodoxy confirms this in its own wooden way. In that view, the Christian hope is a demonic distraction of human energies away from the actualities in which alone human fulfillment is possible. Marx himself was much too sober a revolutionary thinker to have wasted ammunition on a trivial social force. He knew that the Christian hope was anything but that, even in his misreading of it. Popular Christian piety taught him to misread the Christian hope.

CHAPTER FIVE

1. Is our appreciation of the poetic truth of his *Odyssey* supposed to be enhanced by scientific confirmation of his accounts of how many days it takes to go by sail from *a* to *b*?

2. The Freudian age; but here Freud only as the Columbus of the depth continent of the self.

3. There are logical oddities in the concept of the protean self, of recent and fleeting sociological fame. Who or what is it that desires (and aims?) to be many selves? Are the multiple selves a temporal series or are they contemporaneous contenders for the throne?

4. The Pauline theological-political ethic has long been fought-over country. I have not ventured here to survey it systematically; or to take account of such particular problems as the weight of apocalyptic hope in St. Paul's view of the state, and of slavery. It is safe to say in sum that his authority has rarely been invoked by political revolutionists of the left. It is no whit easier to extract from his teaching a doctrine of divine authority to be applied to any or every regime.

5. Some of us cannot but shudder every time we hear a replay of Hitler's megalomaniacal boast to that delirious congregation that the Reich he has fashioned, and is now throwing into war, will last for a thousand years. The shudder itself is a replay: we sensed at the time that the undoing of such monstrous presumption might well bring down our world.

CHAPTER SIX

1. In respect to this the situation of Moses is intriguing. His people have either forgotten the Lord or they are an untutored generation. In either case what sort of authority can the Lord's commands have for them? Moses puts the problem as though it were primarily a matter of his inexperience, his lack of charismatic gifts: the problem of the wrong man for the big job. That is, conveying revelation to people who are not expecting it and may not know what to do with it once it is delivered. But I suspect that Moses had his finger on the theological sore spot: How can an unknown God speak with absolute authority? Especially since he will have none of the heathenish custom of naming deities in order to massage them into good humor or at any rate out of bad ones.

Of course we know how the Lord solves Moses' problem. By mighty deeds, and by speaking directly and decisively to the primordial hunger of the people—namely, a hunger for freedom.

In the story Pharaoh has no trouble identifying the Lord as the author of the mighty deeds, the same being his awful afflictions. But how can he, the oppressor, know that God's intention is freedom?

2. In *The Bacchae* Euripides gives an overpowering account of orgiastic (and in the event, homicidal) participation in the power of Dionysius. But moral trust in him? He (Euripides) has the Chorus say:

Notes

The gods are crafty:
they lie in ambush
a long step of time
to hunt the unholy.
Beyond the old beliefs,
no thought, no act shall go.
Small, small is the cost
to believe in this:
whatever is God is strong;
whatever long time has sanctioned,
that is a law forever;
the law tradition makes
is the law of nature.
What is wisdom? What gift of the gods
is held in honor like this:
to hold your hand victorious
over the heads of those you hate?
(*The Complete Greek Tragedies,*
[Arrowsmith's translation] Vol. IV
[University of Chicago Press, 1958],
lines 887–900.)

3. There is much that is arresting in this situation, this fearsome unthinkable possibility. For any alternative to obeying the protocol commandment looks to be utterly devoid of compensating benefit—who will run with demigods when life with God himself is there to be chosen? Only purblind children and irredeemable fools! But demons and demigods have long innings in history (Cf. C. S. Lewis's account of the age-long conflict between Logres and Britain in *That Hideous Strength* [New York: Collier, 1972]). One can serve them lifelong and die long before they fall. So the options open to Job seem unduly restricted: he can curse God and die—the option his wife recommends, perhaps because she was tired of all that theology—or he can stand fast in faith against every sign that God has forsaken him. But where is that other option, to go whoring after demigods? Surely he must have known that one can preserve the outer forms of respect for the Most High and withal give the love of one's heart unstintingly to no-gods. Not so Job: he stands staunchly within the context created by the protocol commandment and does not even fantasize about breaking out of it. Why, therefore, does he not stand forth as a much more formidable knight of Faith than Abraham, who suspends the ethical expedientially on a variety of occasions? One more measure of affliction for old Job: he has never had a Kierkegaard.

4. This incident, in which King Saul spares his enemy's life, is sometimes regarded as a forward movement of the ethical consciousness. In the story this movement is temporarily arrested: Samuel, full of prophetic fury (not too quickly to be identified with righteous indignation) seizes a sword and hacks Agag to pieces, even as Saul had been commanded to do. Are we to suppose that this is another divine teleological suspension of the ethical? Or were Saul and Agag brother members of a secret society?—Whatever, in the story Saul's humaneness

is treated as a terrible dereliction of duty, and it costs him the kingdom.

5. There is a widely prevalent philosophic notion that *perception* either dismisses the criterion of veridicality or absorbs it. True, we may still be inclined to say of another person, "His perceptions are faulty." And we may be as naturally disposed to say, "Well, after all, those *are* his perceptions." So in the end it is not that a neurotic's perceptions are wrong but that his feelings about his perceptions are inadequate.

Part of the problem here is a category confusion. We often infer the quality of another's perceptions from his or her utterances and other gestures; whereas as often we know in ourselves that utterance may be calculated—whether consciously or not is immaterial to this point—to mask rather than to disclose perceptions, that is, the perceptions of the masker. Suppose, for instance, someone says, "I perceive that mendacity is the rule of the world." What is the appropriate response to this (assuming that it is more than an attention-getting device)? (a) "Come now: you haven't actually perceived the *world*. Philosophers know that the world as such is not, cannot be, an object of perception." (b) "Why do you say such a thing as, 'I perceive that mendacity is the rule of the world'? Are you afraid to tell or trust the truth?"

The (b) move strongly suggests a conviction that in this case there is at least a disparity, if not a tension, between perception and utterance. It would surely be wrong-headed to make a principle out of that empirical generalization. Yet it has a cautionary value. One often has reasons for one's utterances other than one's perceptions, such as convictions, anxieties, and goals upon which perceptions fall discordantly.

6. The *in principle* thing strikes an Hegelian chord. But I do not impute to the theologians who employ that concept any intention to strike that chord.

CHAPTER SEVEN

1. *Encyclopaedia Britannica*, 1948, Vol. XXI, p. 515.

2. Moses Hadad, "Introduction" in *Lives of the Caesars* (Buffalo: The Heritage Press, 1965), p. xi. The quotations from Suetonius are from this edition of his work.

3. John Williams in *Augustus* (New York: Viking, 1972).

4. Thus the self as the subject in scientific cognitivity is animated by a single appetite: the need to know a world in no respect compromised by being known. To try to conceive the self as constituted by that appetite alone is to take a seven-league step toward madness.

5. For a particular form of this phenomenon see Page Smith's discussion of the history of interpretations of the American Revolution in *The Historian and History* (New York; Knopf, 1964).

6. See Arthur Danto, *An Analytical Philosophy of Knowledge* (Cambridge, Eng.: Cambridge University Press, 1968).

7. The problem of causality looms large in modern philosophy of history. In speaking of so-and-so as a cause of an event, I do not mean to beg any real question. So far all that is intended is that we may say, "Lincoln did this and that" when that overt action stands in the record. Moreover, we may say, "Lincoln intended to do that" when the record of his declared intentions is clear. Historians do not need to devise hidden motives to impute to their subjects. If intentions are not exhibited in actions, psychology is a guessing game.

We know how weighty various theories of motivation have become; they have the weight of metaphysics, in fact, except that these incorrigible beliefs are customarily called scientific.

As to persisting conflicts over social causation: there is something quixotic in a thinker postulating that no mere individual is ever a real mover of society. Why not drop all the way back and avow that the individual is an illusion? *Whose* illusion would be the next question.

8. "And they compelled a passerby, Simon of Cyrene, who was coming in from the country, the father of Alexander and Rufus, to carry his cross" (Mk 15:21).

9. In saying "attribution," I do not presume to dismiss out of hand the possibility that the laws of history are read off historical experience. Yet the plurality of such perceptions, if such they be, should give us pause before we accept any one or any set of such laws as reality legislated. This is a prudential matter rather than a logical or metaphysical ukase.

10. Patrick Gardiner, in *The Encyclopedia of Philosophy* (1972), Vol. I–II, p.415B.

11. The history of Western modern science abounds with cases of discoveries denied acceptance in the reigning circles because they were alleged not to fit the laws of nature. See M. Polanyi, *Personal Knowledge* (Chicago, 1958.); also "Alfred Wegener and the Hypothesis of Continental Drift," in *The Scientific American*, Feb. 1975, pp. 88–97. Professor Hallam writes: "Perhaps the long travail of Wegener's hypothesis (now all but universally accepted) can best be explained as a consequence of inertia. A geologist at the 1928 symposium of the American Association of Petroleum Geologists is reported to have said: 'If we are to believe Wegener's hypothesis, we must forget everything that has been learned in the past 70 years and start all over again' " (p. 97).

12. "Prehistoric Agriculture in Tropical Highlands," Linares, Sheets and Rosenthal, in *Science*, Jan. 1975, p. 141.

13. The creator of the messianic Spirit Dance which played so tragic a part in the Indian uprising in 1890.

14. See *This Country Was Ours*, V. J. Vogel, ed. (New York: Harper and Row, 1972) pp. 184–187.

15. The allusion is to Jaspers' theory of world-historical pivotal events. *The Origin and Goal of History* (New Haven: Yale University Press, 1953).

16. So S. E. Morison, in *The Oxford History of the American People* (1965), p. 685.

17. I do not mean to insist upon a hard-and-fast distinction between *importance* and *interestingness*. Nor do I think it greatly matters that *importance* is commonly

a retrodictive judgment whereas *interesting* is much more likely to be an instantaneous assessment of an object or event. In much of social chatter "interesting" is a front-line response to queries about our opinions of dresses, hats, art objects, John Doe's latest mistress or the latest gossip about his old one. "Interesting" is a picket-line behind which one hopes to have forces in strength in case the conversation should take a serious turn.

18. Republican Rome had seen many Dictators. It was an honorable title for many generations; until Caesar, Rome had licensed eighty-eight of them. See Livy, *The War with Hannibal*, Books XXI–XXX of his *History of Rome from its Foundations.* Julius Caesar had a precedent for his usurpation of power: that of Sulla in 82 B.C.; no friend but an invaluable tutor in the arts of intrigue.

19. Lk 9:30; Mal 4:4–6: "Behold I will send you Elijah the prophet before the great and terrible day of the Lord comes." (Cf. also Eccles 48:1–11.)

20. The identity of the murderer(s) of Richard's nephews remains one of the great mysteries of English history. There is no conclusive evidence that they were in fact murdered; none that ties the foul deed to Richard. For a review of the case see Paul Kendall, *Richard the Third,* London, 1955, Appendix I. Richard's conqueror and successor, Henry VII, has occasionally been nominated as the real villain in the piece.

21. I do not intend at all to suggest that the historical plays of Shakespeare have the explicit liturgical function of the Orestes cycle in Greek tragedy, or of Sophocles' *Oedipus.* Nonetheless it is important to note that Shakespearean tragedy is very inadequately interpreted simply by recourse to Aristotelian categories. A cathartic effect may be intended. But above all the perdurable structures of the public order are celebrated as superior in their claims to even the most engrossing and terrible individual suffering.

22. "The Shrubbery: Written in a Time of Affliction."

CHAPTER EIGHT

1. *Early History of Rome*, Penguin, pp. 37–38, Selincourt translation. Cf. the fragment from Dio Cassius, Bk I, p. 15: "Among these . . . were also the founders of Rome . . . who were suckled by a wolf, called by the Italians *lupa;* this name has been aptly applied as a term for courtesans." Leob Classical Library, Dio's *Roman History,* Cary translation.

2. *Op. cit.* pp. 33–34.

3. The poet is Coventry Patmore. The short sonnet does not give off the undiluted optimism the tag line is often taken to represent:

> Here, in this little Bay,
> Full of tumultuous life and great repose,
> Where, twice a day,
> The purposeless, glad ocean comes and goes,

Notes

Under high cliffs, and far from the huge town,
I sit me down.
For want of me the world's course will not fail;
When all its work is done, the lie shall rot;
The truth is great, and shall prevail,
When none cares whether it prevail or not.

4. Alfred North Whitehead, *Religion in the Making* (New York: Macmillan, 1926), p. 50.

5. W.B. Yeats, "The Land of Heart's Desire" in *The Collected Plays of W. B. Yeats* (New York: Macmillan, 1953), p. 45.

6. *The Idea of History*, Oxford, 1946

7. "The canvas of Gibbon teems with life, but the actions represented are always subjected to the control and discipline of the artist. The two great activities of his mind, dissection and analysis on the one hand, and fusion and creation on the other, are carried on concurrently. The simultaneous activity of taking apart and putting together makes his narrative a continual commentary. It is to his interest wherever possible to distinguish with precision the ingredients which make up the whole, or as he puts it in one place, 'to ascertain the separate shares of accident, of fancy, of imposture, and of fiction.' As an artist, however, conducting a tremendous narrative, he must put together and create from the individual parts the living picture." H. L. Bond, *The Literary Art of Edward Gibbon*, Oxford, 1960, pp. 87–88.

8. *The Columbia Encyclopedia* (1963), p. 1965.

9. Bond, op. cit.: ". . . *The Decline and Fall* may be called the epic of the Enlightenment, for it celebrates the triumph of human reason in Gibbon's 'philosophic' age (p. 160) . . . Gibbon is quite explicitly the spokesman for his age in the numerous reflections—political, moral, and philosophical—with which he studs his narrative. His frequent appeals to the reason and judgment of his contemporaries and his confidence in their ready acceptance of his assertions suggest that he was quite consciously playing the role of spokesman for his times" (p. 162). Bond contends that Gibbon deliberately—and in large measure successfully—fashioned his history upon epic models.

10. Though Gibbon probably would have disagreed with this. See Bond, op. cit., Chapter Six.

11. *The Columbia Encyclopedia* (1963), p. 1402.

12. *The Columbia Encyclopedia* (1963), p. 575. Ernest Cary, the translator of Dio's histories in the Loeb edition, files a rather different judgment: "Unfortunately the value of his history is greatly diminished for us as the result of his blind devotion to two theories governing historical writing in his day. On the one hand a sense of the dignity and true value of history demanded that mere details and personal anecdotes should give place to the larger aspects and significance of events. On the other hand the historian was never to forget that he was at the same time a

rhetorician; if the bare facts were lacking in effectiveness, they could be adorned, modified, or variously combined in the interest of a more dramatic presentation." Volume I, 1914, p.xiii.

13. *The Peloponnesian War,* R. Warner, tr. (New York: Penguin, 1954) pp. 24–25.

14. Once again the classic case of Richard III comes to mind. Here I cite the summation of Paul Kendall: "Thus did he remain alive in many men's memories. But memories are mute and the written word was dangerous. Henry had the writers, and what Henry's court said was all that counted. King Richard, such as he was in life—confused and diligent and erring and earnest—was buried beneath the black alluvial deposits of the Tudor historians, who created in his stead a simulacrum—an ogre, atop which King Henry was displayed, rescuing England." *Richard the Third,* London, 1965. Alas for poor Richard, even saddled with a fictitious humpback! Could Olivier have made do without that? A question for art, not history.

15. "This method [comparing the radioactivity of a modern piece of wood with that of a specimen of unknown age] . . . has been checked by comparison with pieces of wood of known age from the tombs of the Pharaohs and has been found to be fairly reliable." *The Penguin Dictionary of Science* (1972), p.320.

16. *History of Civilization in England.* Quoted by J. M. Robertson, *Buckle and his Critics,* London, 1895, p. 529.

17. For a striking use of "archaeology" as a hermeneutical tool, that is, for getting at buried meaning, see Riceour's *Freud and Philosophy* (New Haven: Yale University Press, 1970).

18. I have intentionally bypassed absurdist fiction in these observations. The canons of verisimilitude are deliberately defied or scrambled in such things as Gardner's *The Sunlight Dialogues* (New York: Knopf, 1972) and Pynchon's *Gravity's Rainbow* (New York: Bantam, 1974). Both novelists seem to be reaching for weighty metaphysical counters; perhaps not so explicitly as Camus, say; certainly not with the economy of statement and sophistication of philosophic mentality of Beckett. But here it is, again: the world is a crazy place. So does one have to be "stoned" to get along in (not with) it? Or is being stoned requisite for getting the message of the novelist?

19. 2 Kings 7:3–8. The Old Testament historian says that the Lord produced in the Syrians auditory delusions of great hosts coming up to destroy them. "So they fled away in the twilight and forsook their tents, their horses, and their asses, leaving the camp as it was, and fled for their lives" (v.7). The narrative has a very nice circumstantial air about it. Four lepers, thinking they have nothing to lose anyway, decide to visit the camp of the Syrians only to find it deserted. After briefly enjoying various goodies left behind, they decide to report this marvelous thing to the besieged Israelites. The king decides to put their implausible yarn to empirical test, and of course learns that the Lord has again delivered his people.

20. In speaking of New Testament critics and theologians who cut great swaths with concepts of myth, C. S. Lewis says: "First then, whatever these men may

be as Biblical critics, I distrust them as critics. They seem to me to lack literary judgment, to be imperceptive about the very quality of the texts they are reading. . . . If (such a critic) tells me something in a Gospel is legend or romance, I want to know how many legends and romances he has read, how well his palate is trained in detecting them by the flavour; not how many years he has spent on that Gospel" (*Christian Reflections* [Grand Rapids: Eerdmans, 1974] p.154). I do not believe that Lewis is here pulling rank as a distinguished literary historian.

21. Mt 24:43,44; Lk 12:39,40. Also 1 Thess. 5:2.

22. "Within six months she was completely corrupted. It could not be said that he corrupted her. His own life, for all its anonymous promiscuity, had been conventional enough, as a life of healthy and normal sin usually is. The corruption came from a source even more inexplicable to him than to her. In fact, it was as though with the corruption which she seemed to gather from the air itself, she began to corrupt him. He began to be afraid. He could not have said of what. But he began to see himself as from a distance, like a man being sucked down into a bottomless morass." *Light in August,* Modern Library, p.227.

23. Vintage Book Edition, 1972, p. 378.

24. I do not intend anything prejudicial by "illuminate." If a historian prefers to say "interpret," "explain," "understand," he is welcome to the substitutions.

25. Though we should not immediately agree with Wallace Stevens that this is sufficient reason to

> Treat the philosopher's hat,
> Left thoughtlessly behind,
> As one of the relics of the mind. . . .*

Or is there more comfort in thinking that

> Rationalists, wearing square hats,
> Think, in square rooms,
> Looking at the floor,
> Looking at the ceiling.
> They confine themselves
> To right-angled triangles.
> If they tried rhomboids,
> Cones, waving lines, ellipses—
> As, for example, the ellipse of the half-moon—
> Rationalists would wear sombreros."**

*From "The Prejudice Against the Past" in *The Collected Poems of Wallace Stevens.* Copyright 1947 by Wallace Stevens. Reprinted by permission of Alfred A. Knopf, Inc.
**From "Six Significant Landscapes"; Copyright 1923, 1951 by Wallace Stevens. Reprinted from *The Collected Poems of Wallace Stevens* by permission of Alfred A. Knopf, Inc.

26. It is tempting to make too much of Augustine as a metaphysical genius of the highest order. On one metaphysical topic alone such luminosity radiates: Time. But what topic could be more fit, more central and commanding, for the greatest of postbiblical fountainheads of the philosophy of history in the Western world?

27. Death has become a very lively topic for academic treatment. All sorts of professionals are busy with it, oftimes in bold interdepartmental programs. College seminars on it are high priority elections. All this in a time when meaning-structures are breaking down all over the place. It is said of certain lower animals that they know when the time has come to die. One wonders whether some such "instinct" is at work even in the Academy.

28. *The Violent Bear It Away* (New American Library, 1961) p.159.

29. O'Connor ventures it. Of her boy-prophet, Francis Tarwater, she writes:

He threw himself to the ground and with his face against the dirt of the grave, he heard the command. GO WARN THE CHILDREN OF GOD OF THE TERRIBLE SPEED OF MERCY. The words were as silent as seeds opening one at a time in his blood (op.cit., p.159).